BRITAIN AND THE FRENCH REVOLUTION 1789–1815

Each volume in the 'Problems in Focus' series is designed to make available to students important new work on key historical problems and periods that they encounter in their courses. Each volume is devoted to a central topic or theme, and the most important aspects of this are dealt with by specially commissioned essays from scholars in the relevant field. The editorial Introduction reviews the problem or period as a whole, and each essay provides an assessment of the particular aspect, pointing out the areas of development and controversy, and indicating where conclusions can be drawn or where further work is necessary. An annotated bibliography serves as a guide for further reading.

PROBLEMS IN FOCUS SERIES

Britain and the French Revolution, 1789–1815

EDITED BY

H. T. DICKINSON

M

MACMILLAN
EDUCATION

First published 1989

Published by
MACMILLAN EDUCATION LTD
Houndmills, Basingstoke, Hampshire RG21 2XS
and London
Companies and representatives
throughout the world

Printed in the People's Republic of China

British Library Cataloguing in Publication Data
Britain and the French Revolution, 1789–1815.
—(Problems in focus).
1. Great Britain, 1760–1820
I. Dickinson, H. T. (Harry Thomas), 1939– II. Series
941.07'3
ISBN 0–333–44260–1
ISBN 0–333–44261–X Pbk

Contents

Preface

THE French Revolution, and the Revolutionary and Napoleonic Wars which accompanied it, is one of the most significant events in European, perhaps in world, history. Contemporary observers of the astonishing events in France were soon conscious of the fact that they were witnessing not only the restructuring of French institutions and French society, but also the reshaping of the fortunes and destinies of the other major nations of Europe. As a near neighbour of France and perhaps her greatest rival, as a country which both admired and abhorred what was happening in France, and as a state which offered the most sustained opposition to French efforts to export their revolution by force of arms, Britain could no more isolate herself from the influence of the French Revolution than could those countries which succumbed more obviously to French ideas as they did to French arms. Any attempt, therefore, to understand the full significance of the French Revolution requires an assessment of its impact on Britain as well as on the other major powers of Europe. With the historical profession about to celebrate the bicentenary of the French Revolution it seems particularly appropriate to offer at this time a substantial, up-to-date and well-rounded appreciation of the impact which the revolution made upon Britain.

In preparing this collection of essays I have been very fortunate in my choice of contributors. They all completed their assignments on time and, where necessary, they willingly made minor changes to meet my overall design for the volume. No editor could have had more professional collaborators. I am also very grateful to my colleague, Dr F. D. Dow, for shrewd and helpful comments both on my own essay and on my introduction, and to the Leverhulme Trust, the Carnegie Trust for the Universities of Scotland, and the Clark Library of UCLA, for financial support to undertake this and other recent research.

University of Edinburgh   HARRY DICKINSON

Introduction: the Impact of the French Revolution and the French Wars 1789–1815

H. T. DICKINSON

THE outbreak of revolution in Paris in 1789 was an event of the very greatest importance in the history of France. The subsequent efforts to export revolution to the rest of Europe and the long wars which this helped to provoke had important consequences for every major country in Europe. Although a stubborn opponent of French ideas and also the most persistent foe of French arms, Britain was greatly influenced by her nearest neighbour in positive as well as in negative ways. The French Revolution stimulated new developments in Britain and encouraged existing trends as well as proving an obstacle to change. It is extraordinarily difficult, however, to measure the precise impact on Britain of the French Revolution and the French Wars because during these same years Britain was in the midst of profound changes – rapid demographic growth, major economic improvements and sustained urbanisation – which are usually labelled 'the Industrial Revolution'. This internal revolution was in the process of transforming almost every aspect of British life. It is therefore particularly difficult in this period to disentangle those changes which were the consequence of the momentous events in France. It is obvious that the French Revolution and the French Wars had a significant effect on Britain even if these events just stimulated Britain to resist French ideas and to oppose French ambitions for a quarter of a century. It seems very likely, however, that the events in France had a deeper and a wider impact than this, although it is very difficult to measure it with any precision. In some respects we can do no more than speculate on what caused the major changes between 1789 and 1815.

I

The constitutional context in which British politicians operated in the period between 1789 and 1815 was significantly altered by two major developments; one gradual and almost imperceptible, the other sudden and dramatic. The first involved a slow change in the political influence of the crown, the second was a radical alteration in the composition of Parliament because of the Act of Union with Ireland.

Ever since his accession to the throne in 1760 George III had shown his determination to sustain or to undermine ministers who won his favour or earned his enmity. One of the most blatant and wilful exercises of his royal prerogative had been to bring in the Younger Pitt as Prime Minister in 1783 when he was unable to command a majority in the House of Commons. In the years after 1789 he continued to make his personal political views known to his ministers. Like Burke he came to regard the war against revolutionary France as essential for the preservation of society and he urged his ministers to pursue policies which would suppress radicalism at home and would rally the propertied classes to the defence of the British constitution. He regarded British defeats as setbacks to be endured at present and remedied as soon as possible. There is no doubt that his attitude stiffened the resolve of his ministers and won the admiration of the majority of his subjects. Loyal addresses and mass demonstrations which involved celebrations in support of the monarchy show that George III became identified with the vast patriotic struggle against France. The king's personal views could also continue to have adverse effects as when his hostility to Catholic emancipation helped to bring about Pitt's resignation in 1801 and that of the Ministry of all the Talents in 1807. None the less, despite evidence of his continuing influence on his ministers and their policies, George III played a less significant role after 1789 than he had in earlier decades. This development owed something to the events in France, because the conservative reaction in Britain rallied an increasing number of the propertied elite behind the party of government and so it could rely more on the voluntary support of the majority of MPs and did not need to depend so heavily on those MPs who were recipients of crown patronage. The waning of the king's power, however, owed more to a whole series of legislative and administrative reforms since the early 1780s which had reduced crown patronage and to a series of breakdowns which weakened the king's mental state and eventually left him incapable of performing his royal duties. When the Prince of Wales assumed his responsibilities as regent in 1812 his own character faults, combined with the steady decline of crown patronage over many years, ensured that he could never influence his ministers to the same extent as his father had done though he could cause them moments of anxiety.

Since 1782 the Irish Parliament in Dublin had achieved legislative independence which meant that it could not be so easily controlled as before by either the British government or the Westminster Parliament. Unfortunately, this concession by Britain had merely served to entrench the political influence of the Protestant Ascendancy in Ireland and it had done nothing to conciliate the Catholic majority. Tensions between the propertied elite and the impoverished masses and between the Catholics, Protestant Episcopalians and Protestant Dissenters remained as high as ever. The French Revolution did not cause the Irish problem, but it made a troubled situation worse. Fear of French principles spreading to Ireland encouraged the British government to support concessions to the Catholics, while admiration for French principles stimulated the Society of United Irishmen to demand major political reforms for all their fellow countrymen. Under this twin threat both the Protestant Ascendancy and the Dissenting majority in Ulster reacted strongly in defence of their special privileges. In despair at their failure to achieve reforms by peaceful means some United Irishmen, with a little encouragement from the French, looked to revolutionary France for political support and even military assistance. The connection between radical Irishmen and revolutionary France was never properly coordinated, but their efforts did exacerbate tensions within Ireland and did help to produce sectarian warfare, an ill-organised rebellion in 1798, and attempts to land French forces on the island. Thoroughly alarmed by this crisis, the British government used all its powers of persuasion and influence to convince the Protestant Ascendancy to give up legislative independence and to accept a fully incorporating union with the Westminster Parliament in 1800. The Act of Union significantly increased the size and changed the composition of the united Parliament, but since the king refused to concede Catholic emancipation and the social and economic position of the Irish majority was not improved, the Irish problem continued to cause divisions within both the government and opposition parties and it created major headaches for successive British governments up to the present day.

II

In the period from 1789 to 1815 parliamentary politics in Britain were characterised by four significant developments: a rallying behind the government of most of the propertied elite; reduced support for the Opposition Whigs; a more marked two-party structure; and, after a long period of dominance by the Younger Pitt, a decade or more of ministerial instability. It is quite possible that all of these developments might have occurred even if there had been no French Revolution and no prolonged French Wars. None the less, it is also quite possible to trace important connections between these major constitutional and political changes and the dramatic events in France.

Although the party of government in this period bore many similarities to that which existed before 1789, there were important changes which were influenced by the British reaction to the French Revolution. As Frank O'Gorman claims in his essay in this volume all ministries between 1789 and 1815 were as oligarchic and as aristocratic as any during the eighteenth century. Throughout the whole period an extremely limited number of individuals, most of them from aristocratic families, held cabinet office. This situation promoted cohesion and continuity in the party of government, particularly since so many of these men gained their political education by serving under the Younger Pitt. As with earlier ministries parliamentary support for the administrations between 1789 and 1815 came from a small group of professional politicians, nearly 200 MPs who were attached to the crown by places, pensions or other marks of royal favour, and a number of independent backbenchers who were always ready to support the king's ministers so long as they avoided a major disaster at home or abroad. During this period, however, the composition of ministerial majorities did undergo gradual, though significant, changes, largely because of the threat posed by France.

The popularity of the Younger Pitt's determination to oppose radical change at home and, eventually, to resist revolution abroad encouraged most young men with serious political ambitions to attach themselves to Pitt and the party of government rather than to Fox and the Opposition Whigs. Most rising young politicians looked for careers in a party of government dedicated to preserving the existing political and social order rather than with a discredited opposition. Pitt and his disciples were credited with a patriotic defence of the country and its major institutions. Their actions won over Edmund Burke, the more conservative Whigs led by the Duke of Portland, and, eventually, the great majority of the propertied elite. This governing party proved itself expert in exploiting the power of ideas to defend the existing constitution in church and state. Admiration for the British constitution, combined with growing alarm for its safety in the face of the French threat, led to the articulation and the dissemination of a conservative ideology of considerable appeal, resilience and intellectual power. Edmund Burke launched the first impassioned and sophisticated attack on the moral and intellectual claims of British radicals and French revolutionaries. He warned that, if such men were not opposed, they would destroy the established order in church and state, eliminate hierarchy, social harmony and justice, and incite the impoverished masses to pillage the wealth of the propertied classes. More recent research on the conservative ideology of this period has, however, focused less on Burke and more on the many less profound, but very influential writers (such as William Paley, William Cusac Smith, Robert Nares, Francis Plowden, Samuel Horsley, Samuel Cooper, Richard Hey and John Reeves), who endeavoured to counter the appeal of radical propagandists. These conservative theorists denounced radical claims based on universal natural rights and the sovereignty of the people. They rushed to defend the existing order with appeals to utility, morality, natural law, history and prescription.' Burke and these other conservative propagandists all argued that Britain was engaged in a war of ideas with both domestic radicals and foreign revolutionaries. In order to unite and to strengthen the ruling oligarchy they urged the nation to rally to the defence of the monarchy and the established church.

Whereas events in France increased the parliamentary majority of the party of government in the years after 1789, they also played a major role in dividing the Whig Party in opposition and in condemning the Foxite Whigs to nearly forty years in the political wilderness. The disintegration of the Whig opposition certainly owed much to purely domestic factors. Ever since 1783 Opposition Whig complaints against the royal prerogative had ensured that George III would do everything possible to keep them out of office. The political future for the Opposition Whigs looked very bleak after their disastrous handling of the Regency crisis in 1788–9 and the support of some of the Opposition Whigs for such liberal measures as Catholic relief, the repeal of the Test and Corporation Acts, and parliamentary reform was, by 1790, already putting a considerable strain on a parliamentary coalition which always contained an influential conservative element. Once the king's health was restored in 1789, the Whig Opposition was outwitted, even humiliated, by Pitt. Thereafter the Opposition Whigs suffered from divided counsels and erratic judgement and tied themselves too closely to the unpopular and irresponsible Prince of Wales. The internal problems facing the Opposition Whigs, however, were greatly exacerbated by their inability to unite in their response to the French Revolution and the French Wars. The Opposition Whigs disintegrated between 1792 and 1794 largely because Burke, Portland and other conservative Whigs could no longer accept the Foxite view that domestic radicals and French revolutionaries posed little threat to the political and social order within Britain. The anxiety created by prolonged war proved even more alarming than the political changes within France and it reduced even further the support for the Foxite Whigs both within Parliament and within the political nation as a whole. For the Foxite Whigs the years of the Revolutionary and Napoleonic Wars were, as John Derry shows below, years of protracted agony, when familiar loyalties were shattered, conventional assumptions were undermined and political expectations were repeatedly thwarted.

The Foxite view of the French Revolution was dominated by English assumptions and expectations. They mistakenly believed that the French were about to establish a constitutional monarchy on the English model. Even when the revolutionaries turned to violence the Foxites claimed that it was the absolutist powers of Europe, aided and abetted by the reactionary Pitt, who were more to blame than the French for the descent into anarchy, terror and dictatorship. The war against France was condemned as unjust and unnecessary. Peace could be had if the great powers ceased to intervene in French affairs. Such attitudes as these, maintained in the teeth of the evidence, ensured that the Opposition Whigs would never command a majority among the political elite so long as the French threat remained. At the same time the Foxite Whigs failed to enlist the enthusiastic support of radicals and reformers outside Parliament because their commitment to parliamentary reform was at best ambivalent and was almost invariably lukewarm. They failed to find and extend the middle ground in an age when political opinions were sharply polarised by events in France. Although the Foxite Whigs eloquently argued the case for peace and bravely tried to stem the tide of reaction, their efforts were condemned by the political elite as defeatist and unpatriotic and were rejected by the radicals as half-hearted and insincere. They ended up appearing opportunistic and irresponsible.

In their different responses to the French Revolution and the French Wars the Pittites and the Foxites were divided more than any other recent government and opposition by a yawning political and ideological gulf. No longer divided, as in the 1780s, primarily on the question of the royal prerogative, the two groups now increasingly differed over their attitudes to domestic reform, the French Revolution and the issues of war and peace. These major ideological differences propelled the Foxite Whigs further along the road to improved party organisation on which they had embarked before 1789. The need to put his conservative views into action also persuaded Pitt to accept that greater organisation was needed to rally his supporters in Parliament. This became even more advisable as the reduction in crown patronage and the precarious nature of the king's health meant that royal support could not produce as many ministerial supporters in Parliament as in previous decades. Although the Younger Pitt always regarded himself as an 'independent Whig' critics increasingly applied the label 'Tory' to ministries which defended the royal prerogative, supported the privileges of the Church of England, cultivated patriotic sentiment in the nation at large, encouraged militant loyalists and suppressed expressions of radical dissent. The term 'Tory' was common in many constituencies in the 1807 general election and it was soon thereafter accepted by pro-government backbenchers in Parliament. By 1815 Liverpool's administration accepted the label and the majority of MPs could be assigned to the Whig or Tory parties.[2]

Paradoxically, although the French Revolution and the French Wars did much both to rally a large majority in Parliament behind a conservative government opposed to French principles and French ambitions and to divide and weaken the Whig Opposition, these developments did not always produce a strong administration. The Younger Pitt's ministry did survive the crises of the 1790s, both at home and abroad, but his resignation in 1801 was followed by a succession of five short-lived ministries in little more than a decade. Any explanation for this failure to achieve ministerial stability must assign a significant role to the impact of the French Wars, though purely internal factors were not without their influence.

The ministerial instability of the early nineteenth century was due, in part, to circumstances which might have brought down ministries at any time in the eighteenth century. The resignation of Pitt in 1801 and the Ministry of all the Talents in 1807 owed much to the king's refusal to contemplate Catholic emancipation. Pitt's second administration ended with his death in 1806, while Spencer Perceval's collapsed with his assassination in 1812. Addington's ministry, the Talents' ministry and Portland's ministry all suffered from having too many able politicians in opposition. All the administrations between 1801 and 1812 were weakened by internal divisions and conflicts provoked by the unrestrained ambitions of such politicians as George Canning and the Marquess of Wellesley. In 1805 and again in 1809 political scandals involving Henry Dundas, Viscount Melville and the Duke of York respectively aroused intense public indignation and undermined support for the particular administrations in Parliament.

None the less, although such factors might have weakened any administration in the past, it seems certain that ministerial instability in the early nineteenth century owed much to disenchantment in and out of Parliament with governments unable to make peace or to defeat the forces of Napoleon. In these years Britain signed an unsatisfactory and short-lived peace treaty, faced the alarming prospect of invasion and saw the war in Europe stagger on from military disaster to military crisis. A succession of military reverses, the disastrous negotiations at the Convention of Cintra and the utter failure of the Walcheren expedition alienated public opinion and undermined the confidence of ministers. Even Wellington's peninsular campaigns appeared for many years to be a bloody and expensive sideshow with no prospect of inflicting a decisive defeat on the French. It was military defeat abroad rather than any internal failings that made so many otherwise able ministers appear so inadequate and incompetent. This view is confirmed by Lord Liverpool's success in establishing a durable and stable administration from 1812 onwards when the military tide finally turned and Britain participated in a stunning victory over the French.[3]

III

From 1789 to 1815 events in France stimulated intense political debate within Britain far beyond the confines of Parliament and deeply polarised public opinion on the question of reforming the British constitution. An extra-parliamentary movement anxious to see the reform of Parliament had, of course, existed for several decades before the outbreak of the French Revolution and signs of organised popular conservatism can be detected during the debate on the earlier American Revolution. None the less, there can be little doubt that events in France did much to revive the fortunes of the reform movement in the early 1790s, after it had declined in the mid 1780s. Soon thereafter hostile reactions to the French Revolution created a climate of opinion which seriously weakened the radical cause. It is also beyond question that the conservative reaction to radicalism at home and abroad stimulated the rapid growth of militant loyalism, while the French Wars were directly responsible for the appearance of a new and large-scale peace movement during these years.

The revived radicalism of the early 1790s had much in common with the reform movement of a decade and more earlier, but the stimulus of the French Revolution did produce some changes. Many veteran reformers and longstanding radical organisations gained new heart from the astonishing events in France, but the British Jacobins of the early 1790s drew rather more support from lower down the social scale and spread their influence to more urban areas. In their political aims most radicals still campaigned for the same extensive programme of parliamentary reform that had been first advocated by the Westminster Association in 1780. Most radicals also still based their political demands on the historic rights of Englishmen under the ancient constitution. On the other hand, Thomas Paine and a few others campaigned for the universal and inalienable natural rights of all men and they went beyond a demand for parliamentary reform when they advocated a democratic republic and a written constitution. Some British Jacobin claims went even further, arguing for improvements in the position of women, a more equal distribution of property and a number of social welfare reforms to improve the lot of the labouring poor. Nearly all the radicals of the 1790s followed the example of earlier radicals in appealing to reason and seeking converts through reasoned debate and printed propaganda. Again, only the more militant element attended the Conventions in Edinburgh, where French terms of address were used, or contemplated violent revolution to achieve reforms by force of arms. While most British radicals explicitly renounced the use of force, the 1790s did witness the appearance of new revolutionary organisations in Britain that were prepared to follow the French example of a violent overthrow of the existing political and social order. Modern historians still dispute the political effectiveness of the revolutionary groups in Britain and Ireland, and we are never likely to know the extent of their support, but, as both John Stevenson and Marianne Elliott show, it is impossible now to challenge the claim that a revolutionary conspiracy did flourish in various parts of the British Isles during the period of the French Revolution. It is also quite clear that these militant radicals, especially the United Irishmen, were in constant contact with the French and that they hoped to achieve their aims with the assistance of French arms.[4]

All popular protests and violent demonstrations in these years – from food riots to Luddite disturbances – had several causes, including bad harvests and technological innovations, but the economic distress which was the root cause owed much to the strains and tensions caused by the prolonged and expensive conflict with France. In other areas of popular politics the events in France had a more direct and a more profound influence. It is difficult to believe that the rise and spread of militant loyalism or the large-scale campaigns of 'the Friends of Peace' could have occurred if it had not been for the profound ideological impact of the French Revolution and the particularly severe consequences of the protracted Revolutionary and Napoleonic Wars.

The British people as a whole had long taken pride in their historic liberties and in their constitution, and they had frequently contrasted the benefits derived from these with the political disadvantages of their continental neighbours. They had also long expressed an antipathy towards the French and a willingness to rally to a patriotic defence of the nation's institutions when a French invasion seemed to threaten them. All of these conservative attitudes had been in evidence during the American Revolution, but it was not until the 1790s that the severe threat posed by the French Revolution stimulated the creation of a more organised and more sophisticated popular conservatism. Although the government deliberately encouraged the setting up of loyalist associations and although many of the tactics of the loyalists were modelled on the activities of the radicals, the sheer scale of loyalist activities in the 1790s was without precedent earlier in the eighteenth century. Loyalist clubs and societies, the exploitation of press and pulpit to disseminate conservative propaganda, the organisation of public meetings and street demonstrations, and the creation of Volunteer companies and other armed defence associations were on such a scale that they dwarfed even the activities of the radicals. As with the repressive measures of the government, the militant loyalists were the product of the alarm generated by the French Revolution and the French Wars. Together they combined to swamp the radical cause and to drive the reformers underground. Only when support for the French Revolution had clearly collapsed in Britain, and only after the protracted war with France had produced high taxation, severe economic distress, a bloated military establishment and evidence of political corruption and administrative incompetence, were there signs of a radical revival in Britain. Even then, it was not until after the end of the Napoleonic Wars that circumstances favoured a renewal of mass support for parliamentary reform.

For much of the period of loyalist dominance liberal opinion had little chance of enlisting mass support for constitutional reforms. What it was able to do, however, was to tap the widespread hostility to a bloody, protracted and expensive war that caused immense distress and offered little prospect of success. The 'Friends of Peace' were not a formally constituted party with a declared programme and a definite membership. They were a loose and informal alliance of various groups who espoused liberal opinions on a whole range of religious and political issues. Most of them were rational Christians or liberal Dissenters and they were largely drawn from the middle classes in the larger provincial towns, especially in West Yorkshire and South Lancashire. They did not share the loyalists' dread of the French Revolution, but they were appalled by the social, economic and moral consequences of the Revolutionary and Napoleonic Wars. Their religious principles led them to regard war as immoral, their enlightened views encouraged them to believe a negotiated peace and the brotherhood of all men were attainable objectives, and, on pragmatic grounds, they abhorred the economic damage, the physical suffering, the profiteering, the growth of executive power and the new barbarism which they associated with a war of huge dimensions and unprecedented savagery. They disseminated their views in newspapers, journals and individual pamphlets and they organised widespread and large-scale peace campaigns in 1795, 1797, 1801, 1807–8 and 1812. Their anti-war protests reached a crescendo in 1812, ironically just as the tide of war at last turned and victory suddenly loomed. As with the political radicals their cause was swamped by a patriotic tide which welcomed the prospect of a great and lasting victory over France after twenty years of war.[5]

IV

While it is difficult to calculate the impact of the French Revolution on British politics, both inside and outside Parliament, it is self-evident that the Revolutionary and Napoleonic Wars had a profound influence on the conduct of British diplomacy and the deployment of Britain's military, naval and economic resources during these years. Nevertheless, it is still difficult to assess how different Britain's efforts were in these wars compared to the responses she made in earlier wars with France in the eighteenth century.

Britain's diplomatic response to the French Revolution was certainly dictated by events over the preceding century. Ministers were convinced that France was by far Britain's most dangerous rival and so they welcomed the fact that the Revolution appeared to have weakened her ability to threaten Britain's imperial, commercial and naval interests. When French power revived and France threatened to dominate her near neighbours, Britain sought European allies, as in previous wars, as a means of keeping French military power within bounds. Throughout the

Revolutionary and Napoleonic Wars Britain pursued similar objectives to those she had pursued in earlier conflicts with France. She hoped to exclude French power from the Low Countries, she wished to prevent French armies advancing into Germany, and she tried to prevent the French forging an effective alliance with Spain. Britain's chief aim throughout the conflict was to maintain a balance of power in western Europe, but this did not prevent her seeking to conquer French colonies and to expand her trade to all parts of the world. The desire for permanent maritime security in particular made Britain anxious to destroy France's fleets and naval bases. Unfortunately, the other great powers of Europe did not share all of Britain's objectives, especially her naval and commercial aims, and they had their own pressing interests in eastern Europe. They were therefore reluctant to join alliances with Britain which appeared to serve her interests rather than their own and which forced them to bear the brunt of French assaults. To encourage these powers to keep their forces in the field Britain adopted her usual policy of supplying them with huge financial subsidies.

Many of Britain's diplomatic aims and tactics were therefore similar to those pursued in earlier wars with France. The differences, which were largely forced upon her, were due to the peculiar nature of the threat posed by the French Revolution and to the sheer scale of the conflict. Since French aggression appeared to stem from the character of her internal regime, Britain was more prepared than on any previous occasion to support resistance movements within France and to use external force to change the nature of the French government, though, as Michael Duffy argues below, this policy often seemed unattainable and so in many peace negotiations it had to be abandoned. It was only after all the major powers had concluded that it was impossible to contain Napoleon's ambitions without removing him from power that a coalition was built up which made a Bourbon restoration a serious possibility. The sheer scale of the conflict with France also forced Britain to commit much larger resources to all aspects of the war than had been necessary in past contests. Since France put more of her resources into continental expansion than she had in earlier eighteenth-century wars with Britain, Britain, for her part, had ultimately to involve herself more closely with the affairs of Europe. She learned to take seriously the problems in central and eastern Europe that preoccupied the other major powers and she had eventually to support a considerable body of troops on the continent where they could assist her allies by diverting a substantial number of French troops from the eastern front.

During much of this prolonged struggle with France Britain waged war much as she had done in earlier wars with her great rival. She used her navy and much of her army to secure colonial and commercial advantages overseas, while offering financial subsidies and small expeditionary forces to encourage her European allies to tie down French forces on the continent. In the early stages of the war she hoped to exploit France's internal problems so that she herself could become the paramount naval and commercial power in the world. It was the sheer size, the skill, and the ardour of the French armies that compelled Britain to reconsider her strategic priorities. While securing herself from invasion and preserving her commercial advantages, Britain had to commit much larger resources than she had previously contemplated to the war on the continent of Europe. In adopting this strategy Britain reverted to the strategy adopted in Marlborough's war in the early eighteenth century, although at greater cost.

In pursuing the long struggle with France Britain raised larger naval and military forces than ever before and, as Piers Mackesy shows, she also had to improve their quality. The navy's infrastructure was improved, dockyards and storehouses were reformed, new ships of the line were built and old ones were systematically repaired. The shortage of seamen remained a major problem throughout the long conflict and there were never enough warships to perform all the tasks required of the navy. Despite the strains placed upon it, however, the Royal Navy performed its strategic role with considerable success and without the benefit of any major new innovations in structure, tactics or weapons. It performed similar tasks to those fulfilled in earlier wars, but on a larger scale, for a more prolonged period of intense conflict and with the support of superb officers and ratings. The state of the army, on the other hand, was deplorable when war broke out and more substantial reforms were necessary before any significant successes were possible against experienced French troops. It took some time for the army to remedy its defects. Eventually firm supervision was imposed, the new drill manual was properly enforced, and light infantry tactics were integrated into the regular order of battle. The army was increased to an unprecedented size until by the end of the Napoleonic War there were 187,000 British regular troops, in addition to a large number of foreign and colonial troops and a huge defence force. Even then, this army was usually so stretched over the whole globe that it could not easily deploy a large strike force of troops on the continent. None the less, good training, ample supplies, prolonged experience in the field, and the supreme talents of Wellington eventually combined to enable Britain to perform with considerable credit in the Peninsula.

Britain's ability to sustain war against France for more years than any of her European allies owed much to her island position and to her command of the seas, but it also owed a great deal to her remarkable ability to tap the financial resources of the nation. In all their wars with France since 1689 British governments had shown an admirable ability to raise huge sums of money through taxes and loans which gave them an effective financial weapon to deploy against the French. The protracted and expensive Revolutionary and Napoleonic Wars put a huge strain on Britain's fiscal and financial system, but, as Patrick O'Brien shows, it rose to the challenge with remarkable success though not without considerable strain. This success was not simply the consequence of faster economic growth, since this was not yet markedly superior to that of France, but was principally due to Britain's political and administrative capacity to improve what was already an exceptionally effective fiscal and financial system. This capacity to raise vast sums in order to wage expensive wars was built up by a continuous process of legislative innovation and administrative developments over more than a century. Important changes were also made during the Revolutionary and Napoleonic Wars when an unprecedented financial burden was put on the British state.

The Younger Pitt had made some reforms of the financial system before the outbreak of war, but during the prolonged conflict with France he and his successors had to raise taxes and loans on a scale unheard of and unimagined by previous generations. Such colossal sums were only raised with considerable difficulty and by a series of uncoordinated expedients. Pitt and his successors simply concocted policies as they went along, raising more taxes and larger loans whenever it could be done. One major change, the suspension of the gold standard, was simply forced upon the government, though the change brought some benefits. Ministers eventually decided on a radical departure from long-established methods and determined to finance a far higher proportion of public expenditure from taxation than any previous government in order to contain the growth of the national debt (though this did rise inexorably throughout the wars). Some extra revenue did come from the expansion of the economy, from administrative reforms and from curbs on smuggling, but most of the increased revenue had to come from over twenty new taxes and from higher rates applied to existing taxes. The most productive and controversial innovation was the new income tax, first raised in 1799, which contributed more than a quarter of the extra money raised for the war. By means such as this the government raised enough money every year to fight a war of unprecedented scale, scope and duration, without placing an intolerable financial burden on later generations.

v

Since the French Revolution and the French Wars coincided with a period of rapid demographic growth, major economic changes and sustained urbanisation, it is particularly difficult to detect to what extent perceptible changes in the economy and in society were the product of the Industrial Revolution and to what extent they were shaped by events in France. Those historians who have investigated the economy in particular are convinced that significant changes were underway before the outbreak of the French Revolution. On the other hand, as François Crouzet argues below, the extent to which the French Wars encouraged or hindered further change is an almost insoluble problem because of the difficulty of isolating any particular factor in the process of change. It is impossible to know whether the economy would have stayed on the same course if war had not broken out or to determine whether any deviations during the period of hostilities were the direct consequence of the conflict.

Economic change was invariably the result of several different causes. The expansion of the cotton trade, for example, owed much to technological changes, which reduced costs and hence prices, but it also owed something to the opening of new markets due to the war. When exports fell back after 1800 this was partly due to the war disrupting trade and partly due to a saturation of the market. The war probably pushed up some prices, especially of agricultural produce, but the growing population also pushed up prices by increasing the demand for limited supplies. The huge sums raised by government taxation and loans absorbed a large share of the nation's savings and deprived the private sector of capital, but it is not clear how far productive investment was kept below the level it might have reached if there had been no wars and therefore to what extent, if any, the economy was hampered. The standard of living of the labouring classes did fall at times during the French Wars, but this was not solely or directly attributable to the war. Again, bad harvests and a rising population put severe pressure on prices and adversely affected wages in some years. One direct and obvious effect of the French Wars was the dislocation of international trade and the severe check placed on some exports, especially during the years of the Continental Blockade from 1806 to 1813, when Napoleon tried to defeat Britain by preventing her exports reaching European markets. Britain did undoubtedly reap some commercial gains by acquiring French and Dutch colonies and by opening up trade with South America after 1808, but such gains were either short-lived or less profitable than expected. The needs of the war machine certainly stimulated the iron industry, the clothing industry and shipbuilding, though the effect on building was probably negative. What is clear is that Britain did manage both to win the war and to improve her economy.

The enormous burdens of the French Wars undoubtedly placed a great strain on the social fabric of the nation, but it is not always clear whether these tensions were due to rapid economic change or were the consequences of the wars themselves. Military conflict, for example, highlighted but did not create the divisions between the old and new capitalist elites. The war also probably stimulated ideas of free trade and encouraged business interests to support pressure groups seeking to influence Parliament, but both of these developments were in evidence both before and after the French Wars. The involvement of large numbers of the middle classes in Volunteer companies or the peace movement may also have increased, though it did not initiate, their assertiveness and their criticisms of the landed elite. What cannot be denied is that the financial demands of the war hit some social groups more than others and that the almost insatiable demand for recruits led to the mobilisation of a higher percentage of the male population of military age than ever before. The lower classes bore the brunt of these burdens and, at times, this had a significant effect on the poor rates and on public order. Yet the impact of war was not always negative, as Clive Emsley seeks to demonstrate. He sees some correlation between military participation and social or political advancement, though he is careful not to push the case too far and he concedes that it is difficult to prove that the men who fought the war or who supplied the needs of the armed services were much better off because of their sacrifices and their efforts.

Whereas conclusions on what impact the French Revolution and French Wars had on economic and social developments can only be tentative, it is possible to be much more certain of their influence on literature and religion in Britain. As Iain Robertson Scott's essay rightly claims it is quite clear that most of the principal writers of the period (and, indeed, many of the lesser ones too) were drawn into the intense debate on the French Revolution and into considering the consequences of

Napoleon's military ambitions. The literary world was as divided in its responses as the political world, with some writers supporting the French and even praising Napoleon, while many others were in the vanguard of the counter-revolution. Wordsworth, Coleridge, Southey, Blake and Hazlitt, to list but the most obvious commentators, were caught up in the intense public discussions on the significance of the French Revolution and on how best to respond to the actions of Napoleon. Indeed, it is difficult to understand the changes in the principles and the ideas, perhaps even the development of the literary style, of such writers as Wordsworth and Coleridge, without an appreciation of what was going on in France and how Britain was responding to such events. Many other writers, most notably William Godwin and the Jacobin novelists, were so stimulated by developments in France that they believed they must make a positive contribution to the discussion of French ideas and French conduct. Hundreds of minor poets also observed the events in France, while literally thousands of caricatures made satirical comments upon internal French developments, the threat France posed to Britain and the dazzling career of Napoleon. Even writers such as Jane Austen, whose work appeared to pay no attention to political or military events, can be shown to have been influenced by the French Revolution and the French Wars.[6]

The connection between religion and politics was also particularly close in this period because of the significance of French events for public morality and ecclesiastical institutions. It was a widely held view in Britain that the French Revolution posed a major threat to the traditional authority (even the traditional teaching) of the Christian churches because the revolutionaries launched a frontal attack on the wealth, privileges and authority of the Catholic Church and Napoleon later seriously weakened the power of the Pope and the ecclesiastical hierarchy. Edmund Burke and many others thought that the threat was not limited to France but had profound implications for all Christian countries because French principles were an assault on Christian morality and ecclesiastical authority. The French were condemned for seeking to establish a godless society throughout Europe that would bring social anarchy and widespread immorality in its wake. While it is true that a minority of Rational Dissenters in Britain, most notably Richard Price and Joseph Priestley, welcomed the outbreak of the French Revolution and hoped its example would further the cause of political and religious liberty in Britain, most Christians feared the consequences of the French Revolution for their religion and their churches. In response to this perceived threat, they campaigned vigorously for a strengthening of the old order in church and state and they condemned all those who wished to challenge the traditional authority of established ecclesiastical structures.

Many of the Anglican clergy and their secular supporters had become increasingly conservative in their political views in the years before the French Revolution, largely in response to the demands of those who campaigned for religious reforms and political change. Shocked by the French Revolution and convinced that British reformers wished to emulate the French, they rushed to defend the privileges of the Church of England and they insisted that the established church was an essential buttress to Britain's much admired constitution. Staunch Anglicans, especially High Church clergymen such as George Horne, William Jones and George Berkeley and their lay allies such as John Reeves, John Bowles and John Gifford, played a major role in articulating and disseminating a conservative ideology which stressed the virtues and benefits of the existing constitution in church and state. The established church was praised as a vital bulwark to national unity, public morality and social order. In many areas it was the staunch Anglicans who provided the backbone of loyalist organisations and helped to provoke a backlash against those who supported parliamentary reform and the repeal of the Test and Corporation Acts. Some of them were even prepared to condone the use of violence against radical Dissenters and to rouse popular prejudices against the critics of the established church.

Political conservatism was not confined to High Church Anglicans. The Evangelicals too were particularly active in this period, not only in preaching the importance of strict morality but in defending the existing constitution in church and state. Even the leaders of Methodism, who were beginning to break their remaining ties with the Church of England after the death of John Wesley in 1791, were determined to preach the virtues of political loyalty and the merits of social obedience. Although it is going much too far to claim that Methodism saved Britain from revolution (apart from anything else they were simply not numerous enough to effect such a result) and although some Methodists were active in radical and trade union circles, it is clear, none the less, that the majority of Methodist leaders supported the proclamations of their Annual Conferences that were constantly urging loyalty to the existing constitution and submission to the prevailing social order. This conservative leadership tried, whenever it could, to discipline those members who appeared tainted with radicalism or involved in subversion. This policy caused the Kilhamites and the Primitive Methodists to break away from the main body of the Methodist movement. It is also clear that many loyalist statements emanated from the formal institutions of the older Dissenting groups and that it was only a minority of Dissenters, though a vocal one, which campaigned vigorously for parliamentary reform.

Although there is substantial evidence to justify the claim that religion was largely on the side of reaction in this period, there were still some indications that religion could promote liberal causes. Although the campaign to repeal the Test and Corporation Acts collapsed in the 1790s the liberal Dissenters were not demoralised for long. They played a prominent part for many years in the campaign for peace and by 1812 they had secured the repeal of the Conventicle and Five Mile Acts, which were part of the old Clarendon Code, and they were beginning to revive the campaign for the repeal of the Test and Corporation Acts. Furthermore, throughout this period, the cause of Catholic relief secured greater prominence and wider support than ever before. The Catholic Church, once despised and feared by Protestants, was now seen as a valuable bulwark against revolutionary principles. In Ireland the government made a number of concessions to Catholics, even granting some of them the vote, and full Catholic emancipation was regarded as such a pressing issue that ministers resigned when the king resolutely opposed it in 1801 and 1807. Despite these setbacks the whole question of full toleration for Catholics remained a subject of public debate and even of parliamentary discussion in 1812 and 1813. Thus, in religion as in so many other spheres, the impact of the French Revolution and the French Wars succeeded in both advancing and hindering, often at the same time, some major developments in British society.[7]

1. Pitt and the 'Tory' Reaction to the French Revolution 1789-1815

FRANK O'GORMAN

THE reaction of the government of Pitt the Younger to the French Revolution has usually been discussed in the context of *reaction* and *repression*. The ministers of George III have been criticised by some for their alarmism and their exaggerated reaction to the imagined dangers of a radical agitation that was as innocent as it was moderate. By others, they have been congratulated upon successfully negotiating the treacherous waters of the 1790s and upon bringing home the ship of state into a safe harbour without permanent damage to its structures. Both versions of events have their champions, even today. Such partisan categories of interpretation, however, restrict our understanding of what really happened in British politics in the 1790s. The state *did* take upon itself unprecedented powers and adopt quite novel attitudes and instruments with which to confront its revolutionary enemies. It is the counterpoint between these novelties, on the one hand, and the continuation and extension of existing tendencies, on the other, which provides the major theme of this essay. Its overriding conclusion is that the British state was successful in containing the threat posed by the French Revolution and the wars which accompanied it, a success made possible by the ability, and the political will, of Pitt in straining almost to their very limits the latent powers of the state in the Hanoverian body politic. This success was not, however, achieved at the cost of freezing the political development of Great Britain during this period, an impression too easily fostered by excessive concentration upon the themes of reaction and repression. The oligarchy of George III's England was able, in the last analysis, to adapt itself and its practices to the needs of the revolutionary challenges which it faced and, in the process, to broaden its political base and to mobilise its supporters.

Nevertheless, oligarchic tendencies unquestionably conveyed a certain momentum and imparted a certain continuity of personnel in government. It is almost superfluous to affirm that the most important single defining characteristic of the Hanoverian state was its tendency to confine political, as well as economic and social, power in the hands of a small number of individuals and families. As John Cannon has recently reminded us, an aristocratic monopoly of offices was not a preserve of the *ancien régime* monarchies of the continent. It was no less marked in England.[1] In the age of the French Revolution there was to be no diluting this concentration of power. Although the number of peerage creations began to rise during the administration of Pitt this had little impact upon the composition of the cabinet. Between December 1783 and July 1794 fifteen different individuals held cabinet office, only three of whom were commoners: Pitt himself, Henry Dundas and William Wyndham Grenville, Pitt's cousin, who, in fact, acquired a peerage in 1790. Between the reconstruction of Pitt's cabinet in July 1794 and the fall of his government in 1801 an additional seven further individuals held cabinet office of whom only one, William Windham, was a commoner. Similarly, in Addington's cabinet of twelve, only one, Addington himself, was a commoner. Subsequently, in Pitt's second ministry only two out of fifteen cabinet ministers were commoners: Pitt and Addington, the latter taking a peerage in 1805. In the Talents ministry of 1806–7 four out of thirteen holders of cabinet office were commoners, Fox, Windham, Tom Grenville and Charles Grey. (The latter, in fact, succeeded to the family peerage a few months after the fall of the ministry.) In Portland's ministry of 1807–9 only two cabinet ministers (Spencer Perceval and George Canning) out of thirteen were commoners and in Perceval's ministry of 1809–12 only three (Spencer Perceval, Richard Ryder and Robert Dundas) out of seventeen. Altogether, of the fifty-two individuals who held cabinet office between 1783 and 1812 only twelve were commoners and of these twelve only seven remained commoners: Pitt, Windham, Fox, Perceval, Canning, Tom Grenville and Ryder.

This extremely limited number of individuals who held an office in the cabinet over a period of almost thirty years lent a certain cohesion to its activities and deliberations while the tendency for many individuals to accept office in successive administrations undoubtedly promoted continuity and experience. What this meant in practice was the domination of cabinet appointments by those who had received their political education at the hands of Willliam Pitt the Younger. For example, of the fifteen members of the cabinet in Pitt's second administration only five, Lords Barham, Buckingham, Harrowby, Montrose and Mulgrave, had *not* served either in Addington's ministry or in Pitt's first ministry. Again, on its appointment in 1812 no fewer than ten of the thirteen members of Liverpool's cabinet had served in Pitt's second administration of 1804–6. Similarly, ten had served in one or other of the two administrations immediately preceding Liverpool's. From 1783 to 1812, and, indeed, on to 1827, there is massive continuity in cabinet personnel. This, after all, is what George III had always preferred. He had hated anything resembling a clean sweep and, what might be implied in that, a change of measures. He infinitely preferred a reconstruction of the existing administration even if, on occasion, he had through the exercise of his prerogative significantly contributed to the downfall of the administration which it was then necessary to reconstruct. His differences with Pitt in 1800–1 and with the Talents in 1807 are revealing cases in point.

In normal circumstances, however, these governments of Britain during the revolutionary period were able to maintain themselves in power with a reasonable degree of confidence. This was a remarkable achievement in view of the fact that Pitt the Younger prided himself on his anti-party principles. He did not sustain himself in office with an organised party, preferring to rely upon the Court and Administration group, organised by the Treasury, and by the voluntary support and informal cooperation of the country gentlemen in Parliament. The situation was neatly summarised by the 'Third Party Circular' of 1788.[2] The backbone of Pitt's support was the 'Party of the Crown' (185 MPs). To these could be added in normal circumstances 108 Independent MPs. Pitt's own party numbered only 52 MPs while 'Detached Parties supporting the Present Administration' yielded a further 43 MPs. Two things need to be stressed about this analysis. First, of the 388 MPs upon whom Pitt depended for his majority (out of a House of 558 MPs) only 52 regarded themselves as personally attached to him. The Circular, in fact, underlines the point that the Party of the Crown 'would probably support his Majesty's Government under any Minister not peculiarly unpopular'. The non-party basis of Pitt's support could not be better illustrated. Secondly, of the 52 MPs who are described as 'The Party attached to Mr. Pitt' only 20 would support Pitt out of office. Pitt's party was not, in fact, a 'party' at all. Pitt had not built it up and, indeed, was at times even embarrassed by its existence. It was a small body of men which included close friends of Pitt as well as ambitious career politicians.

Such was the composition of ministerial majorities during the years immediately preceding the revolutionary period. Thereafter, although the basis upon which those majorities was constructed was gradually changing they were at no time endangered during the revolutionary period. The general election of 1790 left Pitt with a parliamentary majority of around 160. The succeeding years of war and revolution enhanced his position. After the election of 1796 he enjoyed a majority of over 250. After the election of 1802 Addington had a majority of almost 200. Both Portland after the election of 1807 and Liverpool after that of 1812 enjoyed majorities of almost 150.[3] None of these governments was in much danger from defeat by votes in the House of Commons. Nevertheless, the continued stability of an administration was not quite as straightforward as these figures might suggest. As we have seen, the king's opinions could weaken and destroy even the strongest government. Furthermore, no administration could guarantee itself against the unforeseen death of its leader. Both Pitt and Perceval died in office. Divisions within a cabinet and, perhaps, the demoralisation of its leaders, could unsettle an administration which still enjoyed a comfortable majority, as happened to Addington in 1804. All governments, moreover, and not just those of the revolutionary period, needed to cultivate Members of Parliament with the greatest care and patience. Their support could never be taken for granted, especially in that most sensitive of all areas, religion.

As the revolutionary period advanced, however, British governments came to adopt the principles and practice of party in organising their support both within Parliament and out-of-doors. So long as Pitt the Younger remained in office, however, such developments were held in check. Pitt had built his political career upon a repudiation of party principles and regarded himself to the end of his days as an independent Whig. His ministry was founded upon his own abilities and his unswerving devotion to the monarchy and to the national interest, not to any party principles or party combinations. The fall of Pitt in 1801 did not, therefore, represent the defeat of any party. The establishment of Addington's ministry represented little more than new management of existing men and resources.

At the level of practical politics, however, necessities were shaping the development of party, even on the ministerial benches. Even at the time of the establishment of Pitt's administration in 1783–84 those who supported George III in his titanic struggle against Charles James Fox 'had been forced to adopt the techniques of party itself – letters of attendance, pairing arrangements, cordinated tactics, organised propaganda, and electoral planning'.[4] Thereafter, the voluntaristic nature of Pitt's support demanded a high degree of organisation and planning. As the years passed, the ministry acquired a confidence and a character which contrasted sharply with the qualities exhibited by the Foxite Whigs on the opposition benches. In particular, the middle years of the 1790s exhibited a sharp ideological gulf between the government and the opposition on a series of issues: war and peace, parliamentary reform, Catholic emancipation. It was not yet the case that a 'Tory' government confronted a 'Whig' opposition. Nevertheless, the days when politicians differed essentially over their attitudes towards the royal prerogative and their perceptions of secret influence were clearly numbered.

The fall of Pitt in 1801 was almost fatal to the unity of the governing order. The governing coalition was fragmented into a number of groups – Pittites, Addingtonians, Grenvilles, Canningites and, later, supporters of Wellesley. During the undignified scramble for office which dominated politics between 1801 and 1812 there were signs that Pitt's own supporters wished to act a more decided part as a group. They were, after all, men of business. They had been reared in the service of the executive and they now chafed impatiently out of office. Pitt himself refused to sanction party activity. Consequently, the establishment of Pitt's second administration in 1804 owed nothing to party action. Nevertheless, the manifest deficiencies of that administration – its narrow basis and its failure to reunite the old Pittite coalition which had governed the country in the 1790s – gave rise to demands for cohesion and unity. After Pitt's death in 1806 his supporters began to act as a group. Within six months they had declared a systematic opposition to the Ministry of All the Talents, something which Pitt would never have approved and which during the ministry of Addington (1801–4) he had deliberately avoided. With the resignation of the Talents the Pittites trooped thankfully back into office. At the general election of 1807 they rallied royalist and Anglican opinion in the country as they vindicated the king's action in resisting the Talents' attempt to force the principle of Catholic emancipation on the monarch. The revival, and the subsequent intensification, of religious prejudices did much to arouse extra-parliamentary opinion, especially on the 'Tory' side, and to align it with parliamentary groupings.

The process by which the old Pittite coalition was reconstituted and transformed into a Tory party was well advanced by 1815. The ministries of Portland (1807–9) and Perceval (1809–12) reunited Pitt's followers and reaccustomed them to the routine of executive government. Although the role of the monarchy remained an influential element in politics, ministries by now enjoyed considerable independence of action. There was little serious discussion about the role of the monarch and his advisers in politics after 1811. The debates and divisions on the Regency in 1810-11 noticeably clarified and hardened political loyalties. When the monarch ceased to play the role of party leader the way was clear for a 'Tory' rather than a 'King's' government, especially when greater political coherence was beginning to inform ministerial politics. In Perceval's administration Sidmouth's connection was absorbed back into the main body of the Pittites. During the ministry of Lord Liverpool (1812-27) these tendencies accelerated. The ministry quickly incorporated the connections of Canning and Wellesley and, eventually (in 1821), even that of Lord Grenville. The repressive policies of the ministry between 1815 and 1820, so reminiscent of those of Pitt, attracted the epithet 'Tory'. By then the word 'Whig' was normally employed to identify the parliamentary opposition and its supporters. A 'Tory' government thus confronted a 'Whig' opposition.

British governments of the revolutionary era combined a genuine loyalty to the monarchy with a growing appreciation of, and attention to, the national interests of the country, qualities which had not always been strongly apparent during the eighteenth century. For example, although many contemporaries found much to criticise in William Pitt's handling of the war in the 1790s, and although many colleagues complained both of his imperiousness and his secretiveness, his ministry was never seriously in danger between 1789 and 1800. His patriotism could not be brought into question. Nor could that of his successors. The administrations of the revolutionary period were more securely based in power than most of their Hanoverian counterparts. They rested on a firm, at times fanatical, basis of opinion in the country combined with the support of the crown. (Only the Catholic issue, on which both of these conditions were lacking, provoked serious ministerial disruptions.)

These governments also enjoyed the advantage of a fatally divided, and, for many years, profoundly demoralised opposition. The coalition of the conservative, right-wing aristocratic Whigs of the Duke of Portland with Pitt's government in July 1794 was something of a watershed in the history of party.[5] Although it would be unwise to exaggerate the success of the coalition - the Portland Whigs at first hoped to preserve their party identity as 'Whigs' even within the government - there were formidable ideological justifications for the coalition: to repel the French abroad by an aggressive military strategy and to subdue the rising tide of domestic radicalism, if necessary by the restraint of popular liberties. Government and opposition were now divided by yawning differences over the prosecution of the war and the desirability of reform. No wonder that a sharper approach to both these issues was quickly evident within weeks of the successful negotiation of the Pitt-Portland coalition.[6]

Although the Foxite Whigs eventually enforced their claim to the terminology 'Whig' it was to be some years before successive governments adopted the converse terminology 'Tory'. After all, Pitt always regarded himself as an Independent Whig and never accepted the legitimacy of party combination either in opposition or, especially, in government. The Portland coalition did not turn Pitt's government into a party ministry. Rather, it extended its range of personnel and opinion until it very nearly achieved the status of a government of national unity. Furthermore, the political and social establishment which Pitt's government was defending was indisputably a Whiggish one based, as it was, upon a constitutional monarchy, parliamentary government, religious toleration, administrative decentralisation and a combination of the minimal superintendence of the lives of individuals with the maximum protection of property. Consequently, party terminology was not widely employed in the 1790s. There were, however, anticipations of what was to come. *The Anti-Jacobin Magazine* in 1800 contrasted 'our High Church and Tory principles' with 'the modern Whigs, and their associates, who see nothing praiseworthy in our present constitution'.

During the next ten years party terminology became much more common. The death of Pitt removed one powerful obstacle in the way of party usage. At the same time, the disreputability of the old word 'Tory', with its connotations of Jacobitism and treason, could not possibly be applied to the intensely loyalist governments of Pitt and his successors. The revival of the religious issue in the early years of the nineteenth century polarised sentiment in the country quite sharply, especially at the general election of 1807, when party labels were heard once again in the constituencies. By then a self-consciously 'Tory' and Anglican establishment, dedicated to the preservation of the British constitution and the conservation of British institutions, had appropriated the language and culture of patriotism in its service and utilised the enormous new power of monarchical sentiment in its support. Furthermore, as Professor Foord has argued,[7] there was more than a little that *was* 'Tory' about the policies of British governments at the turn of the century: the cultivation of patriotic sentiment, the defence of prerogative, the repression of radical dissent, the curtailment of the freedom of the press and, in spite of Pitt's earlier pluralist sentiments, the defence of Anglicanism.[8]

The broad political reaction to the French Revolution in government circles, then, may be summarised in the following terms: Pitt and his successors succeeded, on the whole, in defending both the country and its institutions. In so doing they enlisted the support of powerful and intersecting groups: landed, industrial, commercial, Anglican. Most of all, they mobilised the power of ideas in defence of the constitution in church and state.

There was nothing necessarily new in this. The ruling elite of Hanoverian Britain was accustomed to celebrating its regime and its constitution in favourable terms. Rule by a favoured and privileged minority was part of the natural order of things, sanctioned by God, justified by prescription, enforced through the laws of man and, not least, through the moral authority of the church. After the uncertainty generated through Jacobite rebellions had evaporated there developed what John Cannon has termed 'an almost hysterical regard for the constitution'.[9] A stream of writers gave thanks for the self-regulating balance of the constitution which guaranteed a unique mixture of strong government and popular liberty. As Pitt himself remarked in his famous budget speech of 17 February 1792:

> It is this union of liberty with law, which, by raising a barrier equally firm against the encroachments of power, and the violence of popular commotions, affords to property its just security, produces the exertion of genius and labour, the extent and solidity of credit, the circulation and increase of capital; which forms and upholds the national character, and sets in motion all the springs which actuate the great mass of the community through all its various descriptions.[10]

Constitutional arrangements, therefore, underpinned the social, as well as the political stability, upon which Britain had built her commercial and economic prosperity.

The threat to Britain presented by the French Revolution, a threat at first intellectual, then political and, finally, military, not surprisingly elicited considerable discussion of the legitimacy of the existing power structure. Edmund Burke, for example, renewed prevailing justifications of authority and panegyrics on the constitution but he added a number of novel elements. He repudiated the French Revolution because it was inspired by the philosophy of the Enlightenment and, in particular, its atheism and its belief in the perfectibility of man. Burke always argued in the 1790s that Britain was engaged in a war of ideas, an ideological confrontation, which had to be won at the level of ideas. To treat the wars of the revolutionary period like the traditional campaigns of eighteenth-century warfare, he argued, was entirely to misunderstand the danger in which Britain stood from the contamination of Jacobinism.[11] He fashioned a prescriptive interpretation of English history in general, and a 'Conservative' version of the Glorious Revolution in particular. He exhibited a fresh and sharp awareness of the organic complexity of civilised, social existence. At the same time, his prescriptive approach to laws and institutions endowed the Anglican state of Britain with historic pedigrees of incalculable legitimising force.

Conservative writers of the 1790s like Burke were consciously reformulating an ideology to unite the ruling elite, to defend its political institutions, to protect its power structure and to discredit its opponents. Its key components may be seen in the pages of The Anti-Jacobin, published in 1797-8 while one of Bonaparte's armies was camped on the French coasts opposite Britain. The recurring themes were to emphasise the benefits of living under the British constitution (in contrast to the anarchy and bloodshed of France), to protect the institutions and establishments of the country, in church as well as state, to rally the people, to promote patriotism and patriotic sacrifice, to identify reformers with Jacobins and to repudiate the egalitarian doctrines of Jacobinism, to proclaim the virtues of order and discipline, the demands of family and community over and against those of individualism, to affirm the belief that God intended man to be a social being and that man had 'rights' in, and only in, society. The symbol of the British state in the 1790s, however, was the monarchy. The valedictory issue of The Anti-Jacobin on 2 July 1798 stated in all seriousness that the character and example of George III had helped to save the nation from the prospect of atheism! This idealisation of monarchy was not merely personal. In the 1790s the ideal of a 'balanced' constitution began to give way to the ideal of a monarchical constitution. It became widely accepted that the monarchy was the most ancient element in the constitution, the stock from which its other branches had sprung, the linch-pin of constitutional practice. Some writers revived the notion of the Divine Right of kings. What, indeed, had the Glorious Revolution been about if it had not been about the cause of the indefeasible right of hereditary monarchy?[12]

It was, of course, entirely paradoxical that a 'Tory' ideology was being mobilised in defence of a Whig revolution, a Whig constitution and an administration that still regarded itself as Whig. Nevertheless, it is an interesting exercise in the social history of ideas to witness the transposition of meaning and reality, from Whig to Tory. Increasingly, the personnel, the techniques and, most of all, the arguments employed on the establishment side in the ideological warfare of the 1790s seem less than Whiggish.[13] By the end of the revolutionary period, however, a self-consciously Anglican and a profoundly monarchist establishment, dedicated to the preservation and conservation of the British constitution, and to the repression of radicalism and reform at home, was governing the country. Furthermore, it had succeeded in broadening its appeal and in mobilising anti-radical sentiment within England itself. The development of a popular patriotic and loyalist mentality was to prove a momentous step in the evolution of the British state and nation.[14]

The key element in any discussion of the British government's reaction to the French Revolution was Pitt's hostility to the revolution and, in particular, his repressive attitude towards domestic radicalism. In fact, Pitt had been extremely careful from the first to keep an open mind on the issue of the French Revolution, remaining independent in his foreign policy, unwilling to commit himself either way. He refused, politely but firmly, Necker's request in June 1789 for supplies of flour to alleviate shortages in France on the grounds that 'the precarious prospect of the harvest' threatened comparable shortages in Britain.[15] In the months that followed, Pitt was anxious to maintain his neutrality, especially when harshly divergent attitudes towards the Revolution were expressed on the Opposition benches in Parliament by Charles James Fox and Edmund Burke. Nevertheless, the outbreak of war in Europe in the spring of 1792 and the deteriorating situation in France led to a reformulation of his even-handed attitude. In the winter of 1792-3 the French started to direct threats of revolution against Britain herself, threats which led to the outbreak of hostilities between the two countries in February 1793.

It was in this climate that Pitt's repressive policy occurred. It is important to be clear, however, that this 'policy' acquired several different forms and operated on several different levels. *First*, the government was anxious to utilise existing disciplinary mechanisms as strongly as possible. This meant, above all, alerting the magistracy to its responsibilities and enforcing existing law through Petty and Quarter Sessions. In May 1792 a Proclamation urged magistrates to be watchful of seditious literature and its authors and to stamp out riot and agitation.

This was little more than a useful means of rallying, and to some extent measuring, public opinion but it was not without effect. During the following months the government, through its local agencies, was able to keep an extremely vigilant eye on the mood of the public. The decrees issued by the French government in November promising to liberate the 'oppressed' peoples of Europe together with the intensification of radical activity at home necessitated further measures. On 24 November the government circulated the Lords Lieutenant, warning against the increased circulation of radical tracts and calling for diligent measures against radical authors, printers and publishers at the next Assizes. On 7 December the government wrote to selected firms of solicitors in the major towns of the kingdom, inviting them to act as government agents in the prosecution of seditious literature, especially Paine's *Rights of Man*. A few score rather half-hearted prosecutions for the sale of seditious literature followed during the next few months in which Paine was the most common target. This series of measures culminated on 1 December 1792 in the issuing of a second Proclamation. This deplored the ineffectiveness of the first and ordered the embodiment of the militia, believed to be particularly urgent in some of the northern counties, on the grounds of an imminent insurrection. This second proclamation was an obvious admission that the use of existing disciplinary mechanisms was not likely to be sufficient for safeguarding the peace and security of the country in the age of the French Revolution.

Second, the government was prepared to mobilise the legal system by directly bringing prosecutions against prominent radicals and reformers. In August 1793 a number of trials in Scotland culminated in the disgraceful proceedings against Muir and Palmer, who received sentences of fourteen and seven years transportation respectively, sentences far in excess of comparable proceedings in other cases. This only served to encourage a British radical convention to meet in Edinburgh in November and December 1793. These proceedings of over a score of radical groups from all over Britain were summarily dissolved by the authorities. The convention shocked and alienated much loyal opinion because of its specific defiance of Parliament and its offensive adoption of French terminology and customs. Pitt, at least, was seriously concerned at the revival of radical activity in the early months of 1794 and the rumours of a new convention. In May 1794 the force of the English legal system was turned on Thomas Hardy, John Thelwall, Horne Tooke and ten other members of two London radical societies. If the government had hoped to use the law to intimidate radicalism then it had severely miscalculated. Thomas Erskine, the Whig lawyer, argued successfully for their acquittal. Nevertheless, in spite of losing this *cause célèbre* the government's attitude had the consequences which it intended. The societies *were* overawed and local groups *were* daunted by the sentences meted out to the Scottish radicals and intimidated by a mixture of legal compulsion and social prejudice. They were harassed by magistrates, their meetings and publications threatened. The knowledge that the legal apparatus of the state could be mobilised against them had its effect. The passage of new legislation in 1795 which was specifically directed against their proceedings was the last straw for British radicalism. In most parts of the country radical activity began to decline. 1796 was a much quieter year than 1794 or 1795 had been. A few prosecutions for seditious or riotous behaviour can be found in most of the remaining years of the revolutionary period, but the moment of maximum danger and challenge had passed. The government's direct intervention in the legal system in general, and in the matter of enforcement, in particular, had clearly succeeded in its object.

A *third* and complementary element in the government's repressive reaction to domestic radical agitation was its use of Parliament and parliamentary enactments. At the level of rhetoric and propaganda, of course, ministers had frequently used Parliament as a platform from which to focus and influence public sentiment towards the French Revolution and its supporters and sympathisers in Britain. In 1794, however, a new tactic becomes evident in response to the rising tide of radicalism. In May 1794 the government suspended Habeas Corpus. Eighteen months later, in response to an attempt upon the king's person, the government rushed the Two Acts through Parliament. The first, the Treasonable and Seditious Practices Act, defined treason against the king's person or government as any 'compassings, imaginations, inventions, devices, or intentions' which might be published, printed or written and which might endeavour 'by force or constraint, to compel him or them to change his or their measures or counsels, or in order to put any force or constraint upon, or to intimidate, or overawe, both houses or either house of parliament'. The second measure, the Seditious Meetings Act, passed at the same time, banned meetings of more than fifty people whose object was either to petition Parliament on *or to discuss* any alteration of the establishment in church and state.

The timing of these enactments is extremely interesting. They occurred at times of critical political significance. The suspension of Habeas Corpus came when Pitt's relations with the Portland Whigs were beginning to assume major significance for the future of his government. The Two Acts occurred when the popularity of the war was beginning to show ominous signs of slipping. They are signs that traditional, informal and indirect methods of controlling and containing radicalism were no longer sufficient.

Nevertheless, although the government *was* prepared to take draconian measures to discipline domestic radicalism, it was not prepared to endanger the constitution in so doing. The legislation which it passed was of a temporary nature. The suspension of Habeas Corpus was limited in its initial duration to six months, a limitation which powerfully weakened Charles James Fox's charge that the rights of a free people were in danger. Similarly, the Seditious Meetings Act was for three years, although the most important clauses of the Treasonable Practices Act were to apply for the rest of the reign of George III. Nevertheless, it is important to be clear that while Pitt was ready to strike, and strike hard, in defending the existing constitution, he was not planning any permanent change in the nature of that constitution.

Fourth, the government of Pitt the Younger was prepared to intervene in the labour market to restrict the rights of workers. Two Combination Acts of 1799 and 1800 banned combinations of workers (embryonic trades unions) from taking strike action and facilitated their prosecution by allowing proceedings against them to be heard by a single Justice of the Peace, even if he were an employer in the same industry as those charged. The legislation had been triggered by organising tendencies among the cotton weavers of the North-West who were demanding increases in their wages. In principle, there was nothing drastically new about the Combination Acts. There was nothing new in the principle of legislation against combinations or, it may be said, in the ingenuity of workmen in evading their operation. The Acts of 1799 and 1800 represented merely the culmination of much eighteenth-century legislation.[16]

The Acts had little effect. As is well known, they did nothing to stop combinations to improve wages and conditions. They were rarely enforced. Employers were loth to alienate themselves from their workforces and, to some extent, from the communities in which they lived, by invoking such controversial and unpopular legislation.

Historians have argued for nearly 200 years about the legitimacy and justifiability of Pitt's repression of radicalism. Some have pointed to the draconian nature of the legislation against reformers, who were undeniably loyal and well-intentioned, and the considerable, and often extremely unpleasant harassment and intimidation directed against innocent reformers. Others have drawn attention to the lenient treatment of radicals compared to the ugly penalties commonly meted out in the penal practices of the time and underlined the temporary nature of the repression in what was, after all, an age of warfare, revolution and attempted invasion. Much still hangs on the question: was there really a danger of revolution or, possibly, of insurrection in the 1790s? With the benefit of hindsight we can, of course, argue that there was not. Given the enthusiasm with which the propertied classes rallied round the throne and the church there seems to have been little serious threat to the internal security of the country. Most radicals were sincere men, uninterested in violence and revolution, although inspired, perhaps, by the underlying idealism of the French Revolution. On the other hand, these realities could not be taken for granted at the time. Nobody could possibly guarantee that they would continue to apply in the future. Nobody could know that French invasion plans would be doomed to failure and disappointment, that Ireland would eventually be secured and that the war would, in time, be won. We should never forget that the war was, for long, a wearying, unsuccessful and demoralising uphill struggle. The entire nation, not just the social and political elite, was absolutely horrified by what had happened in France, especially between 1792 and 1794: the outbreak of war, the September Massacres, the execution of Louis XVI, the Terror and the suppression of Christianity. The stirring of reform movements in Scotland and the descent towards revolutionary activity in Ireland aroused more general fears for the preservation of national unity. Finally, the undoubted existence of a fringe element in the English radical movement which *was* devoted to violence throughout the 1790s and into the early years of the new century kept the government on its toes. It also offered to Pitt and his ministers a wonderful set of motives for and justifications of the government's repressive actions in its determination to preserve domestic security. There were few who came to question the government's position: at a time of unprecedented national danger against a malevolent ideological enemy there was every reason to look to the security of the realm, especially as there was a fifth column which openly sympathised with that enemy.

The case against the government's repressive attitude towards radicalism is less convincing than the case for it, but it, nevertheless, deserves to be heard, not least because the case against the repression of small, politically-motivated dissent against the state is always worth preserving. On all but a handful of occasions – December 1792 and November 1795 particularly – the government *knew* that the country was sound, and likely to remain so. Its system of informers and spies enabled Pitt's government to exercise informed vigilance over the domestic scene. The legal processes against chosen radicals were entirely political and alarmist in their purposes. The opinions and the actions of Lord Justice Braxfield in Muir's case amounted to the corruption of a legal system, while the judge in Palmer's trial, Lord Abercromby, virtually instructed the jury to find the accused guilty because he had argued for the reform of Parliament. As Albert Goodwin has written: 'The whole judicial proceedings, even by Scottish standards, were highly irregular... and the verdict of guilty only served to show that, in the minds of both the bench and the jury, the case had been pre-judged.'[17] The government itself was guilty of overkill in England when it prosecuted harmless men whose only crime was their dissent from the orthodox and prevailing view of society and politics. Almost every single radical was a harmless and loyal subject who would have been as horrified as Edmund Burke, William Windham or, even, William Pitt himself, at the prospect of a revolutionary regime in England. Pitt attacked the radicals in order to guarantee the preservation of a peace and order whose security was never in doubt. Pitt was seeking to insure himself against political failure and to protect himself against possible criticism from the king and from important groups like the Portland Whigs. According to this version of events, William Pitt *used* the domestic situation in order to strengthen and preserve his administration and to silence the growing number of critics of his unsuccessful prosecution of the war against the French.

There can be no doubt, however, that Pitt believed that the nation was, *or could be*, endangered if radical groups were left to agitate without hindrance. The French revolutionary period in British history is, perhaps, most remarkable for the climate of public opinion which came to dominate society. In its creation the government played a remarkable role.

There was every reason why it should. Ministers could never assume automatic support from the country, especially during a long and laborious war when the yearning for peace was never very far below the surface. The machinery of government depended upon voluntary cooperation with the political nation and, in its turn, upon the compliance of those beneath. What the government had to do was to mark out the parameters within which the practical cooperation of all social orders could be most safely secured and continued. Lord Grenville, like his cabinet colleagues, wished England to avoid the upheavals which the French were experiencing:

> I am convinced that this can only be done by keeping wholly and entirely aloof and by watching much at home, but doing very little indeed: endeavouring to nurse up in the country a real determination to stand by the constitution.[18]

This, he was convinced, could not be done by the government alone. Government could take the lead, but the defence of the constitution and the protection of property depended upon the unity and enthusiasm of the propertied classes themselves.[19] By 1792 there is much to suggest that the ruling classes were beginning to look to the government for a lead. A completely effective response to the dangers from France required much more than a policy of 'repression'. It required a pooling of resources and of effort, uniting to the influence of the crown, church and government the natural influence of all with property and acres. It needed the comprehensive, yet voluntary, mobilisation of social influence.

This was the achievement of the Reeves societies. Sweeping across the country from late November 1792 onwards, these loyalist associations provided a local focus for anti-revolutionary activity. Meetings of the associations provided well-publicised opportunities for the reiteration of constitutionalist sentiment and for its downward channelling and replication among the lower orders. Such sentiment, indeed, had been building for some years. It is possible, in fact, to trace back to the 1770s, and the perceptible hardening of opinion against the American colonists, a stiffening of sentiment behind the existing constitution. The swing of opinion against Charles James Fox and in favour of William Pitt the Younger and George III in 1783–4 emphasised these tendencies. Similarly, there can be little doubt that successive campaigns for the repeal of the Test and Corporation Acts in 1787 and 1790 met with scant sympathy from Anglican opinion. Popular celebrations of the centenary of the Glorious Revolution in 1788–9 reinforced existing predispositions in favour of the established constitution in church and state. What may roughly be termed *conservative* opinion was rallying, therefore, even *before* the French Revolution came to exert an influence over British society. Thereafter, there can be no question but that historians have severely overestimated the amount of sympathy that existed in England towards the French Revolution. After the middle of

1792 it is the creation of a powerful and popular loyalist and patriotic opinion in the country that impresses the historian. By comparison the radical groups of the decade appear numerically weak and, on the whole, organisationally primitive.[20]

Some historians, especially those of the British labour movement, have attacked Pitt, his colleagues, his successors and their class, for their tyrannical treatment of the radicals and their (allegedly) contemptuous disregard for the liberties of the subject. There can be no denying the anti-Paineite hysteria, the atmosphere of witch-hunt and scapegoat, the harassment of radicals, the violence of language and the blatant use of the law for political and ideological objectives. Nevertheless, ministers did not see themselves as acting tyrannically. They saw themselves as applying desperate measures to protect the constitution at a time of unprecedented crisis. The strain of ministerial pessimism in these years should not be underestimated. What happened in France sent shock waves through English society as an age of revolution appeared to be dawning in Europe. What happened in Ireland, and to a lesser extent in Scotland, and in some parts of the Midlands and North of England, portended the dawning of the age of revolution within the British Isles. In the end, and with the considerable benefit of hindsight, the governments of William Pitt the Younger and of his successors were successful in riding out the storm. They safeguarded the independence of the nation, they sustained its social hierarchy, they protected its property and, on the whole, they maintained law and a tolerable degree of order. This they achieved without permanent damage to the constitution, although they did not flinch from developing to an extent sometimes remarkable the inherent social power of the political establishment. Through careful mobilisation of the social as well as the political influence available to them, Pitt and his successors not only strengthened but broadened the base of government by attaching to it a patriotic alliance of the propertied orders of the nation, alerting them to the latent possibilities of the consequences of the French Revolution for Britain and awakening them to a more thoroughgoing appreciation of their constitution, their liberties and, not least, their monarchy.

2. The Opposition Whigs and the French Revolution 1789-1815

JOHN DERRY

THE French Revolution has often been seen as the catalyst which transformed the Whig Party in opposition, thrusting the development of party politics into new and unforeseen paths and compelling the more conservative Whigs to break with Fox. Some caution is needed when assessing such a judgement. In the spring or summer of 1789 no one, least of all the Opposition Whigs, expected disagreements over the French Revolution to lead to the estrangement of Fox and Burke, the eventual alliance of Portland, Fitzwilliam and their friends with Pitt, and the reduction of the Foxite Whigs to an ineffective rump of about 60 MPs, whose devotion to Fox transcended whatever misgivings they had about what was happening in France. When evaluating the impact of French affairs upon Britain it is worth remembering that the war against the French Republic and Empire had a greater impact on British opinion than attempts to reform French domestic institutions, whether by persuasion or force.

A broader perspective mellows trenchant generalisations. Much attention has been paid to the disintegration of the Opposition Whig Party in the years 1792 to 1794, but surprisingly little has been said about the alliance of Fox and Grenville after the fall of Pitt in 1801. Yet without the combination of Foxites and Grenvillites there would have been no Ministry of All the Talents in 1806, and although that administration was an unhappy and incompetent one Grey and Grenville sought, often desperately, to maintain their political alliance after George III had driven them from office. Once the exhausting French War ended it became impossible to sustain the alliance, but it was, nevertheless, a marked feature of the decade and a half after the peace of Amiens. Initial

Opposition Whig responses to events in France had been mixed, and over a period of twenty years the attitudes of the Opposition Whigs towards international conflict and European upheaval were varied and uncertain, as familiar loyalties were shattered and conventional assumptions destroyed.

In May 1789 the Opposition Whigs were in disarray. During the Regency Crisis Fox and his friends had been out-generalled by Pitt. Once again he allowed them no escape from their errors of judgement. When the news came that the French States General held out the possibility of reform in France the Opposition Whigs were preoccupied with recovering from yet another political humiliation, rather than eager to immerse themselves in French disputes. Pitt's political ascendancy seemed even more commanding. In contrast the Opposition was divided and distrustful of each other. Fox had failed to control his colleagues, several of whom, such as Grey and Sheridan, were detested by their associates. Nor could the party claim to be the guardian of Whig principles. When the French Revolution attracted attention in Britain Fox and the Opposition were looking for some means of restoring their political credibility and of recovering a measure of popularity.[1]

Even more ominous was the isolation of Burke. The Regency controversies had intensified his loneliness, making him, once the apologist for party, indifferent to the fate of a mere party. While the other Opposition Whigs had tried to escape from the consequences of the doctrine of the prince's inherent right to the Regency, Burke had asserted it to the bitter end. He felt that he alone was the custodian of true Whig doctrine, believing it to be his duty to defend the heritage of 1688 even if doing so meant destroying the Whig Party.

The Opposition Whigs viewed French politics with the English experience uppermost in their minds. They ignored essential differences between Britain and France, emphasising superficial similarities between them. Fox saw the French Revolution primarily as 'a good stout blow against the influence of the crown'.[2] Instead of attempting to understand the Revolution as a French phenomenon he sought to assimilate it to a political viewpoint dominated by English assumptions and expectations. Fox was thrilled at the thought that Bourbon absolutism was at an end. 'How much the greatest event that has happened in the history of the world, and how much the best!' he wrote to Fitzpatrick on hearing of the fall of the Bastille.[3] Fox believed that the French were about to establish a constitutional monarchy on the English model, with civil and religious liberty for all. The French were imitating the British example, and the example of France would reinvigorate the reform movement in Britain. Throughout the Revolution Fox sought, without much success but with obsessive persistence, to identify those French politicians who best deserved to be described as Whigs. Eventually he lamented that the French were inferior to the Americans; the French nation was incapable of remaining faithful to the ideals of 1789. In private Fox was often depressed by the violence of the revolutionaries, but he nevertheless believed that the absolutist powers of Europe, aided and abetted by Pitt, were more to blame than the French for the Revolution's decline into anarchy, dictatorship and terror. Ignorant and optimistic in the early stages of the Revolution, Fox assumed that the speedy resolution of French constitutional problems would prove a useful stimulus to the Whig cause in England. But he never wanted attitudes towards the principles of the Revolution or the practice of the revolutionaries to become decisive in determining British political alignments. Preoccupied with preserving the Whig Opposition he failed to give the lead which both conservative and liberal Whigs expected of him. He believed that Burke and Portland, on the one hand, and Grey and Sheridan, on the other, wantonly rejected his advice, thereby exacerbating the stresses and strains within the Whig Opposition by making too much of what was happening in France.

But once Burke published his *Reflections on the Revolution in France* in November 1790 it was impossible to relegate the debate over the Revolution to a secondary position. Burke's intervention transformed an intermittent and lethargic debate into a major ideological confrontation. Burke was not opposed to reform in France; as a Whig he preferred constitutional monarchy and a parliamentary system to any other pattern of government. Believing that every society needed checks and balances against the abuse of power he was resolutely opposed to any centralising tendency. He saw the French Revolution, not as a beneficent reform of French institutions, but as a threat to European civilisation, a portent of violence, injustice and war.

Nevertheless, it was an event in England, not France, which provoked Burke into publishing his misgivings as a manifesto against the Revolution. When Dr Richard Price, a prominent Dissenting minister and a well-known reformer, preached his famous sermon in November 1789 Burke was outraged. Price associated an enthusiasm for the American and French Revolutions with an interpretation of the Glorious Revolution of 1688 which Burke regarded as misleading and dangerous. As a Unitarian Price was particularly resentful over the limited religious toleration granted by the Toleration Act of 1689. Disappointed by the failure of the campaign to repeal the Test and Corporation Acts he saw the example of France as completing what the Revolution of 1688 had merely begun. By linking such claims with the assertion that the English Revolution had established the right of the people to frame a government for themselves and to cashier their governors for misconduct Price inflamed Burke's apprehension that false thinking about the French Revolution was inevitably connected with erroneous thinking about the English Revolution.[4]

It was, therefore, as a defender of the Whig Constitution that Burke denounced the French Revolution and its English sympathisers. Instead of appealing to abstract rights Burke reaffirmed the value of prescription, experience and tradition. He defended property as a security for liberty, and romanticised the English aristocracy as the great oaks of the constitution, arguing that far from Britain having anything to learn from what was going on in France the French had failed to draw the right lessons from the English experience. At the time his book was published many who shared his misgivings thought his arguments exaggerated. It seemed premature and alarmist to talk of the French Revolution as anti-Christian, or to see in it the precursor of dictatorship and war. Yet all of Burke's presuppositions were Whig. Although he defended the constitutional rights of the crown under the law he did not advocate extreme prerogative. Nor was he contemplating political desertion. He still distrusted Pitt. Only months before he had seen Pitt as a dangerous opportunist, exploiting legal technicalities to his own advantage in a manner disrespectful of the principle of hereditary succession. Burke was also disappointed by Pitt's slowness in recognising the evil implicit in the French Revolution.

Burke hoped to rally Whig opinion. He believed that it was his duty to save the party from shallow opportunism and radical infiltration. Nor did he write his book from petty or ambitious motives. During the Regency Crisis he knew that he had little chance of major office, even if the Whigs turned Pitt out. He wrote as the guardian of Whig principles, not as a man who looked for political advancement. Freed from the trivialities of daily politics, and indifferent to party advantage, he defended Whig principles from a new threat, which was more ominous than the alleged revival of the influence of the crown.

Intellectually Burke's intervention was decisive. Although his interpretation was challenged, the *Reflections* determined the style in which British commentators debated the French Revolution for half a century. Yet it needed the experience of events to persuade the majority of the political nation to say ditto to Mr Burke. The flight to Varennes in June 1791 seemed to confirm that Burke's gloomy predictions were being justified by events. The outbreak of war between France, Austria and Prussia in the spring of 1792, the fall of the French monarchy in August, the September Massacres and the Reign of Terror, enabled many who had originally thought that Burke's obsessions were getting the better of him to claim that they had known him to be right all along. Widespread adulation for Burke meant trouble for the Whig Party, especially when in 1792 anxieties over France spilled over into concern for stability in Britain, and when men of property saw evidence of a desire in radical circles to emulate French practice as well as French theory.

Fox had no wish to bring the controversy with Burke to the fore. His own reaction to Burke's prophecies varied. Sometimes he thought that Burke was exaggerating, as he was wont to do. But there were other occasions when he wearily conceded that Burke was right, but that he had been right too soon. Fox recognised that the intensity with which Burke's view of the French Revolution was debated heightened tensions within the Whig Party just when he wanted to play them down. Nor was Fox happy with all of the criticisms directed against Burke. His own attitude towards radicals was hostile, though muted. He read Part I of Paine's *Rights of Man*, disliking it so much that he could never bring himself to read Part II. He loathed Paine's levelling ideas, his lack of respect towards property and rank, his levity towards the English Constitution, his disdain for revered Whig principles. But Burke had done more than provoke a debate over the French Revolution: he had roused the suspicions of the conservative Whigs, who had been dimly uneasy about the reception of the French Revolution in England, but who had been unable to discern precisely how their uneasiness might affect their political conduct. The association of support for the French Revolution with support for a programme of domestic reform in Britain – especially the reform of Parliament and the repeal of the Test and Corporation Acts – made the situation difficult for the more conservative members of the Whig Party, such as Portland, Fitzwilliam and their friends.

The Opposition Whig Party had always been a coalition. It had never been monolithic in structure or united in outlook. In some respects it had been brought into existence by common opposition to the policy of coercion in the American colonies, and a shared belief that the influence of the crown had corrupted the House of Commons. There was, however, a degree of contradiction among Whig attitudes, as well as a thinly disguised hostility between personalities, which rhetoric might obscure but which it could not destroy. Opposition Whigs called for economic reform, arguing that the suppression of places, pensions and sinecures would restore the purity of the House of Commons and inaugurate an era of efficient public administration, but it was always possible to support economic reform while disagreeing over the role of the king in government. This dispute was at the heart of the conflict between Fox and Shelburne, and then between Fox and Pitt. Some Opposition Whigs saw economic reform as the best way of reducing the influence of the crown; others, such as Shelburne and Pitt, were more concerned with improving public administration. Even more controversial was the issue of parliamentary reform. This question was central to the misfortunes of the Whig Party in the 1790s, but it had always been controversial and the party had never been unanimously committed to it. Burke, Portland, Fitzwilliam and Thomas Grenville supported economic reform, but they had always opposed a reform of Parliament. Those Opposition Whigs, such as Fox and Sheridan, and later Grey, who supported a reform of Parliament were careful to differentiate the mode of reform which they favoured from the schemes put forward by radicals. Fox never approved of universal male suffrage, and Grey emphasised that he urged a reform of Parliament as a practical measure, on grounds of utility, not on the basis of radical ideology.

Just as ambivalence characterised Opposition Whig attitudes towards reform, so several of these Whigs muted their misgivings about annual parliaments and a broad extension of the franchise in order to maximise their appeal outside Parliament, in the hope of acquiring some control over radical activities. At the same time the Opposition Whigs tried hard to distance themselves from advanced radicals, such as Thomas Hardy and the London Corresponding Society, while arguing that a moderate reform of Parliament was timely and judicious. The French Revolution did not create these ambiguities, but it brought about a political climate in which it became harder to maintain such a multifarious stance with any degree of credibility. The determination of the younger Opposition Whigs, acting against Fox's advice, to bring parliamentary reform forward in the aftermath of the French Revolution heightened the misgivings of the conservative Opposition Whigs. Burke's warnings against the introduction of French ideas into Britain stiffened their determination to resist constitutional innovations. Even more ominous were the efforts made by radicals to seize the initiative, not only in London but in provincial towns such as Norwich and Sheffield, in order to agitate for an advanced programme of parliamentary reform and the abolition of religious disabilities. Because they saw such activities as manifestations of the spirit of the French Revolution the conservative Whigs in opposition became more hostile towards similar proposals emanating from the ranks of the Foxites. They regarded those who brought forward schemes of reform as seeking to isolate the more cautious members of the party. Yet the last thing Portland wanted in 1792 was to be forced to break with Fox and align himself with Pitt.

Domestic politics were not the only focus for debate in 1790 and 1791. In 1790 Britain came into conflict with Spain over Nootka Sound. The outcome was a diplomatic victory for Pitt. One reason for the humiliation of Spain was the denunciation by the French National Assembly of the family compact between the French and Spanish Bourbons. Sympathisers with the French Revolution seized on the episode as proof of the pacific intentions of the National Assembly, asserting that a constitutional monarchy in France would be able to cooperate with the constitutional monarchy in Britain. A further reminder of the importance of foreign policy came in 1791, when Pitt challenged the expansion of Russian power in the Near East. But the Ochakov affair was an unhappy experience for Pitt. The limits of the Triple Alliance were cruelly exposed and, worse still, Pitt saw his support in the Commons decline. Fox exploited the situation with skill and eloquence, and although Pitt extricated himself he had suffered a sharp reverse. The Opposition Whigs gloated over what they regarded as a well-earned rebuke for his arrogance. But Fox drew the wrong conclusions from the incident. He believed that if Pitt encountered a similar reverse in foreign policy on another occasion it might be possible to unseat him. This led Fox greatly to exaggerate his chances of exploiting the frustrations of the French War after 1793.

In April 1792 the outbreak of war between France and Austria, with Prussia soon joining in as an ally of Austria, ended expectations that the Revolution would inaugurate an era of international peace. Fox believed that victory for the Austrians and Prussians would ensure the triumph of reaction, but Burke and Windham called for British intervention. Fox wanted to defend the French Revolution, Burke and Windham to crush it. In May 1791 Fox and Burke had finally and publicly broken with each other over the French Revolution. This was the total breach which Fox had feared, and which he had tried to avoid. He regretted that Sheridan and Grey had taken a delight in taunting Burke over the French Revolution. Far from inflaming tempers Fox had wanted to cool them. But the debate over Pitt's Canada Bill led to open disagreements between the Opposition Whigs. On 6 May Burke, goaded beyond endurance, denounced the French Revolution in the House of Commons. He urged the British nation to flee from the Revolution. Fox interrupted to say that whatever their political differences there could be no loss of friendship. Burke replied that he sacrificed his friendships to the call of duty. Fox wept, the depth of his feelings making a profound impression upon the House. The scene merely thrust into public view tensions which had existed for at least a year. Once Burke had broken his links with the Foxite Whigs he was eager to persuade Portland and the other conservatives to put the struggle against the French Revolution before party loyalties.[5]

Fox sought, more desperately than ever, to preserve the party. He suspected that Burke would seek to destroy the Opposition Whigs in order to forge a grand coalition to protect society against French infection. He saw Burke's influence behind every problem the party faced. Burke, on the other hand, found Pitt unresponsive to his demands for a more vigorous British reaction to the challenge of the French Revolution. In the summer and autumn of 1792 Fox hoped that events in France would reach a definite conclusion. He hated the possibility of a Prussian victory, asserting that the outrages committed by the revolutionaries were caused by the Brunswick Manifesto and allied intervention in French domestic affairs. But with every month that passed it became harder to identify who were the French Whigs and impossible to recognise the guardians of constitutionalism in France. Fox was horrified by the September Massacres, but hoped, nevertheless, that moderation would prevail. Even when Robespierre came to prominence he thought his power would be checked. He sympathised with Girondins, saw St Just as Robespierre's chief rival, and expected that victories in the field would allow the Revolution to resume a constitutionalist course by removing the threat of foreign occupation. He thought the French had betrayed the ideals of 1789 too often for anyone to have complete confidence in them, but he was apprehensive lest Britain should become involved on the side of reaction. When the French resorted to annexation and aggrandisement Fox condoned their actions by asserting that the conduct of Austria, Prussia and Russia had been worse. He stuck to this stance obstinately. It soothed his conscience, allowed him to defend the ideals of the Revolution, but failed to provide a viable solution to the predicaments which were tearing the Opposition Whigs apart.

After Thurlow was dismissed as Lord Chancellor in May 1792

Loughborough slipped away from the opposition and made his peace with Pitt. He was eventually appointed Lord Chancellor in January 1793. Loughborough had been dubious about the French Revolution from the beginning, but he had no wish to be seen as crudely ratting. He wanted to take other conservative Whigs over to the ministry. This would make his own position in Pitt's government less vulnerable, as well as establishing some credibility for his claims that he had acted out of conviction not opportunism. Burke and Windham also favoured a coalition, and although Pitt was sceptical about the chances of success he embarked upon a cautious negotiation. Even if it failed to strengthen his administration it would embarrass the Opposition, and it would be useful for him to be seen as willing to establish a national government at a time of deepening crisis.

The reception of his proposals showed that, whatever their worries about the French and their exasperation with the Foxite wing of the party, Portland and his friends were not yet ready to abandon Fox. They had not lost their deep loathing of Pitt. They remembered the crisis of 1784 and the acuteness with which Pitt had exploited their difficulties since then. Only the Opposition Whig Party was capable of defending the constitution and securing civil and religious liberties. Whatever their differences over the French Revolution or parliamentary reform Portland and Fox shared a common desire to preserve the party. Both hoped for a speedy resolution of the French crisis, though each hoped for a different conclusion. Whether Brunswick restored the French monarchy, or the French defeated their enemies, Fox and Portland hoped that a providential turn of events would remove the French Revolution from the British political agenda. Both decided to hang on: the break-up of the party would be a triumph for Pitt. Not even the French Revolution justified the destruction of the Whig Party in opposition. But Fitzwilliam complained that he did not like Fox's attitude: in his anxiety to rally the party by denouncing Pitt, Fox was willing to divide the Commons on almost any issue. Fitzwilliam thought such conduct irresponsible. But the conservative Whigs still insisted on terms which made a coalition impossible.[6]

Although Fox gave precedence to the preservation of the party in opposition above every other issue he was incapable of imposing his will upon his colleagues. Fox disapproved of parliamentary reform being raised in a fashion which would make life more difficult for his conservative colleagues. He therefore advised Grey against bringing the issue forward, believing that it would do little good. Recognising the loyalty of the conservative Whigs to the party he had no wish to put it under strain. But he could not prevail upon Grey to hold back. Grey was convinced that by calling for an inquiry into representation he could prevent the radicals from seizing and retaining the political initiative. Once the situation in France was more peaceable the Opposition Whigs might profit from their boldness. Their disagreements over parliamentary reform were not new. The anti-reformers were asking too much if the price of their fidelity was indefinite postponement of the reform issue. When Grey introduced his motion in the Commons Fox supported him, despite his reservations. The House remained opposed to reform. Despite the restraint with which the Opposition Whigs had sought to deal with each other all that had been achieved was another public demonstration of the divided state of the party.

To debate parliamentary reform in the House of Commons was one thing, to embark on daring experiments outside Parliament quite another. Grey and Sheridan, with the concurrence of Romilly and Whitbread, tried to win the confidence of radicals by setting up the Society of the Friends of the People. This was an aristocratic reform society; neither its constitution nor its objectives were democratic. It represented what Grey believed was a middle way between frightened conservatism and foolhardy radicalism. Forming the Society of the Friends of the People was neither a casual after-dinner romp nor a gesture of defiance inspired by a mood of tipsy improvisation. It was an attempt to keep open Opposition Whig lines of communication to moderate reformers in the country, a means of controlling reformist opinion outside Parliament as well as reflecting public feeling. Once again Fox was deeply uneasy and once again his advice was ignored. He warned Grey against forming the society, complaining bitterly that Grey seemed determined to take no one's advice, least of all his. Many years later Grey claimed that one word from Fox would have saved him from the Friends of the People 'and all that nonsense'. This represented a desire to play down the provocativeness of his conduct. It also suggested that he was more deferential to Fox than had actually been the case. As a young man Grey deferred to nobody, not even Fox. He was arrogant, confident of his own ability, and impatient with the counsels of sober experience. Like Sheridan, Grey had been fiercely critical of Fox's leadership, both during the Regency Crisis and since. Fox was a friend of surpassing charm and charisma, but Grey trusted his own political judgement more than he respected that of Fox. Had the war between France and Austria and Prussia ended in 1792 the experiment of the Friends of the People might not have appeared so nonsensical in retrospect. As it was the gamble failed. The radicals were as little inclined to defer to Grey as he had been to listen to Fox. Many radicals distrusted Fox as an opportunist, fond of talking about reform while in opposition, but more committed to attaining office than to affirming high principle.[7] Conservative Whigs and all who sympathised with Burke saw the Friends of the People as further proof of how far the Foxite Whigs had gone down the slippery road to radicalism. Suspicion between the two wings of the party continued to fester.

Fear of war came to be an even greater anxiety than fear of revolution. Pitt tried desperately to remain neutral, resisting Burke's calls for a crusade against the French Revolution. Fox became more gloomy about Britain being drawn into war. But events took matters out of both Pitt's hands and his own. The French antagonised many of their friends. The Edict of Fraternity seemed a wanton interference in the internal affairs of a neutral, whose good will the French had at one time hoped to procure. The French invasion of the Low Countries, their unilateral abrogation of the clauses of the Treaty of Utrecht pertaining to the navigation of the Scheldt, and their establishment of satellite republics in those countries in which their armies had been victorious, offended British opinion. Fox did not condone what the French had done, but he called for time, negotiation, an effort to reach agreement on contentious issues. He urged the government to recognise the French Republic, and criticised Pitt for recalling Earl Gower after the Revolution of 10 August had overthrown the French monarchy. The trial and execution of Louis XVI appalled British opinion. Even radicals believed that the republic was violating its own principles when the Convention rejected Paine's plea that the French royal family should be exiled to the United States of America. On 1 February 1793 France declared war on Britain. Pitt justified the war because of French aggression; Fox replied that the British government had not sought redress of grievance in a sufficiently forthright manner.[8]

Once Britain and France were at war it was impossible to dissociate debate over the French Revolution and the menace of Jacobinism from the conduct and progress of the war. The war was deemed to validate Burke's doom-laden view of the Revolution. The Reign of Terror, and the spectacle of France plunged into civil war as well as international conflict, intensified the conviction that the Revolution was the harbinger of disaster, violence and death. With every month that passed it was harder to discriminate between the ideals of 1789 and the ferocity of the Jacobins. In England loyalism became dominant. There was widespread hostility towards radical societies, and even the most cautious advocates for reform were regarded with suspicion. Fox believed that it was the duty of the Opposition Whigs to defend civil liberties. The party had long claimed that it was the surest defender of religious toleration, freedom of speech, and the right of assembly. In 1792 Fox had the satisfaction of carrying his Libel Bill, which gave additional securities to the press in cases of libel by making the jury the arbiter of the proof of libel as well as of the fact of publication. The closing weeks of 1792 saw a genuine, though short-lived and ill-founded, fear of insurrection in London, a fear which Pitt turned to good political use. Portland and the other conservative Whigs in opposition became ever more anxious about radical activities. But they clung to the hope after February 1793 that the war would soon end and that once the French were defeated politics would return to normal.

Throughout 1793 and 1794 the fortunes of war favoured the French. Jacobinism seemed triumphant in its struggle against the kings of Europe. Apprehensions about the possibility of defeat mingled with anxieties about French influence in Britain and Ireland. Fox eloquently argued the case for a limited war for limited objectives, urging the government to lose no opportunity to negotiate for peace and denouncing every suggestion that the war was a conflict of ideologies, in which nothing less than total victory would suffice. Burke had foretold that the French Revolution would lead to an era of conflict, similar to the Wars of Religion in the sixteenth century. Fox inveighed against the notion of ideological war. A war against the ideas of 1789 would be a war in which bloodshed, savagery and extremism would be unrestained. Fox looked back to the traditional, eighteenth-century concept of limited war. In speech after speech he claimed that if the war had any justification it was for the curtailment of French power. He accused the British government of being doctrinaire in its view of the war. Hypocrisy marred the conduct of Britain's allies: while Pitt asserted that he was fighting a war to defend Europe from Jacobinism, Austria and Prussia had violated Poland and sought to intervene in the domestic politics of France. When the war went badly Fox saw in it an analogy with the war against the American colonists. Just as frustration and defeat had brought down North, so patriotism might turn to disillusionment and opinion swing emphatically against Pitt. Military defeat might well restore the fortunes of the Opposition Whig party.

By July 1794 Portland, Fitzwilliam and their friends were so depressed by the disappointments of the war, and so alarmed by the apparent growth of radicalism at home, that they swallowed their pride and hesitations and joined Pitt in a coalition administration. No longer did they insist, as they had done two years earlier, that Pitt should resign as first minister. It had long been Fox's ploy to say that he would serve with a detested rival – Shelburne or Pitt – but not under him. It was a tactful and effective method of blocking dangerous or unwelcome political negotiations. Now the alarmism of the Portland Whigs and their alienation from the younger members of the party in opposition had reached such a peak that duty necessitated serving under the old enemy. Pitt had acted honourably throughout. The Portland Whigs were given a fair share of offices and favours. Portland became Home Secretary, Spencer Lord Privy Seal, Fitzwilliam President of the Council (within months he was to become Lord Lieutenant of Ireland), Windham Secretary at War. Portland was more eager to curb radical agitation and crush Jacobinism than his predecessors Grenville and Dundas had been. When Fox denounced measures of government as repressive it was ironic that these were the prime responsibility of a former colleague. Fox's party in the House of Commons shrank to between 35 and 60 MPs. The old Opposition Whig Party had been destroyed, as much by their own misjudgements as by the French Revolution. But the Revolution had thrust to the forefront of controversy issues which brought longstanding disagreements and antipathies to a head.

1794 was a decisive year in the history of the Whig Party in opposition. Some would see it as a crucial year in the evolution of a new Tory Party, although Pitt never ceased to call himself an independent Whig and those Whigs who had been recruited to his standard did not see themselves as abandoning their Whig principles. Nor was Fox's faithful remnant a radical or liberal party. Only about half of those who remained Foxites supported parliamentary reform. As the years went by the proportion increased, but the reform of Parliament covered everything from a very limited measure of redistribution to advanced schemes of franchise extension. Fox and Grey never went further than household suffrage and a redistribution of seats from the most decayed boroughs to the counties and under-represented towns. They dissociated themselves from manhood suffrage and annual parliaments. Rather than being devoted, above everything else, to parliamentary reform the Foxites were motivated by several preoccupations. Some, despite caution over domestic reform, felt held by the power and charm of Fox's personality. Despite Fox's proven weaknesses as a leader they remembered the humiliations heaped upon them by Pitt. Some believed that the influence of the crown was the source of the country's ills; others believed that civil and religious liberty had to be defended, whatever the cost and however gloomy the prospect. Others opposed the war against France, not so much out of admiration for the French Revolution as from the calculation that the war was likely to end in defeat. Others detested the absolutist powers of Europe more than they disliked the French. Some could not bring themselves, whatever their anxieties about radicalism, to follow Portland into alliance with the hated Pitt. Others believed that if the war went badly Fox would profit from such an outcome, much as Rockingham had done in 1782. The Foxites flattered themselves that they were the only security against the two dangers threatening the country: reaction on the part of Pitt and the loyalists, and revolution stemming from the activities of the radicals, whom the Foxites regarded with disdain.

Only with the advantage of hindsight can Fox's belief that the French War was analogous to the American War be seen to be wide of the mark. But the taint of defeatism, which was associated with their criticisms of the war, was crippling for the Foxite Whigs. Fox's speeches harped incessantly on Britain's responsibility for the failure of the war effort and the inability to end the war by negotiation. Most contemporaries thought them opportunist and irresponsible: Fox seemed too prone to extenuate French conduct and too fond of rejoicing at British reverses. When the war reached deadlock, with Britain supreme at sea and the French dominant on land, Fox appeared little better than a French sympathiser. But the failure of Pitt's attempts to negotiate a compromise peace in 1795 and 1796 brought no comfort to the Foxite Whigs. The frustration of the party reached a climax when they seceded from the Commons in 1797. This was to revert to a very old-fashioned style of opposition, even more backward-looking than their reliance on the reversionary interest.

The Foxite Whigs were appalled by the Treason Trials in 1794 and by the passage of the Seditious Meetings and Treasonable Practices Acts in the following year. Fox was outraged by Braxfield's handling of the trials of Muir and Palmer in Scotland, and distressed by anything which limited the right of public assembly. The Foxite Whigs claimed that the actions of the government confirmed that constitutional liberties were being threatened by an overbearing executive. They played upon fears of the influence of the crown - an archaic cry, but one which was necessary to give a semblance of unity to the Opposition. Although they were distressed by the proceedings taken against leading radicals, and though Erskine's advocacy secured the acquittal of Hardy, Horne Tooke and Thelwall on charges of treason, the Whigs had no love for those advocating advanced radicalism. They detested legislation controlling public meetings because they believed that the government would exploit such powers against the Whigs even more than against the radicals. Similar suspicions were prevalent among the Whigs at the time of the Peterloo affair in 1819. Sincere though their defence of traditional liberties was, it was as much a reflection of their political situation as an expression of high principle. But in the long term it was advantageous for the Opposition Whigs that they could cite their devotion to civil liberty, however mixed their motives had been.

Civil liberty remained a cardinal tenet in the Foxite creed; another was religious liberty. When Pitt failed to carry Catholic emancipation as the sequel to the Irish Union the majority of Foxite Whigs supported Catholic relief. There was little prospect of Catholic emancipation after 1801, but as Grenville became disenchanted with Pitt and Addington a common devotion to the Catholic cause helped to bring Fox and Grenville closer together. The Foxite Whigs welcomed the Peace of Amiens, asserting that it proved they had been right all along, that peace had been there for the taking. Events exposed the superficiality of such a judgement, but at least the peace allowed Fox to visit Paris and to meet Napoleon. Each flattered the other, but Fox could not convince the Consul that the British press was independent of government direction, a failure which had some bearing on the resumption of the war in 1803.

The experience of the Addington ministry changed the character of the Opposition in a fashion which would have seemed inconceivable only a few years earlier. Throughout the 1790s Grenville had been one of Pitt's closest associates. The triumvirate of Pitt, Dundas and Grenville had been the mainstay of the struggle against the French Republic. As Foreign Secretary Grenville had developed an impressive command of the skills of diplomacy, but he had been so disappointed by the failure of the Second Coalition that he regarded any repetition of such a bold strategy as doomed to fail. Although he had been in awe of his cousin for many years he was a man of firm conviction. He wholeheartedly believed in Catholic relief and, when Pitt allowed himself to be cajoled by George III into promising never to raise the issue of Catholic emancipation again during the king's lifetime, Grenville flatly refused to give such an undertaking himself. He was frustrated by Pitt's lethargy in opposing Addington, especially since he was deeply critical of

Addington's fiscal policies. Dissatisfaction with Addington, a coolness towards Pitt, and a growing anxiety about the possibility of a resumption of the war, together with a common devotion to Catholic emancipation, drew Grenville into collaboration with Fox, caution eventually giving way to harmony. A stealthy realignment took place in British politics. The alliance of Fox and Grenville was as surprising a coalition as that between Fox and North had been. Grenville, the unyielding foe of the French Republic, acted in concert with Fox, the apologist for the French. Parliamentary reform remained a question on which they could only agree to differ, but their willingness to act together demonstrated that parliamentary reform was much less decisive in determining political loyalties than has sometimes been assumed.

When the war was resumed in 1803 Grenville was gloomily defeatist. Fox argued that a determined and skilful negotiation might yet restore the peace. When Pitt finally threw himself into active opposition to Addington's financial policies the ministry fell. Pitt, Fox and Grenville had combined against Addington, but George III asked Pitt to head a new administration. Pitt wanted to form an all-party government, with Fox as Foreign Secretary and Grenville as Lord President, with other Foxite Whigs, such as Grey and Fitzwilliam, joining the ministry. But George III refused to accept Fox and none of the Whigs was prepared to come in without him. Grenville refused office without Fox, and the coalition between Fox and Grenville, which had seemed the accidental product of the unusual situation after Pitt's resignation, was established as an inescapable fact of political life. The Fox-Grenville grouping was a much more credible alternative to Pitt than Fox's little band had been in the 1790s. When Pitt died in January 1806 George III turned to Grenville, more in desperation than enthusiasm, to form a new government. The king knew that this time he would have to accept Fox. It was one of the ironies of the closing months of Fox's life that he and George III got on better than anyone had expected. Fox was eager to prove the king's old prejudice to be as wrong-headed as it had been persistent. Besides, Fox could be magnanimous: he had told his friends to accept office without him in 1804, and he was determined to ensure the success of a new government now that Pitt was dead. Although the exclusion of Fox indicated the continued importance of the king's preference in the choice of ministers, George III's acceptance of Fox as Foreign Secretary in January 1806 revealed that there were restraints upon the king's exercise of his prerogative and that these were becoming more significant. But Fox recognised that the king's opinions remained influential, even decisive, and with this in mind he warned his colleagues against any premature agitation of the Catholic question. After his death the Foxite Whigs forgot his advice, with catastrophic results.

The Ministry of All the Talents was thwarted in its chief hope, that of ending the war by negotiation. It was an objective closer to Fox's heart than to Grenville's. Grenville hoped to end the war, but he was more sceptical about the motives of the French than Fox was, possibly because of his considerable experience as Foreign Secretary during the hard years of the Revolutionary War. The peace negotiations of 1806 had little chance of success. The British negotiators, Yarmouth and Lauderdale, were no match for Talleyrand, and the French were more concerned with dividing the British from the Russians than in securing a peace settlement. After Fox's death in September 1806 Grenville took a more direct part in the conduct of the negotiations. Diplomatic expertise on the British side improved, but the outcome was failure just the same. The Foxite Whigs were left in a humiliating position. Napoleon had called their bluff. For years the Foxites had claimed that only British intransigence had prevented peace with France. They had to mute such claims with Grenville as first minister. Another irony was that Fox had defended Grenville's right to hold various sinecure offices while serving as First Lord of the Treasury, which contrasted with the familiar Foxite threnody about secret influence, the growth of corruption, and the evil consequences of placemen in the Lords and the Commons. The episode marked another stage in radical disillusionment with Fox as a reformer. Once again he appeared to sacrifice principle to the demands of political exigency. The abolition of the Slave Trade gave the ministry a measure of consolation, but even so the issue was not one which conformed to conventional party alignments. Almost everything went wrong for the Talents. They had had to swallow having Sidmouth, first as Lord Privy Seal and then as Lord President of the Council, even though Fox and Grenville had learned to act together in opposition to him as prime minister. To call Grenville's ministry a Whig administration is to prefer simplicity of designation to accuracy in description. Nor did the Talents wage war effectively. Windham was an incompetent War Secretary. Grenville thought that the country should fall back on a cautious defensive strategy to save money and prevent economic exhaustion. This policy was reminiscent of that favoured by Addington in the early months of the war against Napoleon. But the ministry fell, not because the war went badly, but because, like Pitt before them, they offended the king on the question of Catholic relief.

The ministers failed to work out a coherent policy. They made no attempt to introduce a full scheme of Catholic emancipation, by which Catholics would be admitted to Parliament. They wished to carry a limited measure of relief to allow Catholics to serve in senior commissioned ranks in the army. But they antagonised the king when they revised their proposals to include staff appointments and to cover the navy as well as the army. The ministers were confused, the king was convinced that he had been deceived, and when George III objected to the final version of his ministers' suggestions they backed down amid confusion and acrimony. George III was determined to prevent a repetition of the incident. He knew that public opinion was behind him, not his ministers, and he asked Grenville to promise never again to raise the issue of Catholic relief. Grenville refused and the ministry resigned.[9]

Although they had experienced the difficulties of trying to make peace with Napoleon the Whigs never wholly accepted the realities of the war against the French Empire. Their attitudes towards the war were neither coherent nor consistent. Several conflicting emotions pulled members of the party now one way, now another. Those who thought of themselves as Foxites dreamed of peace, but the Spanish Rising against Napoleon led some who had been close to Fox to speak in passionate terms of the glorious nature of Spanish resistance. Lord Holland, who knew Spain well, was a committed advocate of the Spanish cause. Sheridan, who had embarrassed his colleagues in the 1790s by occasional lapses into patriotic enthusiasm, eloquently called for intervention on behalf of the Spaniards, stating that where Napoleon had previously faced the resistance of effete princes he was now confronted with the resistance of a people. Such enthusiasm lured some Opposition Whigs into exaggerating the likelihood of success, and this made reverses in Spain all the harder to bear. Responsibility for failure was usually blamed on the British alone, the Opposition Whigs preferring to idealise the Spanish patriots. Grey was wayward. Whenever he was under Holland's influence he supported the war in Spain, but when he yielded to Grenville's pessimism or Wilson's partisan notions of Peninsular strategy he talked of certain defeat. When the Convention of Cintra cast away the fruits of victory the Opposition Whigs exploited the discomfiture of the government. When Sir John Moore took over command they supported him because his politics were Whig, but they did not understand the strategy of the Corunna campaign and when Moore was killed and the British army evacuated they fell into renewed despondency. Grenville said that no British army should ever again be committed to the continent. Later Grey spoke of Talavera as a defeat. The Whigs in opposition had no comprehension of Wellington's strategy during the defence of the Lines of Torres Vedras, and even when the war turned dramatically to the advantage of Britain and her allies they were ungracious and obtuse in their response to events. This was partly because of their ignorance of military affairs, but Wellington's Tory associations and the patronage extended towards him by Castlereagh heightened the hostility shown towards him by many Whigs. Some Whigs, such as Whitbread and Byron, never overcame their admiration for Napoleon. Whitbread criticised votes of thanks to Wellington, and although Grenville and Grey sought to distance themselves from the more extreme partisanship of their followers it was hardly surprising that the Opposition Whigs were widely regarded as defeatist about the war.

Divisions over the war reflected confusions in the party leadership. Grey and Grenville preferred morose isolation in their country houses to active involvement in the routine business of opposition. Ponsonby and Tierney were ineffective as leaders. Grey tried hard to maintain the alliance with Grenville. But they often disagreed. They differed over parliamentary reform, though during the war years Grey was far from eager to see the issue brought into prominence. Grenville thought firm action necessary to defeat Napoleon during the Hundred Days. Grey thought a quick end to the war unlikely. Once hostilities ceased they agreed about little except the Catholic question. Public order always brought Grenville's innate conservatism to the fore. Though Grey lamented the reactionary policies of the government and the revolutionary intentions of the radicals he failed to exert himself in public life. Opposition had bred a temperament averse to responsibility. The Opposition Whigs had misguidedly rejected offers of a broadly-based administration in 1810, and while the offer of a negotiation in 1812 was less serious they had relied too confidently on the patronage of the Prince of Wales. They hoped that the Prince Regent would dismiss his father's ministers and summon the Whigs to office. But the Prince Regent resented the defeatism of the Opposition Whigs, priding himself that under the Regency the nation was winning military glory. Nor did he forgive the attitude of several of the Whigs to his private affairs, and his relations with Grey and Grenville were sour. His decision to retain Liverpool as his chief minister sealed the fate of the Opposition.

The Napoleonic War was a different type of conflict from that which had been waged against the Jacobins. Despite the horrors of the Reign of Terror it had been possible to see the French as fighting for the right of national self-determination, and for ideals which held out the possibility of the restoration of civil and political liberty in France. There had been a period during the Consulate when Whigs had seen Bonaparte as bringing order out of chaos: left to his own devices he would prove a humanitarian and a reformer. But whatever might have been said about the Consulate the establishment of the French Empire marked the abandonment of republican ideals. Most Britons, therefore, saw the war against Napoleon as a struggle against a tyrant. The Opposition Whigs shifted uneasily from suggesting that the war was unnecessary to arguing that a different strategy would win it, but their alternative strategy amounted to little more than criticising whatever the government did. The probability is that had the Opposition Whigs come into office, either in 1810 or 1811, the consequences would have been disastrous.[10]

When the French Wars ended the Whigs were further from power than ever, despite the fact that they could count on the support of about 150 MPs. Throughout the Liverpool ministry the Whigs were a feeble opposition, and only divisions within the emerging Tory Party, made grievous by the vexed question of Catholic emancipation, set in train the events which led to Grey forming a ministry in 1830. Even so, that ministry was a coalition, for it contained former Tories, Canningites and Independents as well as Whigs. It might seem, therefore, that the French Revolution, and the long war which was the most dramatic consequence of the Revolution, consigned the Foxite Whigs to a generation of political futility, the Ministry of All the Talents being an interlude which confirmed the unfitness of the party for power.

But although the impact of the French Revolution was powerful it is too easy to allow the Revolution to serve as an alibi for Whig failure. It was the response of the Foxite Whigs to a series of events which was their undoing: as well as the Revolution in France the Opposition Whigs had to react to questions of strategy and finance, coalition diplomacy, the Catholic issue, military and naval organisation and recruitment, pressing domestic concerns, and the uncertainties engendered by radical activity and reformist controversies. The Foxite Whigs were not pure and spotless advocates of peace, retrenchment and reform. Their understanding of the French Revolution and their attitudes towards domestic politics were often shallow, inconsistent, opportunistic and wilful. Too often they jumped to conclusions, their conduct dictated by the need to preserve party unity and to dissociate themselves from the government. In 1789 they shared the prevalent mood of condescension and complacency. Like most Englishmen the Opposition Whigs viewed the French Revolution from an English perspective. The Foxite Whigs paid a high price for their misjudgements, but they were themselves responsible for their fate, not the Jacobins in Paris. The French Revolution exposed inherent contradictions within the Opposition Whig party, but it did not create them. Far from converting the Foxite Whigs into a liberal party the Revolution reinforced aspects of their thinking which were backward looking as well as those which were reformist. When the Opposition Whig Party broke up in 1794 the subsequent realignment of parties was protracted, indefinite and far from permanent. The French Revolution exercised a considerable influence on the evolution of the Whig Party, but it was not the only influence at work and its significance should not be exaggerated, even when it is duly recognised.

3. Popular Radicalism and Popular Protest 1789-1815

JOHN STEVENSON

THERE has been a considerable upsurge of interest in recent years in the impact of the French Revolution upon popular radicalism and popular protest. Studies in three main areas, on popular radicalism, popular disturbances, and early trade unionism have fed into an increasingly complex and many-sided debate, with wide repercussions, about the nature of the British response to the French Revolution and its impact upon British society. Pride of place in this reassessment must go to E.P. Thompson's *The Making of the English Working Class*, first published in 1963, but achieving much wider recognition with its publication in paperback in 1968. Thompson's powerful analysis, drawn with a vivacity and panache which left even those who disagreed with it forced to admire its qualities, effectively presented a quite new agenda for research and interpretation. For Thompson, the 1790s were the crucial period for the 'Making' of the title, the crucible out of which a new 'working-class consciousness' was formed. Here, the popular radical societies, rather than the Whigs or Charles James Fox, occupied the centre of the stage, their activities and major personalities fleshed out with greater sympathy and enthusiasm than ever before. They were placed within a context in which Paineite radicalism offered an ideology of revolt which was to sustain the popular radical movement up to and beyond the Great Reform Act. In Thompson's view, this was no story of a fumbling attempt by obscure and ill-educated men, tragically misunderstood by a government in the midst of wartime panic, but the first self-conscious assertion of the political rights of working men and women, in its implications more momentous than the most radical interpretations put upon the debates of the Levellers and Diggers a century and a half earlier. For Thompson, the meetings of groups such as the London Corresponding Society, arranged around earnest, sober discussions of political and constitutional affairs, displayed at least in part 'the first stages in the political self-education of a class', while the composition of the societies bore direct analogy with those participating in the most radical events across the Channel, the *sans culottes* of the Paris sections.[1]

Moreover, Thompson did not deny, as some of his more Whiggish forbears had, that British radicals could develop an insurrectionary temper, particularly after the increasing repression of overt radical activity from the mid 1790s. Further, Thompson's argument that the radical movement did not perish but went 'underground' from the end of the 1790s had a number of important implications. First, it took seriously the hitherto shadowy world of conspiracy and insurrectionary plotting of the years between the late 1790s and the early 1800s as a genuine continuation of the Jacobin legacy of the early 1790s. Deserted by Whig allies and fair-weather radicals, a rump of Jacobin conspirators entered the world of clandestine plotting and treasonable activity, increasingly drawn into a complex web of Franco-Irish conspiracy. In this interpretation, the United Societies and the Despard conspiracy were neither a figment of anti-Jacobin propaganda nor a 'lunatic fringe', but the considered response of one group of radicals to the failure of constitutional and legal paths to reform. The late 1790s were to give rise to an insurrectionary tradition which was to survive Despard's execution and the defeat of the Irish rebellions of 1798 and 1803, to be carried forward into the Luddite outbreaks and by the group of 'Spencean philanthropists' who clustered around Dr Watson and Arthur Thistlewood in the immediate post-war years. Second, Thompson was to argue that the Jacobin movement, although forced underground and debarred from public activity, was to retain a degree of continuity both in ideas and personnel, emerging as more favourable circumstances permitted towards the end of the Napoleonic Wars in the campaigns of the Westminster Committee for the election of Sir Francis Burdett in 1807, in the meetings of like-minded artisans and tradesmen in the craft centres within the metropolis and in places such as Leicester, Newcastle, Nottingham and Manchester, culminating in the great quasi-insurrectionary episode of Luddism. Once forged, the working-class consciousness was not lost forever in the decline of the popular political societies, but even 'in the darkest war years the democratic impulse can still be felt at work beneath the surface'.[2] By the end of the Napoleonic Wars the effect of the Combination Laws of 1799 and 1800 and the quickening pace of industrial change, abrogating the old craft traditions and exposing whole groups of artisans to the rigours of laissez-faire in the difficult economic climate of Orders in Council and the bad harvest of 1812, had served to bring the illegal Jacobin tradition and nascent trade unionism closer together. By the end of the Napoleonic Wars, on the eve of the great burst of reform activity which marked the era from 'Waterloo to Peterloo' there had been 'a radical alteration in the sub-political attitudes of the people'; in spite of the short-term failure and defeat of the radical movement of the 1790s, that decade had seen 'something like an ''English Revolution''...of profound importance in shaping the consciousness of the post-war working class'.[3]

Thompson's controversial and seminal work with its great stress upon the impact of the French Revolution in stimulating the creation of political consciousness amongst the common people, initially largely amongst the artisans and tradesmen of the traditional centres of craft industry, but by the end of the Napoleonic Wars increasingly evident in the growing manufacturing districts of the Midlands and the North, had all the more impact because it gave a prominence and an importance to the popular radical societies which they had never been given before. Here was a genuinely 'revolutionary impulse' which was to have wide-ranging and important repercussions. In the short term this impulse was to be defeated by repression before it could have practical effect. Its desertion by Whigs and middle-class sympathisers in the 1790s created a fissure between the classes which was to dominate the reform movement throughout the first half of the nineteenth century and to create an alienation between classes which would last even longer. The 'panic of property' in the early years of the 1790s broke the 'natural' alliance between the growing industrial and commercial classes and the working class which was the only one strong enough to bring about substantial change in the political system. Instead the popular radical movement was faced by a consolidation of 'Old Corruption' which united landowners and manufacturers in a common front.[4] In that sense Thompson's argument was similar to P.A. Brown's, half a century earlier, but with the important difference that while popular radicalism may have been too weak to effect either reform or revolution alone in the 1790s, it left a permanent legacy which was to survive through the war years and re-emerge after 1815.

Thompson's work, however, did not stand alone. Gwyn Williams's short but stimulating comparison of the artisan movements in France and Britain in the 1790s showed a lively awareness of the points of similarity and also of difference between the popular movements on both sides of the Channel.[5] Like Thompson, Williams gave some prominence to the important provincial dimension of popular radicalism, notably in Sheffield, while elsewhere he gave evidence of the impact of the French Revolution and Paineite ideas upon the small-town Welsh intelligentsia and by the end of the Napoleonic Wars in the industrialising 'frontier country' of Merthyr and the Welsh valleys.[6] The provincial dimension of popular radicalism in the 1790s also received major re-examination when Albert Goodwin's years of research into the reform movements of the late eighteenth century gave rise to his massive, learned exposition, *The Friends of Liberty*.[7] While making less ambitious claims for the creation of a working-class consciousness in the course of the 1790s, Goodwin provided the most thorough exploration hitherto of the rise of the provincial reform societies from the late 1780s through to the years after the French Revolution. Goodwin gave particular emphasis to the role of Dissent and the campaign for the repeal of the Test and Corporation Acts in creating a climate in which the events in France found a welcome. Goodwin's researches, however, remained focused on the early 1790s, the classic architecture of earlier studies such as those concerned with the repercussions of the French Revolution upon the Whig Party. Moreover, Goodwin's principal interest was to investigate at the level of the growing middle class, the largely more well-to-do people, often Whigs, or Dissenters, who formed 'The Friends of Liberty' of his title.

Nowhere, perhaps, was this clearer than in the relationship between the activities of the popular radical societies and the successive waves of popular unrest which affected the Revolutionary and Napoleonic periods, for crucial to the debate on the development of a political consciousness amongst significant sections of the lower classes was the delineation and interpretation of the popular disturbances of the period. Rudé's work on the crowds in the Wilkite movement of the 1760s and those surrounding Lord George Gordon in 1779-80 demonstrated a channelling of crowd activity into political campaigns of national importance. But the implications of Rudé's work went further than placing the hitherto despised 'mob' in a more prominent role in some of the political events of the eighteenth century, for the real impact of his work lay in a greater understanding of the composition, nature and, crucially, the ideology of the eighteenth-century crowd. Careful study of court records revealed that stereotypes of the 'mob' as being composed of criminals, the unemployed and ne'er-do-wells were highly misleading, rather they were found to represent a fairly typical cross-section of the working population, people in work rather than unemployed, a range of journeymen and tradesmen drawn from the various crafts, and even a sprinkling of professional people. Most important of all, however, when examined closely, many riots were revealed as disciplined and highly ritualised forms of protest in which the populace acted in accordance with a coherent set of beliefs and values. The London 'mob' of the eighteenth century revealed a recurrent emphasis upon 'rights' and 'liberties', intermingled with a strong strain of anti-popery and popular chauvinism. Rudé was also one of the first historians to turn his attention to the country food riots of England and France in the eighteenth century, suggesting that they too were selective, disciplined and, often, highly ritualised forms of protest, aimed at securing food at 'just' or 'fair' prices, or forcing the authorities to intervene to obtain the same end.[8] Elsewhere, Eric Hobsbawm's interpretation of industrial protest pointed in a similar direction. In his essay on machine-breaking, Hobsbawm placed such actions within the context of a rational process of 'collective bargaining by riot' – one of the means by which workmen in the eighteenth and early nineteenth centuries could bargain and negotiate with their employers.[9]

Where earlier historians had either ignored the popular disturbances of the period after 1789, except for those such as the 'Church and King' riots of the early 1790s which were explicitly political in content, or treated them as a separate category of events, as part of the response to agricultural and industrial change, it became of some importance to ascertain whether the popular disturbances after 1789 were different in character from those of the eighteenth century in general and whether there was evidence of a change in the ideology of popular protest consonant with the rise of a new popular radicalism in the aftermath of the French Revolution. In *The Making*, Thompson had suggested that most popular disturbances, even those concerned with issues other than politics, could be interpreted as articulating a 'sub-political' tradition which flowed into the early working-class movement. The most characteristic forms of disturbances, food riots, demonstrated a network of ideas and assumptions, a 'moral economy', which increasingly found itself at odds with the growing market economy.[10] These views were elaborated in a major article in *Past and Present* in 1971, but there remained an ambivalence in Thompson's view of the role of the crowd or mob in the political development of the working class during the 1790s.[11] In *The Making*, Thompson had drawn attention to the nature of the London mob which, whatever Rudé had suggested about its rationale and respectability, could still demonstrate as late as 1780 an appetite for outright violence and plunder. The London mob of the 1760s and 1770s, he argued, represented a 'half-way house in the emergence of popular political consciousness', whose true base lay in the debating clubs and tavern societies of the artisan districts. The 'Church and King' disturbances of the early 1790s, such as those at Birmingham in 1791, and the crowds which terrorised radicals and reformers during the following decade illustrated to what extent the traditional 'mob' retained a reactionary and unstable temper. For Thompson, far more significant was the defence of Hardy's house in October 1797 against a loyalist mob. The attack was beaten off by a guard of LCS members, many of them Irish, armed with shillelahs. Hardy's heartfelt comment 'I do not relish the government of a mob', compounded by his bitter experience three years earlier when an attack upon his house while he awaited trial for high treason contributed to the death of his wife, illustrated the distance between the self-conscious artisan movement represented by men like Hardy and the members of the LCS and the still fickle London 'mob'.[12] Whatever the 'sub-political' content of many popular disturbances in the eighteenth century, the rise of a specifically political, organised and self-conscious popular radicalism remained the critical feature in the creation of a working-class movement.

A further development of importance in assessing the popular radicalism of the post-1789 period has been the much more systematic exploration of the early history of trade unionism. Until very recently the eighteenth century remained something of a 'dark age' of trade union history. Eric Hobsbawm's essays on the use of the 'tramping' system and his essay referred to earlier, on machine-breaking, introduced some important evidence about the ability of the early trade societies both to organise themselves and to negotiate with their employers through 'collective bargaining by riot'.[13] The former illustrated an impressive degree of often nationwide coordination amongst groups of skilled workers. The latter was shown to be one of a battery of tactics deployed by workmen throughout the eighteenth century to put pressure upon employers, discipline fellow workers, and draw attention to grievances. Implicitly, these essays suggested a more sophisticated role for workmen in the eighteenth century than had been suggested hitherto. Workmen's organisations have been shown to have been operating on a scale remarkable for their size and effectiveness. C.R. Dobson has located nearly 400 labour disputes in the British Isles between 1717 and 1800, involving a very wide selection of trades and occupations and occurring in almost every part of the country.[14] This record of disputes is certainly incomplete, as almost every local investigation reveals a fresh crop of industrial disputes. Moreover, 'disputes' form only the tip of an iceberg of collective activity by eighteenth-century workmen which never reached the newspapers or court records.[15]

By the end of the eighteenth century, many groups of workmen had displayed the ability to strike, to organise funds, to negotiate effectively, and to represent their grievances by both violent and non-violent means. Moreover the increasing development and complexity of the economy, an overall rise in prices, and fluctuations in trade, accentuated by the American and Revolutionary Wars, gave early trade organisations a renewed impetus. Dobson records the number of trade disputes between 1781 and 1800 as 153, 40 more than in the period 1761–80. The last decade of the eighteenth century accounted for nearly a third of the disputes listed by Dobson for the whole period 1717–1800, with activity in a very wide variety of trades.[16] The years 1791–2 witnessed a veritable explosion of strike activity both in the capital and in the country with 40 disputes recorded, including groups such as the ship's carpenters at Liverpool, the seamen working the east coast from Scotland to the Thames, the colliers at Bristol, Sheffield, Wigan and Newcastle. Disputes continued throughout the 1790s, but especially in 1795, a year of high prices and trade dislocation when shipyard workers, tailors, coalheavers and even some agricultural workers sought wage increases.[17]

On the eve of the Combination Laws then, trade disputes had become increasingly common, backed by various degrees of organisation. In many provincial disputes, organisation appears to have been little more than an impermanent arrangement to prosecute a particular strike. Some groups, however, such as the textile trades, shipyard workers, keelmen, and seamen with a long tradition of labour conflict had acquired the rudiments of a formal trade union structure. The existence of Friendly Societies provided one means by which funds could be collected for use in strikes; an illegal practice which Francis Place frankly admitted was the reason for the creation of a benefit society amongst his branch of the London tailoring trade in the early 1790s.[18] Indeed, it was amongst the skilled London artisans that organisation had proceeded furthest. The importance of this more sophisticated appreciation of early trade unionism is clearly of significance in assessing the extent to which at least some workmen had developed a collective identity and the means of effective organisation. It was to be the artisans, the skilled workers, who were to play the major part in the early radical societies, whose experience of the Combination Laws was, at least according to Thompson, to meld

Jacobinism and trade unionism in a common working-class identity, to erupt so forcefully in Luddism, and provide the basis of the radical working-class movement after the Napoleonic Wars.

How have these perceptions altered our view of the popular movements of the years after 1789? Initially, it is clear that as Goodwin suggested, the most enthusiastic responses to the French Revolution flowed along channels already cut before 1789. To a very large degree, the most active responses were coterminous with the geography of Whiggery and, perhaps even more important, Dissent, especially evident in commercial and manufacturing centres such as London, Norwich, Birmingham, Sheffield and Newcastle.[19] There is little doubt that the French Revolution quickened the pace of activity in a number of these towns, enthusiasm for the early French Revolution was a natural corollary of the campaigns for the repeal of the Test and Corporation Acts and the fortuitous celebrations of the centenary of the Glorious Revolution of 1688. It was striking that in a number of towns, the battle lines already drawn between the established church and Dissent prefigured the acrimony between Dissenters and Anglicans in the early years of the 1790s. The lines were never entirely clear-cut, Whigs and Anglicans were to be found in the Literary and Revolution societies which developed in the period after 1788. In Birmingham Anglican members of the Lunar Society were to find themselves victims in 1791 of the same 'Church and King' crowd who hunted down Priestley and his fellow Dissenters.[20] In Manchester, Archibald Prentice was to recall that the first real divisions of opinion within the town sprang out of the campaign to repeal the Test and Corporation Acts rather than out of the French Revolution.[21] It is this which explains the early appearance in Manchester of a Church and King Club, in the summer of 1790, more than two years before the appearance of the loyalist associations associated with John Reeves and the panic of anti-Jacobinism which followed the September massacres, the radicalisation of the Revolution in France, and the growing circulation of the second part of Paine's *Rights of Man*.

In the immediate aftermath of 1789, the prospect seemed promising for the revival of a reform movement of renewed strength and vigour. But this movement was to receive severe set-backs. The vehemence of anti-Dissenter feeling demonstrated in the Priestley Riots of 1791 strangled the reform movement at birth in one of its major centres, Birmingham. Magisterial hostility and Church and King mobs were also to increase pressure on reform societies and their supporters in Manchester, Leicester and other centres. Most critically of all the rise of popular radicalism and the radicalisation of the Revolution in France were to face many of the more moderate 'friends of liberty' with an acute dilemma, one only compounded by the massive loyalist upsurge which occurred in the autumn and winter of 1792. Moreover, the defeat of attempts to repeal the Test and Corporation Acts in 1789 and 1790 and the failure of Grey's parliamentary motion for reform in 1793 signalled that even with its revival, the provincial reform movement which grew out of the events of 1788-9 was still not strong enough to secure significant concessions.

If one channel of response to the French Revolution lay with middle-class Dissent another lay through the Scots. With the narrowest and most oligarchic representative system in the United Kingdom, and a well-developed civic and intellectual culture, the Scottish counterpart to the English reform movement of the early 1780s was the movement for burghal reform. But whereas the English movement was virtually moribund by the middle of the decade the Scottish movement remained in the field right up to the eve of the French Revolution, 46 petitions for burgh reform being presented to Parliament in 1788 and pursued through the advocacy of the Whig MP, Richard Sheridan, albeit with little success, in the following year. The attempt was resumed in 1791 and again in 1792. By then, however, the influence of the French Revolution was being felt in Scotland. July 1792 saw the formation of the first Society of the Friends of the People in Edinburgh, followed in September by the formation of the Dundee Friends of the Constitution and the Glasgow Associated Friends of the Constitution. Other reform societies spread quickly throughout Scotland by the end of the year. 1792 also saw the first General Convention of the Friends of the People in Scotland, led by Thomas Muir, an Edinburgh advocate.

The Convention, backed by a movement of radical artisans and shopkeepers, deeply alarmed the government. No less worrying were the anti-government demonstrations of June 1792 in Edinburgh known as the King's Birthday Riots when Henry Dundas, Pitt's trusted lieutenant and 'manager' of Scotland, was burned in effigy and the Lord Provost's house attacked by a crowd of upwards of 2000 people. The targets of the crowd's hostility were figures of authority in Scotland, primarily Dundas, 'Harry the Ninth', the figurehead of the Pitt administration north of the border. Similar demonstrations occurred in Aberdeen, Perth, Peebles and Dundee. Towards the end of the year, following the French victories at Valmy and Jemappes, 'Trees of Liberty' were planted in many Scottish towns and cities to demonstrate support for the French cause. At Perth in November it was reported:

> The Tree of Liberty was planted with great solemnity in this town and a great bonfire with ringing of bells and a general illumination upon hearing that General Dumourier had entered Brussels. The Lower Class of People talk of nothing but liberty and equality – 'No Dundas – No Bishops – and no King. Nothing but a Republic for us.' Such is the Spirit of the Times.[22]

It was hardly surprising then that the government gave prominence to events in Scotland in its alarm in December 1792 when regular troops were sent into Scotland, the militia was called out in England and the Tower and Bank of England guarded and fortified against possible insurrection.

By this time, popular radicalism in England had taken on a new dimension. The most dynamic element was the formation of popular political reform societies, during 1791 and 1792, in scores of towns and cities. At least 80 such societies existed in England by the mid 1790s and in the case of the London Corresponding Society, founded in January 1792, comprising as many as 90 'divisions' at its peak in 1795. Although these societies were sometimes dominated by middle-class reformers, in places such as London, Sheffield and Norwich, they were artisan-based. Surviving division lists of the London Corresponding Society show their members as being drawn predominantly from the London skilled trades. Moreover their forms of organisation, with General Committees, treasurers and delegates, and 1d. a week subscriptions, clearly owed a great deal to the traditions of contemporary trade societies. In Sheffield, a town of small masters and artisans, the Sheffield Society for Constitutional Information had an estimated 2000 members by the summer of 1792, drawn largely from its many independent artisans whose talent for organisation had already expressed itself in strong craft unions. The Norwich artisans supported at least 40 small tavern clubs and *The Cabinet*, an intellectual journal which reflected the attitudes of some of the most enthusiastic supporters of the French Revolution. As early as 1793 the principal artisan societies espoused a radical political programme which included universal suffrage and annually elected parliaments. Some of the more detailed lists of resolutions also included economic and social grievances, complaints against taxes, high food prices, the game laws, and the prosecutions of workmen for participating in trade-union activities.

There has been much debate about the significance, ideology and tactics of these societies. Initially, it might be noted that although the popular radical societies have been the subject of much discussion, many of them remain very obscure. Of the 28 provincial corresponding societies listed in the index to Thompson's *The Making*, only a handful have been seriously studied, either for lack of source material or simply because they await their historian. In addition we still know very little in many cases about the antecedents of the popular societies in the years before the French Revolution. Apart from one or two notable exceptions, such as John Money's study of Birmingham and H.T. Dickinson's of the North-East, it is still difficult to appreciate the milieu out of which these societies sprang.[23] As a result historians have been forced to turn to the impact of the French Revolution and, above all, the writings of Paine as the decisive feature in the emergence of a more genuinely popular reform movement. Even in London we know relatively little about the artisan world of tavern clubs and Dissenting congregations in the years between Wilkes and the early 1790s. Fascinating leads, such as Thomas Hardy's membership of the Scottish Presbyterian Church in London and his acquaintance with Lord George Gordon, remain unpursued, while the development of popular politics before 1789 in Westminster, Clerkenwell, Southwark and Spitalfields, areas of major significance in the capital's history, have barely begun to be explored.

The ideology of the popular reform societies has received more critical attention in the light of Thompson's stress upon the influence of Paine and the importance for the development of British 'Jacobinism' in the 1790s. We now have a more systematic and longer-term evaluation of Paine's influence in H.T. Dickinson's exploration of political ideas throughout the eighteenth century, placing the radicalism of the 1790s in the context of its antecedents before 1789. As Dickinson shows, many of the radical propagandists of the decade attempted to shift the basis of the case for reform towards a rationalist appeal to the natural rights of man, from the traditional appeal to the ancient constitution.[24] The central importance of Paine in transmitting a radical ideology of natural rights into Britain is incontestable: both the fulsome tributes to Paine by the radical societies themselves and their active dissemination of his works are evidence enough of his importance. So too is the genuine alarm of a wide spectrum of propertied opinion at the subversive character of Paine's writings. It was entirely consistent with this alarm that it was against seditious publications, notably those of Paine himself, that the government first struck with its proclamations in the spring and autumn of 1792.

But there is a difficulty which consideration of the programme and tactics of the popular reform societies reveals. While radical propagandists may have clearly understood Paine's position and the new basis upon which he justified the call for reform, it is not at all clear that Paine's message was fully accepted in the programme and tactics of reformers. Paine's devastating critique of the British *ancien régime* essentially denied the legitimacy of the monarchy, the nobility and the established church. Conservative readers of Paine were quite correct in regarding it as deeply subversive of the established order. If Paine was taken literally, the logical outcome was some form of republican democracy. But the programme of the major radical societies never extended this far. Time and again, they rejected the charge that they were republicans, the LCS called for *reform* of Parliament on the basis of universal suffrage and annual parliaments, not the replacement of Parliament by a single-chamber assembly. Moreover these demands themselves had been articulated prior to 1789 by the radical wing of the pre-1789 reform movement, notably in Major Cartwright's *Take Your Choice* of 1776. Thus, while there is little doubt that Paine's writings helped to bring reform ideas to sections of the population which had hitherto had little or no public involvement in politics and brought into British radicalism a new emphasis on natural rights, it is not clear that the political programmes of the radical societies fully reflected this change. Indeed, the public statements of the major radical societies in Scotland, Sheffield, London and elsewhere, confirm this view. The first Convention of the Scottish Friends of the People called for moderate parliamentary reform. The London Corresponding Society consistently maintained their aims went no further than a reform of Parliament. In that sense the radical societies of the early 1790s were only Paineite to a limited degree.

Similarly, the tactics chosen by the radical societies in their public phase of activity until the middle of the decade illustrate an essential moderation. The LCS went to great pains to distance itself from unconstitutional methods, even going to the lengths of producing a pamphlet, *Reformers No Rioters*, in 1794 to scotch any suggestion that it was prepared to use violence to obtain its ends. Initially, the societies put their faith in political education to spread their message and the use of traditional methods of petitioning Parliament for reform. The greatest controversy has surrounded the intentions of the radical societies in calling conventions, in Scotland in 1792 and 1793, and the proposal for the London Convention in the spring of 1794 which was to lead to the arrest and trial of the leaders of the metropolitan reform societies on charges of high treason. The weight of evidence remains that in calling a convention the reformers had no intention of mounting a revolutionary challenge to the government. This was precisely the issue in law at the trial of Hardy, Tooke, Thelwall and the other reformers in the autumn of 1794 when most of the multiple counts of treason on which they were arraigned related to their intentions in calling a convention. The government was not then, and historians have not been able since, to prove that the intention went beyond a meeting to discuss and promote the cause of reform. What was, of course, also true was that there was no telling what course a convention might have taken after it met. The threat of an anti-parliament, similar to those proposed in 1819 and in the Chartist period, was one the government took seriously, particularly as the language of some radicals became increasingly defiant in tone.

Careful analysis of the pronouncements of bodies such as the Sheffield Constitutional Society and the LCS in 1794 reveals no more than outraged constitutionalism. The nearest either of these bodies came to a public endorsement of the resort to force was in arguing that if the government went so far as to abrogate and repress all traditional liberties it would have dissolved the compact between government and people thereby justifying resistance. This impeccably Lockean argument, drew as much, if not more, upon the lessons of 1688 and 1776, as those of 1789, still less of 1792. In practice the popular artisan reform societies were unable to resolve the tactical dilemma of attempting to reform an unwilling Parliament by peaceful means. While Paine's message was revolutionary in its context, he did not advocate violent revolution, but neither did he offer any strategic or tactical programme for obtaining reform by other means. Faced with the loss of middle-class allies after the loyalist upsurge of 1792 and an increasingly repressive government the popular reformers had increasingly few options open to them. The crushing of the Scottish and London Conventions was followed by the Two Acts of 1795, one of which, the Seditious Meetings Act, cut the radicals off from their only available means of mass agitation and propaganda, the large mass meetings of the kind attended by thousands of people in London and Sheffield in 1794 and 1795. Francis Place reflected this impasse when he wrote of the 1790s that neither peaceful agitation nor insurrectionary plotting would bring about reform, rather he believed that the government would go on until it was brought down by its own difficulties. It was the duty of reformers to politically educate the people so that they would be ready to make good use of their opportunity when it arose.[25]

But popular feeling towards the radical movement was not always as favourable as it had appeared in Scotland. Although there were pro-French demonstrations in Sheffield and some other places in the autumn of 1792, the most widespread manifestations of popular feeling were the Church and King riots in Birmingham and Manchester in 1791-2 and the spate of anti-Paineite demonstrations in November 1792. Once war commenced, patriotic demonstrations at military successes also became occasions for attacks upon radicals and reformers of all descriptions. Although often orchestrated by the magistracy, or at least sanctioned by them, as in the case of the Priestley Riots, they also often comprised a genuine element of the zealous xenophobia and strident loyalism which had its antecedents earlier in the century. In some areas, such as Wales, historians have argued that in popular protests against recruiting, enclosures and grain prices in the 1790s 'a political thread of Jacobin democracy runs through everything, weaving in and out of the crowd actions'.[26] This is less clear in England where although there were riots and disturbances of many different kinds in the 1790s – over prices, labour disputes, enclosure, turnpikes and recruiting, most can be seen as belonging to the traditional 'sub-political' arena of the 'moral economy' rather than the more conscious world of Jacobin democracy. In Scotland, too, the historian of the Scottish disturbances suggests that while the King's Birthday Riot and the 'Tree of Liberty' demonstrations were something of a half-way house, moving towards a more positive view of the political importance of the common people, many of the other disturbances, against clearance, the militia and high prices, remained largely apolitical.[27]

This is well illustrated by the great wave of food rioting which spread through the country in 1795-6 in response to the gravest harvest crisis for 30 years. Although some agitational literature was discovered and the authorities certainly feared the use to which distress might be put by the 'mischievous and evil-minded', the great majority of these disturbances conformed to the character of food rioting found earlier in the century; in many cases a semi-ritualised bargaining process with local authorities for relief or regulation of the market. Strikingly, too, although we now have detailed studies of several areas where food riots were prominent in 1795–6 and again in the next harvest crisis of 1800–1, widespread as they were, food disturbances were primarily an urban phenomenon or of mixed urban-rural environments such as industrial villages; large parts of rural Britain where the majority of the population still lived remained relatively quiescent. In contrast to the riotous small towns of Devon or the market towns of East Anglia, the more rural counties such as Dorset and Lincolnshire registered hardly any disturbances at all.[28]

London also failed to fulfil the more sanguinary expectations of the days of the Gordon Riots. The most serious disturbances in the capital in the 1790s were the anti-crimp house riots of August 1794 when several houses used as recruiting centres were wrecked by crowds on the suspicion that they kidnapped men for the armed forces. Even though some fiery handbills were anonymously distributed in the riots the LCS steadfastly eschewed any responsibility for disturbances which appear to have been primarily a response to war-time grievances. Similarly in the troubled year of 1795, a recurrence of a mixture of anti-recruiting and price riots in the summer in London was accompanied by some agitational literature; there is little evidence, however, that the radicals had either the desire or the need to encourage what were largely spontaneous reactions to wartime distress. The most famous episode of that year, the mass demonstration and attack on the king's coach on 29 October as he attended the opening of Parliament was blamed by the government on the LCS who, it was alleged, had stirred up the populace to such acts by their programme of mass meetings in the capital, one of which had taken place three days earlier. In fact, there is little evidence that the LCS directly fomented the demonstration, although they may well have contributed to the popular anti-war feeling which emerged in the cries of 'No War', 'No Pitt', 'Give us Bread', 'Peace, peace' which greeted the king.

The conventional picture of the 1790s used to end with the disintegration of the popular radical societies under the twin pressures of disillusionment and government repression. Increasingly, however, discussion has focused on Thompson's argument for the continuity of radical activity and the persistence of a 'revolutionary underground' in the years 1799–1810. We no longer need to doubt the existence of an insurrectionary strand that flowed from the more determined survivors of the LCS and the provincial societies into clandestine and often treasonable complicity with the Irish and French. As Marianne Elliott has shown, the fears of government in 1799–1800 and again in 1802–3 were not entirely groundless as some of the radicals sought the means and assistance to bring about an insurrection. Debate is largely about how widespread and representative these groups were. Certainly on Elliott's evidence their ambitions were on a grand scale, a simultaneous rising of the Irish, the North and London, with assistance from France, if not by full-blooded invasion, at least by a diversionary raid. The so-called 'Despard Conspiracy' of 1802 was only the London end of this grandiose design, aborted by the arrest of the London activists with its other components such as Emmet's Irish rising of 1803 left to go off half-cock and unsupported.[29]

The question of how significant these genuinely insurrectionary movements were has focused on whether events such as the naval mutinies of 1797 and the wave of food-riots in 1800–1 can be seen as evidence of a more radical temper than earlier in the decade. Roger Wells has attempted more than anyone else to explore the revolutionary potential of these episodes.[30] But while it can be shown that some politicisation took place, especially in the Nore mutinies, the main character of the naval mutinies was that of a protracted episode of wage-bargaining. Moreover while the food riots of 1800–1 did witness more agitational literature and generally suggest a stronger strain of anti-government feeling, most of the disturbances continued to show the character of the classic eighteenth-century food riot, with their emphasis on fair prices, resistance to exploitation by the middlemen, and an appeal to the authorities to intervene on their behalf. This is not to deny that a shift of food disturbances towards the manufacturing districts was taking place and that in this context distress and scarcity, combined with radical propaganda, could play an important role in developing more widespread support for political ideas. The extent to which this can be described as creating a 'mass movement' remains questionable, nor can incipient 'insurrection' necessarily be deduced from the presence of inflammatory handbills and reports of nocturnal meetings. The former could and often did emanate from small groups whose activities were not necessarily an accurate reflection of the state of mind of the populace as a whole, the latter were often exaggerated and some at least were concerned with trade union activity rather than politics. These issues have been raised acutely in discussion of the significance of the 'Black Lamp' or 'Black Lump' conspiracy in Yorkshire during 1802. Reports of plans for a general rising, of nocturnal meetings and drilling from both informers and magistrates have been interpreted as evidence of a widespread insurrectionary movement. J.L. Baxter and F.K. Donnelly have seen in this the continuation of the radicalism of the 1790s in the Sheffield area and the West Riding. Some continuity of personnel from the 1790s has certainly been demonstrated and some kind of conspiratorial activity does seem to have been taking place, but, as J.R. Dinwiddy has pointed out, the extent and overall significance of the movement remains obscure and much of the reported activity may have been primarily apolitical.[31]

Detailed work on popular radicalism in London has also led to some judicious evaluation of Thompson's arguments. J. Ann Hone's survey of London radicalism from 1796 to 1821 has demonstrated the manner in which reformers after the 1790s sought new ways of promoting the cause of reform. While some did turn to conspiracy, others engaged in educational projects and legal political activity.[32] The re-emergence of men like Place and some of his fellow members of the LCS in the Westminster election campaign of 1807 was evidence of one strategy of adjustment to the unreformed system. Increasingly, at this level, historians have recognised the revival in radical activity in the latter years of the Napoleonic Wars. The support for Burdett and the championing of his cause by the London mob when he was imprisoned in 1810, illustrates a switch in emphasis to support for upper-class, radical MPs elected as opponents of 'corruption' and self-consciously 'independent'. The writings of a new generation of radical publicists, notably Cobbett, with their attack on Whigs and Tories alike, the founding of the Hampden Clubs from 1812, and the call for varying degrees of extended franchise within the context of the existing parliamentary system represented a revival of the constitutional reform movement which was to form the background to the reform campaigns of 1816–17 and 1819.

Moreover, also within the capital, I. Prothero's study of the shipwright leader, John Gast, has illustrated the difficulty of separating trade union and political strands of activity in one instance. Gast has been shown to be not only an outstanding early trade union leader but one who participated with others from the skilled London trades in the reform campaigns after 1815.[33] In this context, at least, and perhaps elsewhere in places such as South Wales, Yorkshire and Lancashire, the idea of a common 'artisan consciousness' embracing both political and trade union activity is not fanciful. This is clearer too, now that the more exaggerated claims for the repressive effects of the Combination Laws have been modified. There is ample evidence that trade union activity continued under the Combination Laws through the agency of Friendly Societies, clandestine meetings and *ad hoc* combinations. The Webbs themselves pointed out that the London craft trades were never more completely organised than between 1800 and 1820 and several saw a strengthening of organisation, with increased emphasis on wage-bargaining machinery among groups such as carpenters, brushmakers, basketmakers, compositors, silk-weavers and tinplate workers. The wartime years in London have been characterised by Prothero as seeing 'unprecedented inflation, unprecedented wage demands and an unprecedented number of strikes'. As a result the London trade societies emerged from the wars far more strongly than when they had begun.[34]

Elsewhere in the country the Tyne Keelmen organised a successful three-week strike in 1809 to increase piece-work rates. The handloom weavers of the North, increasingly finding their position undermined by the introduction of power looms and by the flooding of the labour market with cheap unskilled labour, tried petitioning Parliament for a Minimum Wage Bill in 1799 and 1800 and again in 1807, when 130,000 signatures were obtained in Lancashire, Cheshire and Yorkshire. News of the rejection of the Bill in May 1807 led to disturbances in Manchester when thousands of weavers assembled and sent delegates to the manufacturers and town officials to demand some redress of their grievances. A strike was begun, and was spread through the cotton district in which the men sought an increase in wages of a third. By June 1808 over 60,000 looms were idle and the employees were eventually forced to come to an agreement. Nor were trade union organisations confined to the older groups of craftsmen. The first organisations of cotton spinners had appeared in the 1780s and 1790s. In 1795 the Manchester cotton spinners conducted two strikes for wage increases, the latter lasting a month and proving successful. Further strikes are recorded in 1799, 1800, 1802, though in 1803 the masters raised a fund of £20,000 to defeat another dispute. In 1810, however, the men took advantage of a surge in production to create a wider organisation. After federating their unions, 30,000 spinners struck work and were organised by a congress at Manchester. Supported by contributions totalling £17,000, collected from spinners still working, the strike lasted four months before funds ran out and the men were forced back to work.

Against this background the Luddite outbreaks which affected much of the North and Midlands in 1811–12 have been increasingly recognised as more than a mere blind and spasmodic episode of resistance to technological change. Historians have debated how far political motives penetrated into what was clearly a complex and many-sided movement.[35] A certain consensus has emerged that the frame-breaking which began in Nottinghamshire, Leicestershire and Derbyshire in 1811 fits most readily within the tradition of 'collective bargaining by riot'. By 1811 attempts by the framework knitters of the area to achieve regulation of their trade had failed to achieve any results at a time when unemployment, wage cuts, and high prices bore increasingly hard upon the men. Although the framework knitters' leader, Gravenor Henson, had little choice but to disavow the violence which took place, frame-breaking was seen by many workers as a continuation of wage-bargaining by other means. Most reports emphasised the selectivity of the machine breakers who concentrated on the frames of masters who either underpaid or produced cheap 'cut-up' stockings, using unskilled workers, and the discipline of the bands, meeting secretly then proceeding from village to village to do the frame-breaking. Many of the documents from the Luddites breathed the familiar language of eighteenth-century trade societies, an appeal to protective legislation of the past and to the authorities to intervene on their behalf. Significantly, violent and more peaceful methods appeared to move in cadence with each other. When the first and major wave of machine-breaking was crushed by the stationing of 2000 troops in the Midlands, a 'United Committee of Framework-Knitters' was formed to promote a parliamentary Bill to regulate the trade. When the Bill was rejected in the Lords and the framework knitters prosecuted under the Combination Laws in July 1814, frame-breaking was resumed.

In Yorkshire, to which Luddism spread in 1812, it occurred in the aftermath of the failure of a joint campaign by the 'croppers' of the South-West and Yorkshire to enforce the Tudor statutes against the use of machinery and unapprenticed labour. The two areas had cooperated through delegates and had put a Bill before Parliament in 1805 backed by several petitions. In the event, the croppers' agitation failed, annual Suspending Acts allowed manufacturers to introduce machinery until a general repeal of paternalistic regulation of the woollen trade was passed in 1809. Frustrated in constitutional and peaceful methods, the Yorkshire croppers turned to machine-breaking in the midst of unemployment and high prices. Although there is *some* evidence of political, even insurrectionary undertones to Yorkshire Luddism, their activities were only a variation upon the other means of resisting the erosion of the bargaining position of the workers. It was significant that in another part of the country in 1812, the Scottish weavers conducted one of the most impressive strikes in early trade union history, bringing 40,000 looms to a standstill for six weeks in an area stretching from Carlisle to Aberdeen. In Lancashire, Luddism was a confused mixture of food rioting, frame-breaking and political activity, in which allegations of widespread insurrectionary plotting were made, but were never, in fact, given any opportunity to reveal themselves as arrests and the deployment of troops ended the unrest.

The defeat of Luddism did not end agitation in the manufacturing districts. After 1815 they were to be part of the nationwide campaign for parliamentary reform which culminated in the Peterloo massacre and the Six Acts. The founding of the first political organisations for working men in the early 1790s clearly began a process of political education and involvement which had major implications for the future. Changes in industry and the economy, as well as the autonomous evolution of popular politics from the days of Wilkes, have to be put alongside the French Revolution as influencing this development. After 1815 less was heard of the ancient or Anglo-Saxon constitution and more of natural rights, though radical agitation was generally directed at a wholesale reform of Parliament rather than outright republicanism. But the effects of the French Revolution also posed an acute political dilemma in frightening off respectable reformers and setting Parliament against any concessions for a full 40 years. Some radicals responded by plotting insurrection, others retained a faith in achieving reform by extra-parliamentary agitation in alliance with parliamentary sympathisers, more than has been realised oscillated between the two depending upon the circumstances. Burdett wept at Thistlewood's execution in 1820 and the cool-headed Francis Place was to be found threatening violent insurrection in 1832. The line between constitutional and revolutionary, between reformer and radical, was never clear-cut. But organisationally, the world after 1815 was a different place. Significantly, the food riot was increasingly giving way to the strike, popular reform societies grew up rapidly in the post-war climate and the thousands of sober, peaceful working men and women who read Cobbett's 'two penny trash' and gathered for reform meetings like that of Peterloo were already a considerable distance from the world of the 1780s.

4. Ireland and the French Revolution

MARIANNE ELLIOTT

In 1789 Ireland's economy was booming. There was a general mood of confidence. Her Parliament had won considerable independence from England, and further political and social reforms were on the cards. By 1815, however, Ireland was a byword for lawlessness, her populace was deeply divided on social and sectarian lines, and there was widespread alienation from the state and the ruling classes. She had lost all political and economic independence, with the abolition of her Parliament and full legislative union with England, and the crisis had produced the two forces which would dictate the nation's constitutional development thereafter: republican nationalism and Orange loyalism. Not all can be attributed directly to the impact of the French Revolution. The calm and confidence masked underlying tensions which the French Revolution unleashed, and politically it was as much the occasion as the cause of developments long in gestation. That said, the French Revolution and the subsequent wars brought these developments to such a head that the history of Ireland and of Anglo-Irish relations was radically altered thereafter.

I

Relations between the Irish and English Parliaments were strained throughout the eighteenth century. Whereas the former acknowledged no superior authority but that of the king, Westminster enshrined her right to legislate for Ireland in statute, appointed and closely monitored Irish government officials, and ensured Irish parliamentary compliance through places and pensions. An opposition patriot movement, aimed at reducing government (and English) influence, had existed in the Irish Parliament since the 1760s. In the 1770s and 1780s its members were enthusiastic supporters of the Americans in their fight for independence. The identity of the American complaint against the mother Parliament with their own and the strong ties through emigration (particularly from Ulster) turned Ireland into a dangerously pro-American colony on England's doorstep, and she acceded to a masterful campaign, by granting Irish legislative independence in 1782–3. Thereafter the victors became complacent. Instead of 1782 initiating a period of further reform – as supporters outside Parliament had expected – the so-called constitution of that year became in itself a barrier to reform, considered by parliamentarians such a perfect expression of their independence that any suggestion of reform was deemed an attack on a sacred structure.

In their campaign the Irish patriots, like their Dutch and French counterparts, had enlisted extra-parliamentary support. In doing so they helped create a middle-class identity which would go on to demand an opening up of the political system. It found its most immediate expression in the Volunteers – a citizens' militia, formed in Ulster in 1778, to defend a country denuded of troops for the American war.[1] The Volunteers were fiercely pro-American and hostile to English dominance in Irish political life. With England requiring little reminder of the dangers of Ireland going the way of the Americans, the Volunteers could claim 1782 as their particular victory. In a series of conventions, which went on to demand parliamentary reform, they became a threat to the very Parliament they had helped to independence. The challenge was faced down, but the lesson that even the patriots were part of a social elite, unwilling to share power with the middle classes, was not lost, and it is no accident that it was the Dublin, but most of all, the Belfast Volunteers who went on to form the ultra-radical Society of United Irishmen in the wake of the French Revolution.

As elsewhere in Europe, the French Revolution erupted upon a situation in which new classes were already campaigning for a participation in power, power which in Ireland was held by a narrow social elite collectively referred to as the Protestant or Anglo-Irish ascendancy. Since Catholics were totally excluded from political power by the penal laws, and Dissenters had only limited access, the ascendancy denoted that class of episcopalian gentry who either sat in Parliament or had control of parliamentary seats and had access to professional preferment. Most were either landowners themselves, or had landowners as patrons. More corrupt and factional than English parliamentary politics, those in Ireland revolved around the pursuit of office and preferment. At a time when crown (or executive) influence was declining at Westminster, in Ireland it escalated dramatically after 1782.[2] The very term 'ascendancy' was novel, adopted initially in 1792 by that elite itself, as a barrier against those clamouring for admission, and thereafter used pejoratively as a badge of bigoted and unreasonable exclusiveness.[3] The rhetoric of polarisation had already taken place before the political fact.

As in France, the breakdown in political consensus was the backdrop to revolution. But the campaign of the mid 1780s, to open up Parliament to other forms of property besides land, foundered on another issue – that of anti-popery. Sectarian identity was deeply ingrained in eighteenth-century Irish society. A long struggle for power between Catholic and Protestant in the seventeenth century had resulted in Protestant victory, major confiscations of Catholic land and a series of laws depriving the Catholics of political rights and penalising their religion.[4] But on the whole the Catholics remained quiescent thereafter, even if Gaelic literature had all the rhetoric of slavery, oppression and deliverance, and sectarian identity remained stronger with the Protestants who had more to lose.[5] Consequently, when religious toleration was already the ethos of many European states, every major relaxation of the penal laws had to be forced upon the Irish politicians by Whitehall. More importantly, it was the Ulster Presbyterians' anti-Catholicism which muted their strong republican leanings and criticism of the existing governing structure.

In Ulster much of the land confiscated from the Catholic population in the seventeenth century was settled by imported English and Scottish tenants. But the Scottish Presbyterians tended to be better off, more mobile, more independent, than the lower class episcopalians. Their better economic standing, their democratic church structure and religion based on the belief of a direct covenant between God and man caused an anti-authoritarianism which was out of step with the contemporary hierarchical and deferential system.[6] They were seen by successive governments as the most volatile in Irish society, more dangerous even than the Catholics. It was the prospect of an alliance between the two which caused Pitt in 1792 and again in 1793 to force upon the Dublin Parliament major Catholic concessions, despite the possible repercussions in England, where Catholics had considerably fewer rights after 1793 than their Irish co-religionists and where there might be a Protestant backlash.[7]

Such an alliance would have been unthinkable before the French Revolution. The Volunteer reform movement had failed because their fear of the Catholics allowed the authorities to call their bluff without risk of retaliation. As the reform campaign of the 1780s foundered on the Catholic issue, one of the Ulster leaders, Archibald Hamilton Rowan, entered into a lengthy correspondence with his former tutor at Cambridge – the unitarian and radical thinker, John Jebb – on the related problems of the Catholic franchise (removed in 1728) and reform. While a reform of Parliament should be the first object of the reformers, Jebb replied, in Ireland that would not be obtained unless all religious persuasions were united in the attempt.[8] It was the same argument used to great effect by Theobald Wolfe Tone, which led to the foundation of the Society of United Irishmen – soon to become Ireland's first republican movement.

II

Erupting upon this soul-searching among the advanced Protestant reformers, the French Revolution attracted most support in Ireland for its religious policies, its dismantling of church power in the state and most of all the sharing of political power by Catholic and Protestant alike. The French example removed the impasse which had prevented the reformers' progression to a demand for radical parliamentary reform, and the mood in Ireland in 1791–2 was one of optimism and hope. Colourful parades took place in Dublin and Belfast on the anniversary of the French Revolution, and in November 1792 even tiny Ulster towns illuminated to celebrate the expulsion of the enemy armies from France. It was not only the expression of admiration for a nation long reviled for its repressive Catholicism, but also of a feeling that France was fighting for liberty everywhere and the Irish reform campaign became identified with the progress of reforms in France.

Yet, apart from a generalised expression of support, reaction to the French Revolution had been slow at first and did not take off into the positive French mania of 1791 onwards until the publication of Paine's *Rights of Man*. Part I was first published in Ireland in March 1791, and was quickly ensured a large distribution by a subsidy from the Dublin reformers which dropped the price to 6d. It went into three editions in Dublin alone, selling the entire stock of 10,000 by May; it was serialised by the radical press and in Belfast had the largest circulation of any pamphlet. Its influence was particularly noticeable among that group of Presbyterian businessmen who would spearhead a major revolutionary organisation from 1795 onwards. Paine's own Dissenting background gave his work a particular appeal. The idea of a direct compact between

God and man, of governments, monarchies, established religions as artificial barriers and of sovereignty resting with the individual accorded well with the Presbyterians' world view and gave them a new bible to justify the antagonism they had long felt towards England and the governing system in Ireland. Paine's glowing and highly inaccurate account of the French Revolution, and his criticism of 'the old aristocratical system', were taken up enthusiastically.

More importantly, Paine had provided the slogans of liberty and revolt which took on their own dynamic. Rioters in the furthest corners of the country called for 'liberty and equality' among more traditional demands. 'The sentiments of Tom Paine [were] garbled in the gibberish of these deluded wretches', wrote the pro-government *Freeman's Journal* of rioters in Cork early in 1794. Meanwhile, the North was reported to be 'completely inoculated by Paine, who persuades every man to think himself a legislator and to throw off all respect for his superiors.'[9] But it was Paine's attack on religious intolerance (and tolerance as its 'counterfeit'), as an offshoot of the barriers which states and state religions raised between man and his God, which most struck home.[10] In October 1791 it was Wolfe Tone's application of such principles to the Irish situation in his best-selling *Argument on behalf of the Catholics of Ireland* which caused him to be invited to Belfast to help found the Society of United Irishmen.

The United Irish Society was the most radical to emerge in the British Isles as a direct result of French revolutionary inspiration. It was founded in Belfast in October 1791 by a group of middle-class reformers: the Dublin lawyer, Theobald Wolfe Tone, his friend, the young army ensign Thomas Russell, and ten prominent Belfast Presbyterians, including the woollen draper, Samuel Neilson, the mill-owner, William Sinclair, the tanners, William and Robert Simms, and the shipbroker, Henry Haslett. The foundation resolutions, drawn up by Tone, declared: 'That the weight of English influence in the Government of this country is so great, as to require a cordial union, among ALL THE PEOPLE OF IRELAND... that the sole constitutional mode by which this influence can be opposed, is by a complete and radical reform of the people in Parliament.... That no reform is practicable, efficacious, or just, which does not include *Irishmen* of every religious persuasion.' The society remained an open debating one until 1794, its main branches in Belfast and Dublin conducting proceedings with all the conventional strictness of a college debating society.[11]

Embarrassed by the introspection which had caused the bitter religious divisions in Ireland and deeply influenced by Enlightenment cosmopolitanism, it was and remained enamoured of early French internationalism. Its newspaper – *The Northern Star* – carried the most French news of any paper in Ireland and its favourable bias is unmistakeable. French rhetoric about fighting the cause of mankind and rejecting wars of conquest was particularly singled out. It was this romantic view of the Revolution, perpetuated by Paine, which permitted them to overcome their scruples and attach their cause to France's war strategy after 1795. Although they later went on to mount a war of independence from England, such cosmopolitanism persisted first in lines put out to radical societies in England and Scotland, and latterly in the development of a pan-British revolutionary movement in the United Englishmen and United Britons.[12]

The United Irishmen are the recognised founders of Irish republican nationalism, which in the nineteenth and twentieth centuries sought independence from England through armed struggle. But in this sense they were reluctant republicans. Their republicanism was rather the post-Renaissance classical republicanism, dominant in the British commonwealthman and Dissenting traditions. Classical republicanism held public good as the end of all government. It sought to establish cheap government by eroding luxury and corruption, and it joined forces with the Enlightenment in its belief in public virtue and its mission of public regeneration.[13]

It was Paine, however, who popularised such notions and it was in Paineite language that they were transmitted to a wider audience. His attack on hereditary monarchies and on the corruption and expense of aristocratic governments, and his celebration of the right of every man to make and unmake his own government, helped distil longstanding traditions into a sustained attack on the evils of the Irish governing system. 'Liberty', proclaimed the address of the United Irishmen to the Volunteers in December 1792, 'is the exercise of all our rights natural and political, secured to us and our posterity by a real representation of the people, to the end that government, which is collective power, may be guided by collective will.' A month earlier their widely circulated and thoroughly Paineite *Address... to the Delegates for promoting a reform in Scotland* proclaimed: 'It is not upon a coalition of opposition with ministry that we depend, but upon a coalition of Irishmen with Irishmen.... We do not worship the British, far less the Irish constitution, as sent down from heaven, but we consider it as human workmanship, which man has made and man can mend. An unalterable constitution... must be despotism.'

The French Revolution they admired because 'that people were thus enabled to choose their own government – which we presume, is the natural and unalienable right of every people'.[14] The execution of Louis XVI they condoned because he had betrayed the trust of the people. It took them some time to apply the same principle to George III, whom they had always considered above politics.[15]

Classical republicanism, however, was not incompatible with monarchy, and the United Irishmen had no difficulty distinguishing between the crown as person/institution and the crown as executive influence in Parliament. Their parliamentary reform plan was radical, but hardly revolutionary, differing little from that proposed by the Westminster Association in 1780, and calling for universal manhood suffrage, annual parliaments, equal electoral districts, payment for MPs, and the abolition of property qualifications for parliamentary candidates.[16] Combined with the removal of tithes and hearth-tax, reductions in excise duties and the vast power of the revenue officers (which were indeed popular grievances),[17] and church disestablishment, the United Irishmen also had a Smithian belief in the general good of free circulation of wealth.

Like classical republicans generally, however, they had no blueprint for revolution if the governing system refused to reform itself. It must never be forgotten that the French Revolution was revolution as fact rather than revolution as act. It was not brought about by any preconceived plan, but by the collapse of royal government. Its novelty lay in the necessary creation of political culture after the event.[18] In Ireland the weakness of the Dublin government in the early 1790s caused a temporary alliance between Whiggish aristocrats and extra-parliamentary pressure groups such as that which had occurred in France and in the patriot revolution of the Netherlands. But with the containment of the Catholic emancipation campaign and the declaration of war in 1793, the political elite closed ranks. A newly-strengthened government was able to resist reform demands for the duration of the war and clamp down on organisations like the United Irishmen, whose francophilia had graduated from being an irritant to near treason.

Unexceptional the Society's parliamentary reform programme might appear, but the devastating attacks it launched against the entire governing system through a sophisticated and highly successful propaganda machine were profoundly revolutionary in implication. In terms consciously designed for the common man, the United Irishmen had attributed every wrong to biased privilege, and held out all manner of benefit to be expected from parliamentary reform and Catholic emancipation. They conceived their role to be one of public educators and a flood of handbills, squibs, popular ballads, broadsheets and pamphlets issued from their numerous presses. At the Society's weekly meetings these papers were left in bundles for free distribution by members. They were distributed by hawkers and pedlars or by their lawyer members on circuit, used as wrappers for commercial goods, left gratis at cabin doors, and found circulating at public events. Ireland's highly mobile populace made the task of swift public re-education easier than in revolutionary France. The United Irishmen, by subsidising their propaganda, were far more adept populists than the French Jacobins, who expected the *sans-culottes* actually to pay for their song-books.[19] The United Irishmen had thus created a revolutionary culture long before they themselves became active revolutionaries. The question they had to answer by 1794 – when their organisation was suppressed by government – was whether they were prepared to follow through their rhetoric by leading to armed resistance a public they had helped educate to such an eventuality if their expectations were denied.

For theirs was the dilemma of all classical republicans – what to do when governments took their revolutionary rhetoric seriously and were strong enough to suppress it and its purveyors alike. The United Irishmen were to claim repression as the main cause of their transformation from an advanced reform movement into a revolutionary one by the end of 1795. Certainly on the eve of the declaration of war in February 1793 they had confidently expected a grant of full Catholic emancipation and extensive parliamentary reform. Instead enough was held back from the 1793 Catholic Relief Bill to sustain dissatisfaction. The reform issue was constantly deferred and finally defeated in 1794. With stunning suddenness a package of measures was rushed through Parliament in 1793 to ban the kind of extra-parliamentary mobilisation which had rendered the Catholic Committee and United Irishmen alike so effective since 1791, a secret committee report all but damned such activities as treasonable and over the next year severe prison sentences were handed out to several prominent leaders for publications deemed unexceptional only a year earlier. The war, the turn of events in France after the September massacres of 1792, and most of all the royal executions had eroded moderate support for reform. Attendance at the main Dublin United Irish Society dwindled from 160 in January 1793 to 20–40 by the time of its suppression in May 1794.[20] A rump group continued to meet but there was an absence of any sense of direction and a despondent waiting upon events.

The necessity of taking any radical decision about their future was deferred by renewed expectations of major concessions with the arrival in January 1795 of a new Whig Lord Lieutenant, Earl Fitzwilliam (a product of Pitt's coalition with the Portland Whigs). His pro-Catholic sympathies were well known and as he proceeded to dismiss some of the most hated ascendancy figures from government it looked as if the United Irishmen might be spared an unsavoury resort to arms. But Fitzwilliam was reprimanded by London and abruptly recalled, and the riots which greeted his successor at the end of March were a token of the intense alienation of the populace from government which would be the hallmark of the rest of the war. Certainly the 'journeymen, artificers and tradesmen', who had dominated some of the northern societies, had already been pushing the middle-class members to assume control of a renovated revolutionary movement – a request to which they finally consented after the Fitzwilliam fiasco.[21]

In composition the United Irishmen came in time to represent all sections of society in Ireland's towns and villages. However, it was Ulster middle-class Dissent which provided the most dynamic leadership in both constitutional and revolutionary phases of the movement. Otherwise leadership was composed of a breakaway element of the very ascendancy they were attacking, a number of veteran radicals from the 1780s, several printers and pamphleteers, and a dominant group of professionals, denied the career advancement accorded those with ascendancy connections. As such its personnel did possess similarities to the French revolutionary models of Robert Darnton's down-at-heel literati and Lynn Hunt's 'nearly "ins"' on the periphery of power.[22] The ascendancy members had all the confidence and recklessness of their class and tended to be the most extreme and incautious. Long before it became Society policy, Lord Edward Fitzgerald (a veteran of the American war and later to become United Irish commander-in-chief) was corresponding with Tom Paine in Paris about the possibility of effecting a French-supported revolution in Ireland.[23] The first French agent to arrive as a result of this initiative (May 1793) found the United Irishmen stunned and demoralised at the latest turn of events and dismissive of the idea that a French invasion could alter things. The next agent – the Anglican minister, the Rev. William Jackson – arrived in April 1794 to find the leaders still hesitant, but more willing to entertain such an idea. More importantly, with Jackson's arrest and trial (a year later in April 1795), several key United Irish leaders, including Rowan and Tone, were openly implicated with treason and decided to make a virtue of necessity. The formal inauguration of the new revolutionary United Irish Society took place the following month, and Tone, about to go into exile in America, was commissioned to travel on to France to ask for the military aid proferred so readily by successive French agents.

III

It was, however, the attachment of the middle and lower levels of Catholic society which turned the United Irishmen into a mass revolutionary movement. Jebb had told Rowan in 1784 that the Catholics were naturally inclined to authority and suggested that in the case of the remaining Catholic aristocracy property would prove a stronger bond with the Protestant ascendancy than religion. Certainly the aristocratic leaders of the Catholic Committee had shown themselves as unwilling to share power with their middle-class coreligionists as their social peers of the ascendancy. It was this recognition which, in the new climate of opinion created by Paine and the French Revolution, led a group of Catholic middle class and gentry to reject the aristocratic leadership of their committee and the practice of humble petitioning which had been the tactic since mid century. In an aggressive campaign, which adopted the volunteering tactic of organising through extra-parliamentary representative institutions, the new Catholic Committee helped break the mould of deference which had kept many Catholic tenants in the hold of their gentry.

Yet, despite major concessions in 1792 and 1793, all the avenues to political power – including seats in Parliament itself, and more immediately municipal power, as corporations refused to implement legislation granting Catholics the right of admission – remained closed to Catholics, and they finally threw in their lot with the United Irishmen in 1795.[24] The Paineite rhetoric, through which reform and emancipation campaigns had been fought, had already broken down barriers between the middle-class Catholic and Protestant. 'One consequence of these publications is a strong union between the better classes of Papists and Dissenters', wrote Leonard McNally, a leading United Irish lawyer and government informer, 'They have been brought to think alike'.[25]

The same cross-religious cooperation, however, occurred only patchily in urban and northern areas and rarely in rural parts, where United Irish propaganda had been reinterpreted as an opportunity 'to knock the

Protestants on the head, and...take their places'.[26] In acquiring a necessary popular base, the United Irishmen were introducing into their movement the very sectarianism they had set out to destroy.

If a significant proportion of the middle class of all denominations was already alienated from existing governing structures, the alienation of the Catholic lower classes came about as a direct result of the events of the 1790s. The 1780s and early 1790s witnessed a period of unprecedented prosperity and expansion. But against a background of equally unprecedented population rise (with population doubling since mid-century) these developments created their own tensions. Though generically referred to as peasants, large numbers of Ireland's rural population did not earn their main livelihood from the land, but rather from widespread domestic industry. Rising rents, food prices and taxation led to a dramatic downswing in the economic standards of the artisan, skilled trades and labouring classes generally, particularly in the first year of the war when a banking crisis and export embargo threw thousands out of work, notably in the textile trades. Linen, on which the prosperity of Ulster, and to a lesser extent north-east Leinster and the midlands was based, was particularly vulnerable to the dislocation of the wars and the loss of markets, and fell off steadily from 1795 onwards.[27] Though only part of the reason, economic distress was an important element in the increasing attraction of such elements into secret organisations, notably the Defenders and, from 1795 onwards, the United Irishmen.

The economic and social tensions of these years are particularly important in explaining the rise of the Defenders and the sectarian attacks which would determine the character of the 1798 rebellion. Ulster, already the most densely populated part of the country in the eighteenth century, registered the largest increase in the general demographic explosion of its closing years. The Ulster economy was also dominated by those very textile trades which were particularly hit by wartime slumps and restrictions. Economic rivalries between Catholics and Protestants were intensified by the Catholic Relief Acts of 1782 and 1793, giving Catholics the right to own land and to vote. Linen-induced prosperity for the first time enabled them to compete with Protestants for scarce holdings. Meanwhile, the 1793 grant of the Catholic franchise removed the edge a marketable vote had given Protestant tenants over Catholics in the land market, at the very time when a downswing in the fortunes of the domestic weaver was eroding confidence generally. The loss of such economic superiority was an important element in increasing

Protestant attacks on Catholics from the mid 1780s. The outcome was the opposing movements of Catholic Defenders and Protestant Orangemen, which were to radiate out from their origins in the historic sectarian conflicts of Armagh to affect much of the country by 1798.[28] The impact of the French Revolution was to politicise both and give sectarianism those conflicting badges of loyalism and republicanism which have persisted to the present day.

IV

The resistance of the Protestant ascendancy to sharing power with the middle classes and Catholic gentry destroyed its credibility, even with England. England considered the connection with Ireland fundamental to her own security and to that of the empire.[29] Yet in 1785 the newly self-confident Irish politicians rejected certain readjustments necessitated by their Parliament's new status. It was Pitt's most serious failure in his first two years of office and he never forgot it. He was particularly bitter against those who were government supporters, whom he felt should do as they were told. After war broke out in 1793, his government browbeat them into passing unwelcome reforms, and in 1798 simply ignored them altogether when rebellion and invasion confirmed Britain's belief that Ireland's inability to govern herself posed a danger to the entire empire. London was dismissive of ascendancy claims that the Catholic majority was disloyal and equally of its tendency to run to London for military support against its own populace – a tendency which increased dramatically during the French wars.[30] The Irish landed establishment was expected to be a mirror-image of the English squirearchy and look after its own internal defence. But as Ireland became a war zone in a way that England never did, so Ireland's ability to contribute to the imperial war effort dwindled, and the bulk of military expenditure after 1793 was incurred in her own defence. By the end of the decade Irish government expenditure had increased five-fold and it became dependent on British government credit to keep it afloat.[31] There was little left of its independence when it was finally killed off by the Union in 1800.

England's belief that the ascendancy was responsible for its own plight had some foundation in fact. Nevertheless London's considerable lack of understanding of the niceties of the Irish situation contributed to its deterioration in the 1790s. The war opened with a sign of things to come when, after over a year of attrition, England pulled rank in 1793 and forced the Irish governing party to admit the Catholics to the elective franchise. The self-confidence which was such an important element in the liberalisation of attitudes by the early 1790s was eroded, and the violence of reaction against rising discontent in the country was in part dictated by the ascendancy's own sense of insecurity.

Its reaction to serious anti-militia riots shortly after this forced acceptance of the 1793 Catholic Relief Act was the first example of the landed class's use of military reprisal as first resort. The riots were largely the outcome of normal popular opposition to conscription and the authorities over-reacted. Five times as many lives were lost in two months than in disturbances over the past twenty years. The same reaction continued through a Convention Act – outlawing the kind of gatherings which had won legislative independence and more recently the 1793 Catholic Relief Act – draconian sentences against Defenders and United Irish leaders, an Insurrection Act in 1796, which surprised even Whitehall by its ferocity, and the creation of an exclusively Protestant yeomanry which effectively placed in the hands of the Orangemen the task of subduing the country. Government, the landlord class which composed it, and English rule generally were seen as engines of biased authority. The social processes which had kept Ireland peaceful for much of the century were a classic example of the workings of the 'moral economy'. Until the 1760s agrarian protest was rare, and even then was targeted at restoring old conventions and practices. Economic pressures were already eroding it by the 1790s, but it was finally destroyed by the violence of that decade and the identification of landlord and government generally as the enemy. The 'moral economy' was in tatters, and the readiness with which magistrates resorted to force in the years leading up to 1798 made resistance justified.[32]

Yet the story was not all one-sided. The French Revolution and revolutionary wars may have caused the London government to trample on the sensitivities of the Irish ascendancy in pursuit of a popular pacification, which it destroyed by simultaneously destroying Protestant confidence. But the influences of events in France had also given a novel direction to popular dissatisfaction which frightened the authorities and in turn called for novel responses.

In a society which modern scholarship has shown was considerably more literate than most other peasant societies of the period,[33] the campaigns of the patriots, Volunteers, reformers, Catholic Committee and latterly the United Irishmen had created the novelty of Irish public opinion, and given a focus to the vague sense of wrongs suffusing the oral Gaelic tradition. In the informal education system by which most Catholic children received some, it not all, of their education, the poor and often disaffected teachers frequently used such radical literature as readers. Moreover, such literature received widespread circulation through a rash of reading and political clubs among tradesmen and artisans and a highly mobile rural workforce. The result can be seen particularly in the Defender oaths, which reveal a knowledge of Paine and of the significance of events in France.

The Defenders were already a secret oath-bound movement, speaking of French invasion and armed revolt long before the United Irishmen contemplated either. The Catholic Committee's campaign, reaching a crescendo with the nationwide elections to a Catholic convention in November 1792, played upon dormant, almost forgotten Gaelic aspirations for a restoration of the confiscated lands and revenge on the Protestants who had taken them.[34] The background to the convention and parliamentary campaign was a Defender war which took the form of arms' raids on Protestant houses and signs of quite definite plans for a French-assisted insurrection. It fuelled the shrillness and anti-popery of the subsequent parliamentary debates, genuinely frightening many Protestants, but further repelling radicals and Catholics alike from government. The rise to Orangeism and an upsurge of particularly bitter sectarian attacks on Catholics in Armagh in 1795, which were tacitly sanctioned by the local magistrates and landlords, helped complete the picture of the law and the landlord system as enemy.

v

The war between France and England reacted upon longstanding Catholic traditions of France as the deliverer. A sizeable number of their penalised gentry, after all, had sought in France military careers and education denied them at home. It was, however, a telling reminder of their re-education in the early 1790s that officers of France's Irish brigade (now part of the royalist emigration) were repulsed as enemies to the French Revolution, when they came to recruit in Ireland with England's blessing.[35] Rumours of French subversion and arms' landings were rife, even before war broke out in 1793, and tended to arouse the kind of English concern which Dublin might have liked shown to its other many complaints. Certainly Ireland was a glaring weakness in Britain's defence, which no enemy could afford to overlook.

Yet France treated the claims of the many foreign revolutionaries looking to her for help with scepticism and the Terror ushered in an intensely chauvinistic period which sent many foreign revolutionaries to the guillotine. The first United Irish exile to arrive in France, Hamilton Rowan, almost met the same fate and fled instead to the safer climate of America. Yet such was the confusion of France's conduct of foreign affairs that her secret service took on a life of its own and a number of agents who travelled to Ireland in these early years of the war made contact with Defenders, leading Catholics and United Irishmen alike and created the illusion of French assistance there for the asking.

The suppression of the United Irish Society, the final rejection of reform in 1795 and continuing crackdown brought its constitutional phase to a close and opened a new one as Ireland's first republican movement. A number of the original leaders remained – notably the Belfast Presbyterians, now joined by members of the Catholic Committee. A formal alliance was negotiated with the Defenders and from being an elite propagandist organisation, the United Irish Society was on its way to developing a popular base. By late 1796 it was an oath-bound movement, theoretically based on 36-man cells, delegating representatives to superior committees, which in turn fed into a Directory in Dublin. Until 1797, however, it had neither the military wherewithal nor the manpower to conduct a successful revolution. For this it looked instead to French assistance.

When Tone arrived in France early in 1796 the political climate was favourable to the idea of assisting the Irish.[36] The English-supported civil war in the Vendée had been subdued and Anglophobia was riding high. England rather than Austria was now seen as the principal foe and France's top general, Lazare Hoche, recognised Ireland as the main weakness in England's defence. After negotiations with Tone and two other United leaders, despatched in June, Hoche pursued plans for an invasion of Ireland with a crusading zeal, heightened by his rivalry with the up-and-coming Bonaparte. In December a major invasion force sailed for Ireland, with nearly 15,000 troops on board, and a further 15,000 to follow. It was one of the largest expeditionary forces to sail from French shores during the revolutionary war and it sailed unimpeded into Bantry Bay on Ireland's southern coast. Despite a British blockade on the French ports, its destination came as a total surprise to England and the land forces in Ireland were as unprepared as the navy. Only an incredible series of accidents – notably a dramatic change in weather conditions – prevented a successful French invasion of Ireland that Christmas.

News of the attempt caused a dramatic expansion of the United Irish movement, bringing with it a whole new set of problems. The restiveness of the new recruits threatened spontaneous rebellion, when the leaders sought to reserve strength for another French attempt. The proximity of the French aroused fears of a French takeover among the moderate leaders and led to a major rift in the movement some months later.

The crescendo of revolutionary activity in the wake of the attempt likewise intensified loyalist fears of encirclement. The perennial excuse for England not to send military reinforcements to Ireland had been the protection afforded by British naval supremacy. The Bantry Bay attempt, followed by the Nore and the Spithead mutinies, exploded that myth and intensified the loyalists' sense of isolation. As in 1793, London's apparent unconcern for their plight reinforced their feeling that they must trust in themselves alone for their defence. The upshot was the notorious and bloody disarming of the country under General Lake in 1797-8 which brought forward United Irish plans for rebellion before they could be effectively coordinated with France.

Such Protestant fears had already led in 1795 to the upgrading and extension of Protestant revenge gangs into the Orange Order and for the next three years the country was torn by fratricidal conflict between Orangemen and Defenders. Fears of genocide, genuine economic distress and a growing Catholic belief in a French invasion as a panacea for all ills, were combining to produce an alarming escalation of lawlessness from 1795 onwards. The Irish government was obliged by the panic pressure of its supporters to intensify its severity and the task of subduing the country was placed increasingly in the hands of the almost exclusively Protestant yeomanry force. By 1798 it accounted for over half the country's armed forces and became the particular tool of a magistracy which was socially inferior to its English counterpart and frequently motivated by local, often sectarian issues.

The Catholic populace generally, and anyone remotely suspected of subversion, became the object of intensely sectarian repression. Accounts flooded into government of juries packed with Orangemen and of yeomen sporting Orange emblems. Nor were the United Irishmen squeamish about playing upon this Orange fear to fill their ranks. Signs that increasing numbers of Catholics were joining the Defenders and United Irishmen in response to such tactics only intensified loyalist panic. The country seemed caught in an uncontrollable spiral of violence. The brutal disarming of Ulster in 1797, with Lake's indiscriminate house-burning, torture and arrests, was followed by an unprecedented number of capital convictions at the autumn assizes. Signs of billowing smoke on the horizon, as Lake's shock tactics were progressively extended to other parts of the country, were a factor in pushing adjacent provinces to rebellion in 1798.

The United Irish Directory had been organising for a rising for over a year, but with its policy of holding back until supported by a French invasion, it allowed its strength to be shattered by escalating military suppression, not least the arrest of most of the military leaders. The rising when it came in May and June was a totally uncoordinated affair, confined to the south-east and north-east, where military repression had been greatest – 'a rural civil war', as Louis Cullen has referred to it, rather than the organised revolution and military campaign of United Irish plans.[37] It turned into the bloodbath of their worst dreams, Catholic and Protestant fighting with a suicidal recklessness born of mutual fear of genocide. Some 20,000, the vast majority on the rebel side, lost their lives. The atrocities on both sides were barbaric, perpetuating new and more emotive reasons for sectarian division into the next century and making republicanism and loyalism exclusively Catholic and Protestant respectively.

Fears of such a bloodbath had caused the United Irish leaders to pin their fate to an increasingly unsympathetic foreign power. After the disillusioning experience of Bantry Bay and the premature death of Hoche in September 1797, the French Directory had returned to its more normal policy of helping those foreign revolutionaries who helped themselves. Rise first and we will help, it told Irish agents in France at a time when United policy was quite the reverse.

When the Irish rebellion did occur, the bulk of France's military strength had already left for Egypt with Bonaparte. The force which eventually did land in Ireland in late August was accordingly pitifully small, the rebellion was long over, and the place chosen – Killala Bay in Mayo – was one of the remotest parts of the country, scarcely touched by United Irish organisation. Its local population consisted of a largely Gaelic-speaking, impoverished and fanatically Catholic peasantry, who had taken no part in the rebellion of the summer. The sudden incursion of a hardened French soldiery, with campaigns in the Vendée and in Italy to their credit, into such a community was a tragi-comic episode. The peasants reacted in carnivalesque style, showing off their new French attire with childish arrogance, devouring their rations with the lack of ceremony of men who had probably never before tasted meat, and using their ammunition issue to shoot birds and rabbits rather than the foe.

The French were contemptuous of their new allies and particularly annoyed by signs that the peasants viewed them as allies in some kind of religious crusade against their Protestant neighbours. The Irish in turn were shocked at their treatment by the French, particularly when several were executed for misdemeanours. When the joint force was crushingly defeated at Ballinamuck on 8 September, it was the Irish who suffered most casualties. There was a general feeling among the Catholic peasantry that autumn that they had somehow been deserted by those Protestant leaders who had urged them to rebel in the first place. The loyalists too felt abandoned and Lord Cornwallis, the new military Lord Lieutenant sent to salvage the situation, did not hide his contempt for the Protestant politicians whom he held responsible for much of the crisis.

Despite the wholesale execution, imprisonment or exile of the bulk of the United Irish leadership, the movement itself was not finally destroyed until 1803. But the experience of 1798 changed it, as it did every other sector of Irish society. In 1799 it was reorganised from prison by the rump of the original leadership. The idea of a vast popular movement was abandoned in favour of a military command and a French army. The movement to all intents and purposes went into exile. The English underground, cultivated intermittently from 1797 onwards, assumed a new importance, and the interrupted plans – commonly referred to as 'the Despard Conspiracy' – were to have been a diversionary tactic.[38] But most effort was concentrated on securing another invasion by the French, a difficult and ultimately fruitless task under the Consulate and Empire. Bonaparte was no Hoche, and the growing recognition by the exiled leaders that their struggle might simply replace English with French domination was part of the motivation of Emmet's rebellion in 1803. It foundered because the United Irish Society could not simultaneously reject its popular base and the French military assistance which substituted for it. The remnants of the organisation disintegrated rapidly thereafter.

The legacy of the French Revolution's impact on Ireland was a deeply polarised populace and the running sores of militantly sectarian republicanism and loyalism. The major participation of Irishmen in the English underground raised and maintained anti-Irishness at a new level, and the Union had brought a hundred Irish MPs to Westminster, bringing to the heart of English politics that 'Irish Question' which came in time to dominate them. An entire world separated the nineteenth century from those years when Ireland had seemed to be moving towards a gradual resolution of her problems. The French Revolution itself may simply have reacted upon the underlying tensions, but it is unlikely that the upheavals which consumed any chance of lasting solutions would have occurred without it.

5. Popular Conservatism and Militant Loyalism 1789–1815

H.T. DICKINSON

IT IS generally recognised that the French Revolution polarised political opinion within Britain, but the nature of this polarisation has not always been fully appreciated. Most historians who have studied the impact of the French Revolution on British politics have concentrated on either the conservative reaction among the propertied elite or the growth of popular radicalism in London and other urban centres. Within the ruling class the forces of reaction forged a more coherent conservative ideology and eventually refashioned a new Tory Party committed to the defence of monarchy, the established church and private property. Meanwhile, 'out of doors', the campaign for parliamentary reform, galvanised by the French example and stimulated by a new generation of writers and activists, secured greater popular support than ever before. Thus, according to many traditional historical accounts, the propertied elite moved to the right while the majority of ordinary people were won over to the cause of reform. The failure of the radicals is therefore blamed upon the panic reaction of the propertied classes and the creation of a ruthless machinery of government repression. This rather simple picture of political developments has been challenged by recent research. It has been shown that the machinery of repression set up by the government was neither as effective nor as ruthless as was previously thought. While the government certainly persecuted most of the leading radicals and intimidated the more faint-hearted reformers, it is clear that traditional liberties were not entirely destroyed and that the rule of law still prevailed. It has also been shown that radicalism was less popular and less securely based than once thought.[1] Moreover, it is now being recognised that one of the most significant impacts of the French Revolution on British politics was the enormous boost it gave to popular conservatism.[2]

Further investigations of popular politics have revealed that a large proportion of the population appreciated the benefits provided by the existing political and social order. It can be shown that there was a very popular and pervasive belief that British liberties and British prosperity were the product of parliamentary monarchy, the rule of law, and the prevailing social order. This conviction helped to make many ordinary people resistant to the arguments for change put forward by radicals at home and revolutionaries abroad. The violence and anarchy witnessed in France, a protracted war which devastated all Europe and threatened the economic interests of Britain and her very security and independence, and the suggestion that some British radicals were prepared to conspire with the French to destroy their own constitution, convinced large numbers of Britons that reform was dangerous and existing benefits ought to be cherished.

To appreciate the nature of this conservative reaction among the nation at large we need to examine the appeal that conservative ideas could have for ordinary people, the ways in which such ideas could be propagated in order to involve a mass audience, and the ways in which loyalist attitudes could be demonstrated and organised in order to mobilise mass support. At each stage, however, we need to consider whether the various manifestations of popular conservatism were the genuine and spontaneous demonstrations of ordinary people or were the artificial creation of a cunning governing elite who successfully manipulated the people to serve their own selfish interests.

I

The Popular Dimension in Conservative Ideology

In the 1790s and beyond, belief in the virtues of the existing political and social order, reinforced by the fear of dangerous enemies at home and abroad, led to the development and articulation of a conservative ideology of considerable appeal, resilience and intellectual power. Edmund Burke's celebrated *Reflections on the Revolution in France* (1790) was the first serious warning to Britons that, if radicals at home and revolutionaries abroad were not resisted, the consequences would be the destruction of the established order in church and state, the undermining of social harmony, the elimination of justice, and an incitement to the impoverished masses to plunder the possessions of the propertied classes. In the long run Burke's fears and prophecies won him many admirers and adherents, but it is a mistake to think that all the leading conservative writers of the age were simply repeating or embellishing Burke's original arguments. Many influential conservative propagandists, including William Paley, Robert Nares, Samuel Horsley and John Reeves, joined Burke in denouncing the radical appeal to universal natural rights, but they justified the existing order in many different ways by appeal to utility, morality, natural law, religion, history and prescription.[3] Arch-conservatives such as Samuel Horsley and John Reeves went much further than Burke in upholding the prerogative power of the king and the special privileges of the Church of England. Indeed, they probably deserved the accusation that they were reviving Tory principles. Taken as a whole, there seems little reason to doubt that the writings of the host of sophisticated conservative thinkers seriously undermined the intellectual appeal of radical ideas among most men of property and reinforced their admiration for the existing constitution.

These sophisticated arguments certainly influenced those numerous propagandists, including John Bowles, William Jones, Hannah More and, for a time, William Cobbett, who wished to convert the people as a whole into militant loyalists who would defend British institutions and traditional values from both domestic radicals and French revolutionaries. These writers did not simply produce a modified version of Burke for a mass public. Their more virulent conservative propaganda relied upon more pragmatic arguments in order to appeal to the middling and lower orders. It was also written in simpler, more impassioned tones in order to elicit a militantly loyalist reaction.[4] In almost all these writings a stark contrast was drawn between the benefits enjoyed by British citizens and the horrors being experienced by the French. They endeavoured to show that it was not just the aristocratic elite who had a great deal to lose from following the French example. The French ruling class might appear to be the most obvious victims of the Revolution, but conservative propagandists in Britain sought to impress upon the British people that millions of ordinary French citizens had also become the victims of political upheaval, social anarchy and military aggression. The middling and lower orders in Britain therefore would have nothing to gain and a very great deal to lose if they were seduced by French principles and if they tried to imitate French practices. Conservative propagandists in Britain sought to ram home this message by concentrating on the ideas, institutions and men supporting revolution and by adversely comparing them with those which sustained the political and social order in Britain. While it is impossible to be certain how far this propaganda was absorbed by the people at large, it is instructive to note that conservative publications were not only distributed in huge numbers, but that the ideas they propagated were reiterated in the hundreds of addresses and resolutions drafted by those in the middling and lower orders who wished to demonstrate their loyalty to the existing order.

Conservative propagandists continually warned the British people that the new order in France was built on the most abstract general principles and the wildest speculative theories, whereas the political and social order in Britain was the product of long history, practical experience and sound commonsense. In their appeals to inalienable natural rights and to the abstract concepts of liberty, equality and fraternity, the French were placing far too much reliance on human reason and were ignoring divine providence, the actual nature of man and the hard lessons of history. French revolutionaries were acting under the dangerous delusion that social arrangements and political institutions were simply the artificial products of human reason. A generation of enlightened men could therefore create these anew and could base them on the most rational principles. British conservatives rejected this confidence in the power of reason. Instead, they urged that the social and political order in any particular country was, in part, the creation of divine providence and, in part, the result of the product of innumerable changes, adjustments and even sheer unplanned accidents occurring over hundreds of years in that country's history. The French revolutionaries were denying the dispositions of God and were ignoring the fallibilities of man. Very conscious of both, conservative propagandists in Britain taught the people that their social arrangements and political institutions were sanctioned by religion and had clearly stood the test of time. In their blasphemous rejection of the dispositions of God and in their arrogant reliance on the power of human reason, the French first produced social anarchy and unrestrained terror and then an authoritarian dictatorship which threatened the liberty and independence of all the nations in Europe. In marked contrast, by acknowledging the superior wisdom of the Almighty and by cherishing the benefits gained by practical experience, the British were able to protect private property, preserve their political liberties and secure their religion. Whereas the French found themselves subject to the unrestrained will of man and the authority of a military dictatorship, the British were governed by a natural aristocracy guided by religious principles and seeking to serve the common interest.

Conservative propagandists stressed that the radical desire to promote equality would inevitably lead to a dangerous assault on private property

and an alarming descent into social anarchy. Although they were prepared
to acknowledge that all men shared a common humanity, they insisted
that men were so unequal in their physical, mental and moral attributes
that it was both natural and inevitable that some would prosper and others
would not. Inequality occurred naturally and was, indeed, divinely
ordained. Great care was taken to inform the poor that God had created
both rich and poor as a way of rewarding the industrious and punishing
the lazy. Moreover, providence had so arranged it that the rich had to
bear the burdens of responsibilities and to face the temptations of luxury
and excess, whereas the poor enjoyed a simpler existence and could
more easily live a sober, virtuous and frugal life. Both rich and poor
were also dependent upon each other. The rich could not prosper without
the labour of the poor, while the poor benefited from the direction, the
employment and the charity provided by the rich. Since these were the
facts of life, the poor were urged to be content with their lowly station
in life and they were advised not to be jealous of their superiors. The
middling and lower orders were taught that only the very dregs of society
could possibly benefit from an attack on the existing social order in
Britain. Attempts to level the natural distinctions in society would hurt
the industrious poor as much as the rich. The unrestrained pursuit of
equality would certainly lead to the plunder of the rich, but it would
also produce social anarchy and would threaten even the small possessions
of the honest labourer.[5]

    In opposition to those who claimed that all men possessed an inalienable
right to liberty and that this right required that they should all possess
the right to vote and to a share in the decision-making processes of the
state, the conservative propagandists insisted that what was most
important was the practical enjoyment of justice, the rule of law, and
freedom from state oppression. Whereas the French, in their pursuit of
liberty, lurched from crisis to crisis and experienced mob rule and then
military dictatorship, the British had long enjoyed the greatest degree
of individual liberty consonant with the preservation of political stability.
The British should undoubtedly cherish their constitution which had for
so long been the admiration of the civilised world. This marvellous and
intricate system of checks and balances provided firm leadership,
important limitations on the power of the state, and a legislature which
represented property and all the important social and economic interests
in the nation. Under it, all British subjects enjoyed equal justice and the
rule of law. They were also largely free from government interference
in their daily lives. Radical appeals to popular sovereignty would risk

unleashing the will of the impoverished and uneducated masses and would endanger the delicate balance of an admirable constitution. Since all British subjects already enjoyed the substantial benefits bestowed by the best constitution which human wisdom and long experience could contrive, it was highly dangerous to criticise it and absolute folly to change it so that it accorded better to the speculative designs of some impractical theorists.[6]

Conservative propagandists insisted that French principles and practices were just as much of a threat to the church and the Christian religion as to the state. The French were accused of encouraging open atheism and blatant immorality and of forsaking the truths and virtues long taught by the Christian religion. As their political guides they had substituted human reason and the unrestrained will of man. The practical results were not simply dangerous attacks on church property and the undermining of organised religion, but a precipitous descent into social anarchy and personal immorality. To prevent this happening in Britain many conservative propagandists stressed the practical benefits of religion and helped to promote a religious revival across the country. They taught the people that both the existing social and political orders were sanctioned by religion. They also went on to insist that religion, not political reform, was the people's best guide and greatest solace. Although the poor could not expect to achieve great power or substantial material rewards in this world, they would assuredly reap their just reward in heaven. In the meantime they were encouraged to cultivate such moral virtues as sobriety, frugality, industry, obedience and submission. Some of the more militant conservatives believed that it was not enough to preach such virtues at home. Since the French contagion was being spread across Europe by military aggression, the British were duty bound to contain it by waging a veritable holy crusade against French principles.[7]

By sheer repetition and by highly emotional attempts to elicit a simple patriotic response, conservative propagandists tried to instil in the people an almost unthinking acceptance of social distinction and an unquestioning pride in the existing constitution in church and state. Perhaps even more incessant were the attempts to praise the abilities and virtues of the British ruling class and to blacken the character of those who sought radical change. Appeals were made to history, experience and commonsense to prove that the propertied elite were the men best equipped to exercise political power. The British ruling class enjoyed the benefits of leisure and education, they were used to commanding others, they had most wealth to lose in the event of political and social disaster, and they had presided for decades over an unprecedented extension of British power, prosperity and prestige. In contrast to this praise was a tide of conservative propaganda designed to arouse a profound loathing of British radicals and a deep hatred of French revolutionaries. Crude propaganda, often reprehensible in tone, blackened the character of honourable British reformers and created a hideous caricature of the rapacious and bloodthirsty French revolutionaries.

In conservative propaganda British radicals were invariably condemned as men of weak heads and bad hearts. They were depicted as traitors to their own country and as dupes of a foreign enemy. Frequently portrayed as dangerous and ambitious demagogues, they were accused of being jealous of the deserved honours of the governing elite and of the merited wealth of their social superiors. To scare off potential recruits to the radical cause the aims of these reformers were deliberately misrepresented and the consequences of adopting their principles were grossly exaggerated. The British people were warned that the radicals would destroy the monarchy, ruin the aristocracy and level all social and economic distinctions in society. In a message deliberately designed to appeal to the middling ranks and also to the industrious lower orders, the public was warned that the only beneficiaries of radical reform would be the idle and the dissolute, the thieves, cheats, drunkards and propertyless beggars at the very bottom of society. At the same time conservative propaganda deliberately appealed to the rampant xenophobia and the virulent anti-gallicanism that had long been a feature of British society. Frequent references were made to those French attempts at universal dominion since the reign of Louis XIV that had embroiled Britain in a succession of expensive wars. Now, once more, the French were spreading carnage, oppression and desolation across large areas of Europe and Britain was again compelled to take up arms in defence of her trade, her constitution and the balance of power in Europe. Patriotic Britons must be prepared to make enormous sacrifices if they were to preserve the liberties, privileges and economic advantages that they held so dear. Conservative propagandists created a caricature of the brave, honest and freedom-loving John Bull being called upon to take up arms against the French, who, in turn, were depicted at first as bloodthirsty and lawless terrorists and then as brutal military aggressors. Only a loyal and united people could preserve property, liberty and religion from the scourge of French principles and French practices.[8]

II

Demonstrations of Popular Conservatism

Research on popular radicalism has revealed its success in disseminating political propaganda to a wide audience. It has also shown how it effectively mobilised public opinion or sought to intimidate its opponents through addresses, petitions and large-scale demonstrations. What has often been neglected, however, is the abundant evidence that popular conservatism employed the same tactics and achieved an even greater measure of success.

The variety, the sheer volume and the social and geographical distribution of conservative propaganda was certainly much greater than that disseminated by the radicals in the years from 1789 to 1815. Conservative newspapers and periodicals undoubtedly outnumbered and outsold those produced by the radicals and they remained in existence for much longer periods. In London conservative views were propagated by the *Star*, the *Sun*, the *True Briton* and the *Observer*, whilst in the provinces they were disseminated in such newspapers as the *York Courant*, the *Liverpool Phoenix*, the *Manchester Mercury*, the *Leicester Journal*, the *Newcastle Courant*, the *Caledonian Mercury* and the *Edinburgh Herald*. In towns where there were both radical and conservative newspapers, as in Manchester, Leicester and Newcastle, it was the latter which survived the political contest. The triumph of conservative periodicals was even more pronounced. Some, such as *The Looker On* (1792-3), *The Tomahawk* (1795-6) and *The Loyalist* (1803), had a rather precarious existence, like their radical rivals, but others were pronounced successes. *The Anti-Jacobin* (1797-8) was a very popular weekly, at least among the educated classes. It not only reached very satisfactory weekly sales of 2500 copies, but was subsequently gathered into a collected edition and republished four times. Its successor, the monthly *Anti Jacobin Review and Magazine*, reached sales of about 3250 for each issue and it continued publication until 1821. The *British Critic*, another conservative monthly, started five years earlier, in 1793, and thrived even longer.

The many individual political pamphlets and treatises published by the radicals were certainly disseminated in large numbers, but there were more conservative tracts and they were distributed even more widely. Burke's *Reflections* certainly sold fewer than Paine's famous rejoinder, *Rights of Man*, but selections from Burke were printed in provincial newspapers and, in the intense Burke-Paine controversy, there were more contributions on the conservative side.[9] Moreover, it is often forgotten that the undeniable popularity of Paine's *Rights of Man* was easily eclipsed by the enormous distribution of the series of moral tales written by Hannah More and her associates for the *Cheap Repository Tracts*, which reached the astonishing total of over two million copies between 1795 and 1798. Though often bought in bulk and distributed free to the army and the navy, and to schools, hospitals, workhouses, prisons and places of employment, they were almost certainly read by a higher proportion of the lower orders than any radical publication. Although they were not overtly political, those moral and religious tracts were designed to persuade the poor to accept the existing social order with its inequitable distribution of wealth and power.[10]

Interested individuals and organised loyalist associations undoubtedly distributed a greater range of political tracts to a larger potential readership across the entire country than the radicals managed to achieve. The Crown and Anchor Association alone published about 50 different tracts on its own initiative and it paid to distribute tens of thousands of these works throughout its network of provincial associations. Many thousands of these tracts were also bought and distributed in such places as Maidstone, Blandford, Fulham and Salford, while the Bull's Head Association in Manchester handed out 10,000 copies of its loyal address of March 1793 and, in 1795, it distributed no fewer than 16,200 pamphlets and broadsides.[11] The massive dissemination of loyalist propaganda in 1792–5 was repeated, though in a less organised way, during the years 1802–5 when Britain was threatened by invasion. Hundreds of pamphlets, poems and caricatures joined the existing newspapers and periodicals in a vast and successful campaign to convince the nation of the need for unity, courage and sacrifice in the face of this alarming danger. New periodicals such as *The Loyalist*, *The Anti-Gallican*, and Cobbett's *Annual Register* (later the *Weekly Political Register*) were established and one publisher produced new editions of nearly 50 different publications because of 'the very great demand for spirited and loyal patriotic papers'.[12] James Asperne, at the 'Bible, Crown and Constitution' in Cornhill, London, published dozens of cheap broadsides which he encouraged gentlemen, magistrates and even women of all ranks to buy in bulk for circulation among the lower orders.[13] At the same time the liberal *Manchester Gazette* also urged unity in the present crisis and it ceased to claim that the war was unnecessary and unjust.

Throughout the whole period of the French Wars the burden of a great range of publications capable of carrying a political message, including verse, popular ballads, novels, broadsheets, and caricatures, was heavily weighted in favour of the conservative side of the political debate.[14] More important than all of these in disseminating conservative views, however, were the many thousands of sermons delivered (and often printed) by the clergy and ministers of the various Christian churches in Britain. The clergy of all denominations serviced the most widespread, popular and influential institutions in the state and the majority of them were united in defence of the constitution and in outspoken criticism of French principles. While it is true that High Church Anglicans were the most staunchly loyalist, other religious groups were not far behind.[15] Many leading Evangelicals contributed to the enormously successful *Cheap Repository Tracts* and even those Anglican clergymen who were usually on the liberal wing of the established church, such as William Paley and Bishop Richard Watson, urged the people at large to accept the benefits of the existing social and political order.[16]

Other religious organisations were scarcely less active than the Anglican church in demonstrating their attachment to the constitution. Numerous individual Scottish presbyteries, as well as the General Assembly of the Church of Scotland, submitted loyal addresses to the crown on many occasions.[17] The conservative leaders of the annual Methodist Conference regularly proclaimed their loyalty to the constitution and firmly resisted the efforts of the more radical spirits in the movement to voice their grievances. By the end of the 1790s official Methodism had become, on political matters, little more than a vehicle for loyalist propaganda.[18] Even though the Rational Dissenters were the intellectual elite of the radical cause, the official leaders of the older Dissenting churches proclaimed their loyalty. The leading Dissenters in several towns, including London, Manchester, Southampton and Folkestone, expressed their sincere attachment to the constitution. In 1790 the delegates of Dissenters in several midland counties declared that the constitution was their pride and glory, while, at the national level, the Committee of the Dissenting Deputies and the General Body of Protestant Dissenting Ministers of the Three Denominations issued a succession of declarations of loyal support for the king and the constitution.[19]

Evidence that huge numbers of the people accepted the conservative message preached to them in this great outpouring of political propaganda and religious sermons can be found in the huge number of loyalist addresses, resolutions and petitions which were sent to the king in the years between 1789 and 1815. These addresses were certainly more numerous and were undoubtedly more widespread, both geographically and socially, than those organised by radical groups. They revealed a deep well of sympathy and support for the king himself. In 1789 more than 750 addresses congratulated George III on his recovery from his serious illness. In 1795–6 and in 1800 there were hundreds of addresses of loyalty after attempts on the king's person. On all these occasions the addresses emanated from leading magistrates in towns and counties across the kingdom, from every kind of religious denomination, from all the universities, from groups of merchants and manufacturers, from various clubs and societies, from militia and Volunteer companies, and from groups of ordinary citizens.[20] When the king entered the fiftieth year of his reign, in October 1809, there were elaborate celebrations in many parts of the country and another flood of congratulatory addresses. There were similar celebrations on the centenary of the Hanoverian succession on 1 August 1814. Clearly, the brutal treatment of Louis XVI in France had only served to encourage the British people to cherish all the more the institution of monarchy and the person of their venerable king.[21]

On several other occasions there were similarly impressive demonstrations of a widespread popular determination to preserve the constitution from dangers at home and abroad. The response to two royal proclamations, in May and December 1792, against the spread of seditious writings and of radical activities, produced nearly 500 loyal addresses. In December 1792 resolutions in defence of the existing constitution secured 8032 signatures in London, more than 11,000 in Liverpool, 5033 in Bath and several thousand in Bristol. In other, smaller, places support for loyalist addresses was also impresssive: 1129 signatures were collected in St Albans, over 1500 in Newark, Prescot and Halesworth, 1700 in both Kidderminster and Wakefield, and 1996 in Huntingdonshire. Many other places recorded support in the hundreds and even in excess of a thousand signatures. In distant Cromarty 280 out of 300 heads of families signed and, it was confidently asserted, had a little more time been given, all but three men would have demonstrated their loyalty in this way.[22] Hundreds of loyal addresses were sent to the king at other times: on the occasion of naval victories, when the war was reluctantly renewed in 1803, on the discovery of the Despard conspiracy in the same year and when George III once more refused to bow to ministerial pressure to grant Catholic relief in 1807.

The more militant loyalists were not simply content to demonstrate their loyalty to king and constitution by supporting addresses and petitions. They were also prepared to take more positive action in order to frustrate the propagation of radical views and to stifle any hint of seditious activity. Many thousands of them were ready to join various societies, armed associations and Volunteer companies in order to assist the government to oppose radical views, to suppress disorder, to protect private property. As early as 1790 there was evidence of formed opposition to both the Dissenters' demands for the repeal of the Test and Corporation Acts and to the radical campaign for the reform of Parliament. In several provincial towns, most notably in Birmingham and Manchester, Church and King clubs were formed to combat religious change and political reform. By late 1792 conservative opinion in Britain was thoroughly alarmed at the revolutionary violence in France and the outbreak of a war which threatened to involve Britain herself.

A much larger and more widespread organisation was created to rally loyalist opinion throughout the country in an effort to overwhelm the radical cause at home. On 23 November 1792 a public announcement in the *Star*, a pro-government evening newspaper, announced the founding of an Association for the Preservation of Liberty and Property against Republicans and Levellers. This Association was founded at the Crown and Anchor tavern on 20 November by John Reeves. Within days of it being publicised in the London press, John Reeves and the Association's secretary, John Moore, were inundated by a flood of letters from sympathisers from all over the country. Many correspondents offered to set up loyalist associations in their areas, advised on how the lower orders might be reached with effective propaganda, and offered to write or distribute loyalist tracts.[23]

By December 1792 several other associations had been established in the metropolis and throughout the neighbouring counties. Early in 1793 loyalist associations spread first to the west, then to the Midlands and finally to the north and east. Although rather weak in Norfolk, Lincoln, Cumberland and Westmorland, the Association movement soon became the largest political organisation in the country.[24] The Reeves papers, now in the British Library, record nearly 200 associations, but there were many more associations than those which established correspondence with the parent organisation at the Crown and Anchor. Recent research has shown that the Association movement was clearly much stronger in such places as Scotland, Essex, Yorkshire,

Worcestershire, Sussex and Lancashire than the correspondence in the Reeves papers would suggest.[25]

The total number of loyalist associations undoubtedly ran into hundreds and may well have been as high as the 2000 societies which Reeves himself claimed to have fostered. Active membership, so far as this can be ascertained from the list of committee members, was largely confined to local men of property, though there can be no doubt that these associations did enlist the enthusiastic support of many thousands of humbler men. In many rural areas substantial landowners, yeoman farmers and the Anglican clergy played a prominent role on the organising committees, whereas in urban areas the activists were mainly merchants, manufacturers, professional men and, again, the parish clergy. Many of these men were also involved in local government and church affairs. A large proportion of committee members were lord mayors, aldermen, common councilmen, JPs, parish clergy, church wardens, overseers of the poor, governors of the poor house, etc.[26] Although the lower orders do not bulk large on the organising committees, there is abundant evidence to suggest that they attended the initial meetings setting up these associations, engaged in subsequent loyalist demonstrations, and supported loyalist addresses sent to the king.[27]

The totals of those attending meetings or signing addresses indicate that the Association movement reached beyond the propertied middle classes into the humbler ranks of society. This can be demonstrated quite explicitly in some areas. In Cheapside the journeymen and servants of Robert Pickering, a paperhanging manufacturer, 'resolved that feeling ourselves equally anxious to show our loyalty and approbation of the constitution of King, Lords and Commons, as those of a superior order, we do hereby publickly express those sentiments, and declare our willingness to conform to the laws of the kingdom.'[28] When a gentleman of Oundle went around that town and its neighbourhood, seeking out support for a loyalist address in December 1792, he not only enlisted the local farmers and yeomen, but 'in going round to the different clubs the night before (clubs formed by the lower ranks for the purpose of assisting such of their members as are disabled by sickness) though he was not expected, he found they had already taken up the business among themselves, and were eager to testify their loyalty.'[29] In Newcastle and North Shields, in the same month, the members of lodges of Free and Easy Johns also testified to their zeal for the constitution and their opposition to those who promoted sedition; and similar declarations were made by friendly societies in Gateshead and Castle Eden.[30] Even the debtors of the King's Bench prison were anxious to proclaim their attachment to king and constitution.[31]

In most places where these associations were established the loyalists easily outnumbered the local radicals. Even in places where the radicals were quite strong, such as London, Birmingham and Manchester, the militant loyalists appear to have gained the upper hand. Only in Sheffield do the loyalists appear to have been forced onto the defensive, though even here they made a respectable showing. Most of the loyalist associations were so dominant that they ceased active operations because they had so easily overwhelmed the local radicals. Where the reform movement proved more resilient the loyalist associations had a longer life. In Manchester the powerful and militant Bull's Head Association survived until 1799, while in the metropolis Grove Taylor decided it was necessary to create several new associations of Loyal Britons in October 1793 when the radical cause showed signs of reviving.[32]

As the radical cause waned in the mid 1790s, the activities of many of the loyalist associations lost focus and direction. Since the threat of invasion increased at this time, however, some loyalist groups turned their attention to helping the war effort. Militant loyalists increasingly joined forces with those whose prime purpose was to defend the country and to win the war against France. Loyalists' associations in many parts of the country offered bounties to men who would volunteer to serve in the Royal Navy, collected funds to relieve the dependents of men killed or wounded in the war, and purchased warm winter clothing or extra supplies for the army. Tens of thousands of pounds were collected for these purposes in London, Portsmouth, Southampton, Manchester, Newcastle and other towns.[33] As the war expanded and the threat of invasion grew, the loyalist associations even became a source of recruitment for an armed defence force designed to resist any invasion and to intimidate the remaining radicals within Britain.

As early as December 1792 some sympathisers with the Association movement were suggesting that they should be armed to repel invaders or to protect property from the depredations of a lawless rabble.[34] The government was reluctant to encourage such a move at this time, but by March 1794, it was more willing to listen when William Ogilvie urged the government to allow the rich to arm themselves: 'By the rich I would be understood here to mean not only the rich so called; but every man who has any property; the merchant, the manufacturer, the shopkeeper, the tradesman, the farmer, the housekeeper, in opposition to those who have nothing, neither settlements, possessions nor property.'[35] That same month the government agreed to authorise the raising of armed Volunteer companies. To pay for the arms, uniforms and equipment of this volunteer home defence force the government turned not to Parliament for revenue, but appealed directly to the loyalists in the hope that they would raise the necessary funds by public subscriptions. The government was not disappointed. Many thousands of pounds were raised. The largest contributions came from the landed elite, but considerable amounts were raised from the middling ranks of society. In several towns, including London, Birmingham, Manchester, Exeter and Bradford, the loyalist associations raised their own Volunteer companies and transformed themselves bodily into armed associations. In many other areas the loyalist associations provided much of the finance and many of the senior officers for the new defence force. Large numbers of men were recruited within months and the Volunteer force continued to expand until it was about 450,000 men strong when Britain faced a serious invasion threat in 1804. It was undoubtedly the largest organisation in the whole country and it was dedicated to resist French principles and radical demands for political reform.[36]

The value of the Volunteers as a weapon capable of resisting a French invasion force with any success can be called into question, but it must be remembered that their primary significance was as an instrument of propaganda. The Volunteers undoubtedly demonstrated the readiness of the propertied classes to use force to preserve their privileges. Anglican clergymen of all types were quite prepared to preach loyalty and submission to the members of these armed associations. There is no doubt that, at least at first, every effort was made to enlist only the totally reliable poor, and then only under the command of their own landlords and employers. The government discouraged the arming of the very poor or the disaffected in certain areas. The willingness to serve at any level was used as a test of loyalty to the existing regime. The parades, the military exercises and the patriotic speeches at celebration dinners were all designed to demonstrate the strength, unity and commitment of the Volunteers. Recruited to intimidate the radicals and to promote patriotism, they 'rendered disloyalty unfashionable, sedition dangerous and insurrection almost impossible'.[37]

The loyalist recruits to armed associations and Volunteer companies were quite prepared to use force to preserve order and to intimidate the radicals. Many leading loyalists favoured more subtle forms of intimidation. They initiated prosecutions of those printers and booksellers who distributed radical works and they offered financial rewards for any evidence which would lead to the arrest of seditious persons.[38] In several places the magistrates were persuaded to refuse licences to the owners of inns and alehouses if they allowed their premises to be used for radical meetings; in many places the innkeepers caved in to such threats.[39] Other forms of intimidation included the refusal to employ radicals, the threat to dismiss them from employment, the withdrawal of custom from radical tradesmen and shopkeepers, and the expulsion of radicals from benefit clubs and friendly societies.[40] Perhaps most insidious of all were the efforts of several militant loyalist associations to pressurise every local householder into signing their addresses and resolutions. A refusal to sign, especially when these abstainers were in a decided minority in their community, obviously required considerable moral courage. Few men would have the nerve to stand out against the majority of their neighbours in this way.[41]

There seems little doubt that many of these efforts to intimidate the radicals were initiated at the local level and were not directed or coordinated by the government. Of course, the lead was often taken by the local propertied elite; by JPs, town magistrates and the Anglican clergy in particular. There is every reason to believe that a majority of the property-owning middle classes approved of such measures and there are even indications that many of the lower orders welcomed these efforts to intimidate the radicals. One proof of this assertion is the large number of crowd demonstrations which enlisted widespread local support for ritual or actual physical assaults on leading radicals. In the winter of 1792–3, in particular, there were dozens of public demonstrations of popular hostility to the seditious views of Thomas Paine. He was burned in effigy across the length and breadth of the country. There were at least thirty such incidents in the north-west of England alone, and almost as many occurred in Northumberland and Durham even though the north-east was one of the least militantly loyalist in the country. Many of these demonstrations involved considerable numbers of people in activities that were elaborate in their ritual and symbolism. The crowds were assembled, stimulated and excited by the processions, bands, songs, banners, slogans, cockades, triumphal arches, bonfires, fireworks and burning effigies, as well as by the considerable drinking and public merriment.[42] These street demonstrations were both popular manifestations of support for the existing political order and a form of psychological intimidation of local radicals. On occasion loyalist crowds were prepared to go much further and to employ considerable physical force against the radicals. The most serious riots, in support of Church and King, occurred in Birmingham in July 1791 and in Manchester in June and December 1792. On 14 July 1791 the Dissenters of Birmingham planned to celebrate Bastille Day and they combined their political declarations with injudicious attacks on the established church. This conduct provoked a serious riot which resulted in the destruction of a Unitarian meeting house and the private property of Joseph Priestley and several other leading Dissenters and reformers in the town. The violent mob was openly encouraged by the local Anglican parson and several prominent local magistrates deliberately turned a blind eye so long as the rioters restricted their attacks to Dissenting property.[43] In Manchester, too, it was the activities of Dissenting radicals which provoked an Anglican backlash and large-scale rioting in both June and December 1792. Popular support for this kind of violence is indicated by the scale and the geographical spread of such disturbances. Recent research has revealed at least 25 violent attacks on the radicals in the north-west of England between 1792 and 1795 and one of these riots, at Thorpe, on 21 April 1794, involved several thousand local people.[44] Attacks of this kind occurred in many other parts of the country, including Warwick, Yarmouth, Exeter, Cambridge, and even the radical stronghold at Sheffield.[45] Although there were several instances of incitement by the local elite, there were simply too many crowds, capable of enlisting considerable local support, to support the claim that they were merely hired bands of ruffians or simple-minded folk easily incited and manipulated by their superiors. It seems quite evident that there was considerable popular hostility to radicalism in many parts of the country, encouraged mainly by fear of French-style anarchy and of French military aggression.

III

The wealth of evidence now available about the popular dimension of conservative ideology and about the large-scale involvement of the middling and lower orders in a whole range of loyalist activities suggests that the conservative reaction at the time of the French Revolution

was not confined to the propertied elite. Fear of anarchy and of invasion
in particular succeeded in rallying a majority of the nation behind
the protracted campaign against revolutionary principles and French
arms. This much seems incontrovertible, but it might still be claimed
that this popular reaction was largely the consequence of the propertied
elite's skilful exploitation of a barrage of conservative propaganda of
addresses, associations and demonstrations. To challenge this assertion
requires evidence that conservative ideas were not entirely under the
control of the elite and that loyalist demonstrations and organisations
were not simply the result of government initiatives. We need to show
that popular conservatism was largely a spontaneous reaction to genuine
and widespread fears of the consequences of supporting radical demands
or failing to resist French aggression.

The writing and dissemination of conservative propaganda was
undoubtedly welcomed by the propertied elite and sanctioned by the
government. Popular conservative writers such as John Reeves, William
Jones, John Bowles and Hannah More had links with the government
or with the leaders of the established church. The government also
subsidised a number of newspapers and periodicals and tried to win
over writers and caricaturists to the conservative cause. There is no
evidence, however, of an over-arching government scheme to
orchestrate an ideological campaign. On the contrary, there are many
indications to suggest that many individual writers and most conservative
publications appealed to the people at large without the bidding or
the guidance of the government. Within days of founding the Crown
and Anchor Association, for example, John Reeves was besieged with
offers from all over the country to write, print and distribute loyalist
propaganda free of charge.

The scale of the conservative propaganda exercise, the passion with
which it was promoted, and the huge market which it reached, all
suggest that a very large number of people indeed was producing and
reading conservative literature. At the very least this propaganda
campaign reveals the political convictions of the large number of people
who were actively engaged in it. It is difficult, however, to assess
what influence this material had on the people at whom it was aimed.
It seems very unlikely that it had no impact at all and it seems
unreasonable to suggest that it had less influence than the smaller body
of radical propaganda that was disseminated throughout the nation.

An examination of loyalist demonstrations and organisations suggests
that not only were many of the middling and lower orders involved

on their own initiative, but that the governing elite failed, in fact, to retain complete control of them. The hundreds of loyalist addresses in 1792–3 were welcomed by the government and they were, in part, a response to ministerial prompting. On 21 May 1792 a royal proclamation called upon all loyal subjects to resist the radical attempts to subvert regular government and it requested JPs and magistrates to make diligent enquiries to discover the authors, printers and disseminators of seditious writings. This appeal encouraged over 150 meetings of magistrates throughout the country to declare publicly their loyal support for the king and the constitution. A similar proclamation on 1 December 1792 urged magistrates to take precautions to overcome the threat of disorder and to defeat the aims of those ill-disposed persons who were seeking to subvert the law and to undermine the constitution. Again this helped to procure the desired response.[46] None the less, many of the loyalist addresses in 1792–3 were not organised by those to whom the proclamations were directly addressed and the large number of signatures appended to many of them suggests that many ordinary people welcomed this opportunity to proclaim their loyalty, their hostility to the rising tide of radical propaganda, and their alarm at the growing violence in France. Moreover, on most other occasions when the king received overwhelming testimony of regard for his person and expressions of support for the constitution, there is no reason to believe that these were simply local responses to judicious prompting by the central government. Much the same can be said for the large number of street demonstrations and public attacks against local radicals. The government did not encourage them. Although there is evidence that some local parsons and magistrates turned a blind eye to attacks on radicals, they only very occasionally incited them and many of the loyalist demonstrations clearly enlisted considerable local support. Indeed, where rioting was most pronounced it was often the latest stage in a long-running local dispute for political and religious control of the area. This was certainly the case in Birmingham and Manchester where the radicals and Dissenters were an active minority who eventually provoked a popular backlash by the conservative and Anglican majority.

The government was not displeased by the creation of the major loyalist organisations, but it is not clear that they were established directly as the result of government initiatives. They were certainly never fully under government control. How much the government knew about John Reeves's plan to establish the Association for the Preservation of Liberty and Property against Republicans and Levellers at the Crown and Anchor tavern on 20 November 1792 is still shrouded in mystery. John Reeves himself claimed to be acting independently, but he was on close terms with the officials in the Home Office and he was employed as the government's paymaster of the Westminster police judges. There is a hint of collusion in the suggestive letter Reeves sent to Evan Nepean of the Home Office on 2 August 1792 and in the draft paper in the Home Office papers, dated 17 November 1792, suggesting the advantages of an 'Anti-Levelling Society'.[47] There is also some evidence of Lord Grenville's interest in such an association.[48] There is no doubt however that once it was launched the Association was actively publicised on government instructions.[49] Two early members of the Association, Charles Townshend and Sir John Dick, were junior ministers, but, perhaps to distance themselves from the Association's activities, they declined to serve on its committee.[50] Whatever its origins, however, the rapid and quite astonishing spread of the Association movement rested not upon government backing, but upon the genuine appeal that such a loyalist organisation had for a large number of people at this critical juncture in both British politics and European affairs. This overwhelming response was not orchestrated by the government and indeed it probably took the ministers by surprise.

Much the same can be said about ministerial involvement in the Volunteers, an even larger loyalist organisation that was never fully under the command of the government. Indeed, suggestions for setting up armed associations, made as early as December 1792, were resisted for more than a year by the government. It was only when its manpower resources to put down internal disorder or to resist a French invasion were stretched to the limit that the government was willing to listen to such advice. Furthermore, as the Volunteer force expanded enormously, ministers became increasingly worried about their ability to command and direct such a force. Despite all the efforts of the propertied elite to ensure that only the most reliable of the lower orders should be recruited, there were some worrying indications that popular loyalism could not be equated with a willingness to obey every command of the elite who commanded this force. While some Volunteer companies, for example, were ready to act against food rioters,[51] it is evident that some plebeian recruits were reluctant to turn out against food rioters and they even occasionally joined the rioters. This was the case at Honiton in 1795, Teignmouth in 1797, and in various parts of Devon in 1800–1.[52] In Wolverhampton the Volunteers informed a magistrate that they had enlisted 'to protect the King and Constitution and that they held such offers sacred; but that it was never intended by them to give security to the human oppressor, whilst the poor are starving in the midst of plenty'.[53] Several contemporaries also expressed concern that Volunteer recruits were not sufficiently deferential. Several companies asserted their right to remove unpopular officers and even insisted on their right to elect their own officers and they sometimes made inappropriate choices. One corps in Devon, for example, chose a butcher as its captain, while the colonel of a London Volunteer company kept a bakery shop.[54] William Cobbett, himself a former regular soldier, actually condemned the whole Volunteer system as being too republican and democratical. He protested that some Volunteers were prepared to criticise government ministers and he claimed that the whole force was getting out of the government's control.[55] By 1801 the government itself acknowledged the problem and replaced the Volunteers with a new Permanent Local Militia Force under tighter discipline and selected by ballot.

Clearly, there is ample evidence to justify a rejection of the claim that popular conservatism was originally the creation or later the servile creature of the government or the ruling elite. Though welcomed and encouraged by the government, most manifestations of popular conservatism were the result of pervasive and deeply-held opinions. This conclusion is reinforced once it is recognised that the popular conservatism so evident at the time of the French Revolution was a virulent outbreak of political prejudices which had existed throughout the eighteenth century but which only emerged in times of severe crisis. Recent research on a variety of fronts is beginning to confirm that conservative attitudes were widespread among large sections of the population in eighteenth-century Britain. Work on political ideology has revealed an impressive degree of popular support for the traditional institutions of monarchy, aristocracy and the Church of England.[56] A recent attempt to explain why Britain avoided revolution in the later eighteenth century

has acknowledged not only the pervasive influence of conservative ideas and popular support for traditional institutions,
but also the widespread recognition by British citizens that they
enjoyed the inestimable benefits of social cohesion, increasing
prosperity, improvements in the Poor Law and other forms of
charitable relief, and the ability of the poor to secure some
improvement in their conditions by riots, trade union activities
and the spread of friendly societies.[57] Moreover, numerous studies
of popular protests in the eighteenth century have concluded that
rioters with economic grievances were very often motivated by
hostility to recent changes and by a desire to return to traditional practices and that most religious disturbances involved a
defence of the established church and attacks on religious minori-
ties. When these various factors are borne in mind, it is not
at all surprising that, when Britons witnessed first the anarchy
and Terror in France in the early 1790s and then the expansionist
policies of Napoleon in the early nineteenth century, a majority
of them should rush to defend a political and social order which
seemed superior to that of France and was being threatened at
home and abroad.

The desire to preserve the British constitution from its domestic
critics and foreign enemies was not restricted to the propertied elite
who had most to lose from reform and revolution. A majority of the
middling and lower orders also rallied in defence of the constitution.
While the repressive measures of the government played their part
in weakening the radicals, it is also true to say that the radicals lost
the battle for the hearts and minds of the British people. Popular
radicalism was occasionally in the ascendant, but it never achieved
the levels of support which loyalism secured, in 1792-3 and 1803-5
in particular. Although food riots in 1795 and 1800-1, the Luddite
disturbances in 1811-13 and the peace movement of 1807-12 were
all campaigns capable of enlisting considerable popular support, none
of these protests made a radical reform of the constitution into a central
objective. Economic distress was certainly widespread in these years,
but it was not successfully channelled into a mass movement for
parliamentary reform. Popular radicalism did not revive significantly
until after 1812 and it was not again to be a major force to be reckoned
with until after 1815. Thus, popular conservatism and militant loyalism
kept domestic radicalism at bay so long as it could be convincingly
linked with the anarchy of the French Revolution and the military

aggression of Napoleon. Ironically, once the expensive and protracted war against the French bogey had been won, and won in large part because of the popular appeal of conservative ideas and loyalist prejudices, the removal of the French threat and the economic depression of the post-war years gave an enormous fillip to the radical cause within Britain.

Ironic?

6. British Diplomacy and the French Wars 1789-1815

MICHAEL DUFFY

BRITISH foreign policy towards the French Revolution was largely dictated by events of the century preceding its outbreak. Despite intermittent periods when their interests coincided, there was a general conviction that France was by far Britain's most dangerous rival, and that rivalry was played out over five wars occupying thirty-seven of the previous hundred years. It was far from clear in 1789 that Britain had achieved any superiority or security, indeed the evidence of their most recent war between 1778 and 1783 pointed the other way. French intervention in the American Revolution had been instrumental in the loss of Britain's thirteen rebel colonies while Franco-Spanish fleets had sailed the Channel unmolested. It had been a stunning display of French maritime power, assisted by the Spanish and Dutch, while Britain's international frailty had been clearly revealed when she could find no allies and when the Baltic Powers combined into an Armed Neutrality to resist British regulation of neutral trade. Britain's naval and financial strength had barely enabled her to survive and she had emerged from the war with a greatly reduced empire, exhausted and shaken.

After the American war the Younger Pitt's government struggled hard to recover the initiative, and it achieved a notable coup in 1787-8 when it broke out of its diplomatic isolation by cooperating with Prussia to wrest back from France a predominant influence over Holland. Thereafter ministers nervously awaited a French counter-stroke and hence the French Revolution, which seemed to nullify – at least temporarily – French international power, was greeted with delight and relief.[1] When France set aside opportunities for intervention in the Belgian revolt against Austria in 1789 and in the Anglo-Spanish crisis over Nootka Sound in 1790, ministers decided that they could discount any French threat in the foreseeable future – Pitt's speculation in February 1792 was for the next fifteen years.[2]

Revolutionary France's apparent withdrawal from great power politics presented Britain's leaders with their ideal diplomatic situation of having full freedom to choose between intervening or withdrawing from European affairs whenever they wished. The choice initially, partly precipitated by their acquisitive Prussian ally, was to intervene to press British interests throughout Europe. They ran, however, into that constant limitation on any adventurous British foreign policy – the national wish to withdraw. The nation would back action to protect immediate interests such as the preservation of Austrian rule in Belgium and rights against Spain in America, but it was reluctant to follow Pitt's efforts to settle a Russo-Turkish war in which, to the public at least, British interests seemed remote. The shock of loss of public support in April 1791 led Pitt into the alternative policy of withdrawal to concentrate on building up national resources and prosperity internally. Such a policy seemed the more attractive when signs of radical agitation began to appear, and domestic anxieties came to predominate over foreign policy. As late as 7 November 1792 Pitt's Foreign Secretary, Lord Grenville, could declare his conviction that only by keeping 'wholly and entirely aloof' abroad, by vigilance at home, by nursing up support for the constitution, and by increasing wages and reducing taxes could they hope to delay an internal crisis that was perhaps ultimately inevitable.[3]

Between May 1791 and November 1792 therefore British diplomacy effectively lapsed. No effort was made to strengthen relations with other powers. In September 1791 ministers refused to become involved in an Austro-Prussian proposal of international intervention to free the French royal family. Even when France took advantage of the British withdrawal to declare war on Austria in 1792 ministers, convinced of French weakness, were not alarmed. One of Grenville's under-secretaries wrote that while it was difficult to guess where the conflagration would stop: 'It is however to be hoped our salt water entrenchment may preserve us from it, and I think our being implicated in a war of this sort as unlikely a contingency as can well be foreseen.'[4]

France underwent further revolution in August 1792 and declared herself a Republic, and in September she repulsed an Austro-Prussian invasion, but British complacency was not shattered until French victory over the Austrians at Jemappes on 6 November led to a whirlwind occupation of Belgium. The event in Europe most dreaded by British governments had happened. Its possibility in 1789 had made ministers far more alarmed about the Belgian revolution than that in France, and Pitt had then declared the need to keep Belgium independent of France as 'worth the risk or even the certainty' of war.[5] While Frenchmen looked to a natural frontier at the Rhine as a solid defensive security, Britons saw it as a natural jump-off point to winning political, commercial and maritime domination over Holland and, through Holland, over north-west Europe. This seemed confirmed by French actions after Jemappes. Decrees on 16 and 19 November opened the River Scheldt to international traffic, despite Dutch treaty rights, and promised fraternity and assistance to all oppressed peoples desiring their liberty, while another on 15 December established revolutionary government in all conquered territories. The French seemed to be consolidating their hold on Belgium as well as threatening Britain's recently regained Dutch ally and even Britain herself where French actions had encouraged radical celebrations. Ministers decided that only a firm front at home and abroad could ward off the blow. Undoubtedly they moved to confrontation reluctantly: Pitt protested angrily at the collapse of his peace policy that it was 'indeed mortifying to be exposed to so many interruptions of a career the most promising that was ever offered to any country'.[6] Nevertheless a series of warnings was sent to France culminating in Grenville's blunt declaration on 31 December 1792 that:

England never will consent that France shall arrogate the power of annulling at her pleasure, and under the pretence of a pretended natural right, of which she makes herself the only judge, the political system of Europe, established by solemn treaties, and guaranteed by the consent of all the powers. − This government, adhering to the maxims which it has followed for more than a century, will also never see with indifference, that France shall make herself, either directly or indirectly, sovereign of the Low Countries [Belgium], or general arbitress of the rights and liberties of Europe.[7]

Efforts to resolve the crisis were hindered by the fact that neither Britain nor France would give way significantly on the issues involved. Grenville thought the particular danger in negotiating with a revolutionary power was to show weaknesss, which would only increase French pretensions. He was prepared to seek an international pledge not to intervene in French internal affairs and even to recognise the Republic if the French also gave a non-intervention pledge and withdrew within their own frontiers, but he was not prepared to make this offer openly: the French must concede first. Moreover, when their firm action at home and abroad rallied public opinion to their side, ministers saw the chance of domestic and foreign support for an advantageous war against an isolated France which might deal permanent damage to French naval power. The French government, in more tenuous control, was even more concerned that showing weakness might bring its domestic downfall. Sensitive to securing international respect, the new Republic was determined that public British recognition, hitherto delayed, should come before concession, though it is unlikely it would have conceded the maximum Britain demanded. Hopeful that domestic discontent would prevent the British government from fighting; in possession of Belgium; and aware of Dutch vulnerability, they felt that the bargaining power was on their side. In these circumstances serious negotiation never really took place. Each side became more concerned with a war of words by which it sought justification in the eyes of its own public. From the end of December British ministers were convinced that France would not give way and Grenville concentrated on manoeuvring the French into appearing the aggressors who made the actual declaration of war, a task successfully achieved on 1 February 1793.[8]

Twenty-one years later another Prime Minister, Lord Liverpool, was to assert that the defence of Holland and Belgium was the only object on the continent of Europe of sufficient magnitude to British interests to reconcile the country to embarking on a war.[9] In 1793 there would have been no war without it and when in the summer Pitt's War Minister, Henry Dundas, outlined British war aims he declared 'the most prominent object of the war' as the safety of Holland. They must ensure Dutch independence from France, a necessary corollary of which was to secure Belgium in Austrian possession 'as the only secure barrier to the United Provinces [Holland] against the power and ambition of France'. But once the war began British aims expanded to include objects which would not have led to war by themselves. Dundas declared possession of the French West and East Indies 'of infinite moment, both in the view of humbling the power of France, and with the view of enlarging our national wealth and security'. Permanent maritime security would be achieved through destroying France's fleet and naval bases in the war and by acquiring in particular France's Caribbean colonies (which sustained two-thirds of French ocean-going merchant tonnage) so as to prevent any effective restoration of French seapower thereafter. This would be 'the principal object proposed by the war in favour of Great Britain as compensation for our charge in it'. Lastly, whether publicly professed or not, Dundas thought it 'certainly the most material object' to end the anarchy in France and see such a government established 'as may guard the interests of mankind in general from the outrageous consequences which necessarily result from the principles which have been acted upon in that country for some years past'. [10]

It was the task of British diplomacy to secure the cooperation in these objects of the other powers of Europe and of those Frenchmen opposed to the extremities of the Revolution. The support of the great military powers of Europe was essential since Britain, with a population less than half that of France, lacked the manpower resources to clear the French out of Holland and Belgium. She had indeed the naval resources to conquer France's overseas empire but she needed European assistance to distract French resources from the naval struggle and also to prevent them from renewing their maritime resources by plundering or dominating their maritime neighbours. Lastly, since the French opponents of the Revolution were too weak to succeed on their own or with British backing alone, European help was needed if Britain was to do what had never been done before – to crush France's resistance entirely and overthrow her government.

As if this task was not formidable enough by itself, Pitt and Grenville's disadvantages were increased by joining a war already in progress, in which Austria and Prussia had already decided on indemnification for their efforts that was diametrically opposed to British wishes. Prussia would join Russia in a second partition of Poland, and, far worse, Austria would exchange Belgium for Bavaria. Having worked to put France in the wrong in the west, ministers had no wish to disrupt their morally justified position by involvement in the east in plundering the 'neutral and unoffending nation' Poland. Grenville therefore applied himself to encouraging the warring powers to seek their compensation at France's expense and in particular to persuading Austria to retain Belgium by holding out the prospect of extending her frontier into French Flanders. To do this he had to pledge British military assistance, and Anglo-Austrian cooperation became the attempted fulcrum of the First Coalition. [11] However, until he could secure general agreement between the powers on their indemnities, Grenville had to be content with a series of agreements between individual powers and Britain in 1793 pledging to continue fighting until France restored her conquests. This was not incentive enough to induce the powers to continue fighting until Britain's more positive objects were secured. When Grenville explored such incentives further, the collective allied demands effectively returned France to her pre-Louis XIV borders and this raised the further problem that no patriotic Frenchman, however much he disliked the Revolution, would willingly abet such a devastating reduction of French territory and power.

Fears of such a fate undoubtedly hindered co-operation with French royalists and helped rally France behind the Republic in 1793-4. French revolutionary strength developed faster than allied unity, and Grenville was still searching for territorial agreements as the coalition collapsed around him. Holland was knocked out of the war in January 1795 and shortly after forced to join the French side. Prussia withdrew in April and Spain in July – the latter to join France in the following year. Autumn 1795 found ministers thinking seriously about making peace before all their allies left them, and a year later they sent Lord Malmesbury to Paris to negotiate for themselves and Austria any peace that would safeguard Belgium. When that failed and Austria too agreed to make peace in April 1797 ministers even temporarily abandoned Belgium and sought a peace of minimum colonial security, but negotiations at Lille failed and in September 1797 Britain stood alone.

From this position of isolation Grenville tried to rebuild a new coalition, with the chance now of avoiding the mistakes that had plagued the first. He sought general agreement on aims and objects in advance of renewed European war. He looked to cooperation with Russia to secure the participation of Austria and Prussia and he hoped to minimise the effects of the rivalry of the two German powers by turning Austrian attentions to gains in northern Italy and limiting Prussian gains in Germany. In order to conciliate French opinion, France would only be reduced to her pre-war frontiers and even retain much of her overseas empire (now of limited value as a result of slave revolt in the Caribbean). In the new project Britain would derive her European security partly by bolstering states neighbouring France – Belgium would be joined to Holland and Genoa to Piedmont – but more particularly by a guarantee of the settlement by a quadruple alliance of the great powers: Britain, Russia, Austria and Prussia. Britain's maritime security would come from retaining France's Indian bases and Ceylon and the Cape of Good Hope, conquered from France's Dutch ally (thus removing some of the danger from any French dominance over Holland).[12]

Again, however, discord amongst the potential allies prevented these aims being achieved. Prussia held aloof, and Britain was still squabbling with Austria over repayment of financial aid given in the First Coalition when Austria and Russia resumed the continental war in March 1799. The Second Coalition was even less concerted than the First and soon fell apart. Russia left it in 1800 and Austria was knocked out in February

1801. This time France under her new ruler, Napoleon, was prepared to make peace with the isolated Britain on terms which allowed her the minimum of colonial accessions (Ceylon from Holland, Trinidad from Spain) to set against French power in Europe.

It soon became apparent, however, that Napoleon intended to exploit the peace by expanding French influence in Europe and restoring her maritime power in the Caribbean and the eastern Mediterranean. When Britain began again to look around for allies and refused to evacuate Malta, war was resumed in May 1803. However, it took another year and a half before any of the European powers responded to repeated British overtures and it was not until 19 January 1805 that a new detailed British plan for the resettlement of Europe, drafted by Pitt, emerged in response to Russian enquiries. It was this plan that Lord Castlereagh, as Foreign Secretary, again sent to the Russians in April 1813 and which he laid before Parliament on 5 May 1815 to justify the Vienna settlement.[13]

The basis of the plan was that of 1798–9 with France reduced to her former limits and the final settlement mutually guaranteed at the peace, but it went further in refining 'a more effectual barrier in future against encroachments on the part of France' by the formation of two lines of buffer states. In Italy, Piedmont as a first line, backed by Austrian possessions. In Belgium, Prussia as a first line backed by Holland. Generally Pitt elaborated the policy, initiated by Grenville in 1798–9, that any small state or province unable to defend itself against France lost any automatic right to restoration and might be amalgamated with another state better able to resist. France would be restrained in Europe not by reducing her former size but by increasing the size of larger and medium powers surrounding her at the expense of the smaller ones.

The degree of detail with which Pitt listed states to be absorbed or restored and expanded reveals how far by 1805 British attention was becoming preoccupied with the dangers of French expansion in Europe. Britain's own overseas expansion was reduced to subordinate importance, although Pitt's offer in summer 1805 to surrender all British conquests for the sake of a European settlement was quickly qualified by insistence on retaining Malta or Minorca and the Cape.[14] Even more subordinate was the overthrow of the French government. Indeed Pitt told the Russians that while a Bourbon restoration was desirable it was 'only a secondary object in the concert now to be established and one which could in no case justify the prolongation of the war if a peace could be obtained on the principles which have been stated'.

The overthrow of revolutionary government in France was always the most expendable of British objects since territorial and maritime advantage was a better, fail-safe, system of security than reliance on anything that happened within France. Ministers were prepared to declare openly their preference for a monarchical restoration and even provided pensions for the *émigré* Bourbon princes,[15] but they were careful to avoid officially recognising the Comte de Provence as King of France, which would have inextricably committed them. There were obvious advantages in supporting the French royalists. Firstly it enabled Britain to recruit much needed manpower from the French *émigrés*. A dozen 'White Cockade' regiments were formed in 1793-4, more were taken over from the Dutch in 1795 when ministers also acquired the Prince de Condé's 4700 strong corps from the Austrians. Secondly, assistance to royalist risings within France weakened the republican war effort and, once contact had been made and routes set up in 1793-4, there was an intermittent flow of money and arms to the insurgents. The landing of large amounts of military stores on an enemy coast was not easy and the biggest attempt at Quiberon in 1795 ended in total disaster, but enough aid was put into western France to help keep at least the basis of a resistance movement going until 1800 and an intelligence network linked to the Channel Islands was sustained until 1808.[16] Thirdly, suppression of the Revolution would destroy what Grenville described as 'the centre... for propagating over all the rest of Europe principles subversive of all civil society'.[17] And lastly, the re-establishment of a regular government in France and in particular the personal pledge to good faith of a legitimate monarch gave the best chance that any negotiated peace would actually last.[18]

Ministers soon found, however, that supporting royalism was to enter into a whole minefield of contentious issues which rendered such support ineffective and even counter-productive. The Revolution had caused so many political divisions that it was impossible to get even the royalists to agree amongst themselves on the shape a restored monarchy should take. Although ministers tried to keep out of the controversy, their sympathies were undoubtedly on the side of the constitutionalists as against the absolutists. Grenville considered an entire re-establishment of arbitrary monarchy neither practical nor desirable. He accepted that the injustices of the system had caused the Revolution and that to recreate it would only eventually recreate revolution. The 'odious personal exemptions' and oppressive feudal rights should likewise go. However, the States General had been a chaos and the 1791 constitution had swung too far towards democracy – they also had facilitated rather than prevented further revolution. Also unacceptable was the principle of confiscation of private property avowed by the Revolution – in British eyes private property was the very basis of stable, responsible government. Crown, church and *émigré* property should be restored, though with some compensation to its purchasers during the Revolution.[19]

What the British government wanted therefore was an entirely new experiment in constitutional hereditary monarchy in France. They refused to spell out the precise form themselves since to last it would have to evolve from a consensus of the French propertied classes. To avoid divisive debate they sought to rally the French people around a general platform of opposition to the extremities of the Revolution and support for the principle of hereditary monarchy, leaving its form to be decided later. Such a solution in practice proved impossible. Absolutist and constitutionalist royalists remained committed to their own former programmes and would not work together. They intrigued against and sabotaged each other's efforts and speedily disillusioned British leaders. After talking to the constitutionalist Mounier in 1793, Grenville was struck 'to see how little these theorists have profited by experience'. He was even more contemptuous of 'the conduct, principles and supposed resentments' of the ultras surrounding the French princes. Moreover, as a British envoy dealing with the royalist factions acutely observed, 'however they hate one another, they *all* in the bottom detest *us*'.[20] Indeed, the fundamental obstacle to British efforts at stimulating a royalist restoration in France was the inescapable fact that it was far easier to unite all Frenchmen behind a common detestation of Britain than of the Revolution.

The other major obstacle to counter-revolution was the practical weakness of the counter-revolutionaries within France. This was discovered on each occasion Britain made significant efforts to support them. Proclamations in the autumn of 1793 called on the French to rally to the cause of hereditary monarchy and offered military assistance, but the two major efforts by insurgents to secure British help were only made when they were so obviously lost causes as to be unable to be propped up by the limited and – for logistical reasons – belated resources which Britain could provide: such was the fate of the Toulon rising and the Vendéean raid to Granville. The same proved true of the two-pronged royalist attack sponsored by Britain in 1795. Arms and *émigré* troops were landed in western France at Quiberon in the hope of rekindling revolt in Brittany and the Vendée, while Condé's *émigré* corps was to strike down a train of revolt through south-eastern France prepared by the British envoy in Switzerland, William Wickham. Despite royalist confidence, there was not enough active internal support for the *émigrés* to succeed by themselves. Each needed further foreign aid, but Pitt had prepared no large-scale back up for the Quiberon landing (none had been asked) which collapsed before it could be assembled, while the eastern invasion never began because of Austrian inaction.[21]

In 1797 therefore a subtler initiative was tried. Wickham was authorised to spend £30,000 to help secure a royalist majority in the French elections. This met with considerable success only to reveal starkly the essential conflict between British objects. Ministers could not use the royalist deputies, once elected, to obtain both a counter-revolution and a peace settlement that limited French power and guaranteed British security. The prejudices of the deputies were so much against the latter that to press it would only wreck chances of the former. The scheme collapsed finally, however, because of the fundamental military weakness of the royalists – the Directory brought in the army to crush them in the Fructidor *coup d'état*.[22]

All these factors combined to place support for the French royalists at the bottom of British priorities. In 1799 Grenville had greater confidence in the success of a rising of Dutch Orangists than of French royalists. When they too failed, ministers did turn again to rearming the royalists over the winter in the hope of effecting a landing in western France in 1800, but the royalists then rashly rose and were crushed before British troops could be sent. That was the decisive point. Thereafter ministers despaired of internal success by royalist insurgents and they did not resume their efforts when war was renewed in 1803. This attitude was firmly expressed to Louis XVIII's agent by Castlereagh, while War Minister in 1807, when he declared that it was not deemed 'consistent with the interests of His Majesty's service, or with the personal safety of the loyalists in the western departments of France, to give any encouragement whatever to insurrectional movement in that quarter'.[23] Restoration, it was considered, could now only take place in the wake of victory by the allied powers and, desirable though it was, it would not be insisted upon but would depend on the consent of the French.

As the wars continued one fact became ever more inescapable: that if Britain was to achieve any of her objectives she needed the support of European great power allies. To attract that support in 1793–4, 1798–9 and 1805 ministers sketched out in ever more detail their proposals for the resettlement of Europe. Yet the more clearly they refined their programme the further they seemed to be from being able to implement it. Undoubtedly this was due to the intrinsic strength of France herself, supplemented so enormously by the Revolution's mobilisation of the energies and talents of the French people and then redoubled by the genius of Napoleon. But much was also due to European discontent with Britain's attempted leadership of a massive anti-French effort.

The major problem for British statesmen was that while they clung to their ideal of a resurrection of the successful Grand Alliance of William III and Marlborough's day, the circumstances which brought that hallowed edifice into being had long since passed away. None of the other great powers of Europe now saw France as either their most immediate or their greatest threat. Prussia and Austria vied for predominance in central Europe and cast anxious glances at Russia's westward and southward expansion, so that the great military powers to whom Britain traditionally turned were reluctant to concentrate on the French war unless it yielded advantages also in their eastern rivalries.

Moreover the military powers saw as much danger as did the other maritime powers in Britain's growing maritime strength: indeed in 1800 her envoy at Berlin reported that Britain was 'evidently giving more alarm and jealousy to Europe than France'. There was a widespread feeling that, while others shed the blood and took the knocks in Europe, Britain by her overseas conquests was gaining a monopoly of colonial wealth and by her naval supremacy was controlling the seaborne commerce of the world. Such complaints were loud enough for Britons abroad to be picking them up as early as 1794, and by the following year even Francis II, ruler of Britain's main ally, Austria, approved a memorandum accusing the British of seeking to 'involve all the powers of Europe in a war to weaken them and then, by its supremacy on the seas and in commerce, make itself arbiter of all international transactions'. Skilfully and remorselessly exploited by French propaganda, this 'universal jealousy, envy and indisposition' (the words are the British envoy's at Vienna in 1800) persisted after even the worst Napoleonic depredations. As Napoleon's Grand Army fell back from Moscow the Russian commander, Kutusov, preferred to offer the French a *'pont d'or'* out of Russia since, as he bluntly told a British military observer, he was 'by no means sure that the total destruction of the Emperor Napoleon and his army would be a benefit to the world; his succession would not fall to Russia or any other continental power, but to that which already commands the sea, and whose domination would then be intolerable'.[24]

Once they were possessed of such fears, much of what Britain proposed and did seemed extremely self-centred and was resented by the European powers. British ministers refused to involve themselves in the concerns of eastern Europe and demanded that everyone whole-heartedly concentrate on France. As far as they could, they tried to pretend that the Polish problem which dominated the attention of the military powers between 1793 and 1795 did not exist. In 1795, when the quarrel over the final partition was clearly obstructing the campaign against a temporarily exhausted France, the furthest that Grenville would go was to hope that news of the triple alliance he had formed with Austria and Russia would get the business over by inducing the Prussians to give way. He firmly refused subsidies to bring Prussian concession by armed force, while Pitt was still looking to offer subsidies to Prussia to liberate Holland.[25] Even Pitt's 1805 plan, which Castlereagh thought a 'masterly... outline for the restoration of Europe', extended no further east than Italy and the Rhineland, whereas Russian enquiries had looked for a policy for the whole of Germany and the Ottoman Empire as well and the Russians were also envisaging a recreated kingdom of Poland within their own empire.[26] In part British governments were trapped by domestic opinion which saw only the French war and, as in 1791, refused to see British interests and resources involved in eastern Europe, but this inevitably led the military powers to seek solutions between themselves and France to the exclusion of Britain's western interests.

There was discontent also at Britain's practical assistance to her war allies. The military powers continually demanded help by a powerful British military diversion in the west – which either failed to materialise or arrived too late or in areas too peripheral to constitute a serious diversion. European land powers always underestimated Britain's real problem in launching and sustaining amphibious operations against any strongly defended coast. On the other hand they continually overestimated the liquidity of Britain's wealth in their requests for financial assistance. On the British side there was resistance to becoming, in Grenville's words, the 'milch cow' of Europe and a tendency to underestimate the financial weakness of European states,[27] but until Pitt and Addington revolutionised Britain's tax revenue by the income tax after 1798 and until British trade expanded sufficiently to provide credit and European exchange, Britain was actually short of money to offer. Yet, convinced of British profit from the wars, continental states seemed to think that British ministers had merely to stamp their feet to produce endless guineas and their subsidy demands invariably exceeded Britain's capacity. In 1796 Austria asked £3 million when Pitt could only advance £1.2 million; in 1805 she wanted £6 million when Pitt had only that sum for Austria, Prussia and Russia combined; in 1809 she needed £7.5 million when Britain's Iberian commitments left her only £1.2 million spare. At the end of 1806 Prussia asked for £3 million to fight on after Jena while Russia requested a £6 million loan: that only half a million pounds had been received before his defeat at Friedland, together with the lack of a British military diversion, hastened an alienated Tsar Alexander I towards his anti-British Treaty of Tilsit with Napoleon.[28] The insidious 'Pitt's gold' of French propaganda was in limited supply: between 1793 and 1802 £9½ million in subsidies and £6¼ million in loans to the European Powers. Between 1803 and 1812 an improved structure of government finance released £23¼ million in subsidies and £600,000 in loans, but it was never enough to meet all the demands on it.[29]

Lastly, Europeans were aggravated by British commercial policy. Britain's problems here were immense. Her main strength was her commerce and her ability to use her navy as an economic weapon to increase her own resources and reduce those of an enemy. The more French power increased, the more Britain had to rely on that economic weapon for her own survival, but the more that weapon then impinged upon the commercial intercourse of all the other powers besides her enemies. Her need to generate the wealth and foreign exchange for subsidies led her to demand from the European powers an open access for British manufactures, which threatened their economies and revenues, at the same time as she offered them alliance and subsidies.[30] Moreover, while she sought to expand her own trade, her methods of economic warfare limited everyone else's. British regulation of trade with her enemies had precipitated the Armed Neutrality of the Baltic powers in 1780 and caused problems as soon as war began with Revolutionary France. In 1794 Denmark and Sweden threatened a new Armed Neutrality and relations with the United States deteriorated sharply. The Americans were temporarily bought off by the commercial and territorial concessions of Jay's Treaty while the Baltic states were checked by Russian acceptance of British methods in the 1793 Anglo-Russian Convention – one of the few early successes of Grenville's diplomacy. However, after the death of Catherine the Great, Russia's line altered sharply. In 1801 she formed a new Baltic Armed Neutrality which occasioned British hostilities with Denmark and was halted only by the assassination of Tsar Paul. Yet Russian prejudices on maritime rights remained. They were pressed on Pitt as the price of alliance in 1805. In 1807 they helped lead Russia into Napoleon's Continental System, and the Russians were still pressing them in 1813–14.[31] In the meantime British methods had produced fresh confrontation with the United States from 1806 culminating in an American declaration of war in 1812.[32]

All these factors put British diplomacy at an immense disadvantage in endeavouring to rally European coalitions against France. A further important bargaining counter was lost in 1796–7 when France refused to follow former precedents (such as 1748) of trading conquests with Britain and reaching a European settlement by Anglo-French agreement. Instead she preferred to deal directly with the European powers. Thereafter Britain was forced increasingly to look to Russia as the most secure and disinterested of the great powers to act as the focus around which a coalition might be formed: in 1798–9, 1804–7, and again in 1812–13. This, however, left British policy at the mercy of Russia's own aims and methods as when in 1805 the latter unilaterally offered George III's Hanoverian electorate to Prussia as the price of Berlin's support. Moreover, Russia would only move in her own time, and only Austria in 1800 and 1809 tried, disastrously, to act without her. Everyone had to reckon on the certainty of massive retaliation by France if they joined Britain.

Hence Britain lost her ability to rally coalitions against France. Without the diplomatic initiative she was reduced to the desperate expedient of seeking military advantage through first strike – against France in 1803, Spain in 1804 and Denmark in 1807 – which further reduced diplomatic options, put her at a disadvantage as the official aggressor, and added immediately to her enemies. Denmark was so embittered as to be the last power to abandon Napoleon in 1813. Eventually French dominance grew so great that British diplomacy was effectively excluded from mainland Europe as Napoleon persuaded more and more states into his Continental System and into breaking diplomatic relations and declaring war on Britain. By 1812 only five British diplomatic missions survived, all on the southern fringe of Europe, in Portugal, Spain, Sicily, Sardinia and Turkey. Without the capacity to search for allies, Britain could only wait for others to approach London and lacked any ability to be selective according to her war aims. Canning really confessed British diplomatic impotence in his 1808 declaration that: 'We shall proceed upon the principle that any nation of Europe that starts up with a determination to oppose a power which ... is the common enemy of all nations, whatever may be the existing political relations of that nation and Great Britain, becomes instantly our essential ally.'[33]

For nearly twenty years therefore Britain found herself outplayed in Europe by a France which could assert far more military leverage; which had conquered European territory to offer other powers; and which was able to exploit central European rivalries and fears of British maritime predominance in a skilful game of divide and rule. How then was Britain able to emerge so well in 1814–15?

Partly it was because of her dogged ability to keep fighting – by herself if necessary. She was sustained in adversity by that very isolationism that so handicapped her diplomacy and exasperated Europeans. She was never so committed to the European powers as to be demoralised by their defeat, never so dependent on Europe as to be prostrated by French dominance. Statistical information, hitherto lacking, now emerged out of the search to organise what was by far Britain's greatest yet war effort, and it showed that Britain's population and resources were growing apace so that there was growing confidence that she had strength enough to maintain her own effort almost indefinitely.[34] There was considerable economic hardship at times, but opponents of government policy focused solutions on peace with the United States rather than France.[35] Success overseas was held to counter-balance defeat in Europe, and even in Europe Britain was never alone for more than two years at any time in the war. There was always hope of a European Power coming forward and Prussia (1806), Spain (1808), Austria (1809) and Russia (1812) all took up arms against France while they were still officially at war with Britain. So long as Britain was still fighting, the other powers had the encouragement that she would in some degree assist them and this made them prepared to pay at least lip service to some of her aims to ensure that assistance.

The position had been reached by 1807 where the only two powers who could alone sustain the war by themselves, Britain and France, faced each other like two great colossi or like Carthage and Rome, with which contemporaries frequently compared them: the one supreme on the sea; the other on land. Neither had the power to defeat the other by herself; neither could do so with the limited alliance systems that they had used for so much of the eighteenth century: Britain with Austria or Prussia and periodically Holland; France with Spain and also periodically Holland. So indestructible had each become that the only force sufficient to defeat either was the strength of all Europe. After 1805 France seemed the most likely to achieve this European unity and, ironically, perhaps Britain's diplomatic weakness was eventually her salvation. She had to work by persuasion and example. She never had the strength to cajole any but small seaboard states like Holland, Sicily and Portugal, whereas Napoleon did – and eventually the temptation to hurry matters along by using his strength rather than his diplomacy proved irresistible. His impatience to achieve the European unity necessary to defeat Britain, combined with his inherent dynastic acquisitiveness for himself and his family, led him to overthrowing existing monarchs – most sensationally in Spain in 1808 which precipitated an Iberian revolt that Britain was able to turn into a continuing military diversion – and to trying to coerce the remaining military powers which culminated in his disastrous invasion of Russia in 1812.

Even 1812, however, did not redeem the British position far. Russians like Kutusov still looked to balance French and British power. Likewise the Austrian Metternich, whose army now held the balance of military power in central Europe, still looked to maintaining a strong France as balance to the irruption from the east of a strong Russia. In consequence the European powers repeatedly offered Napoleon peace in 1813 on terms which would have left France her natural frontiers – including Belgium and Napoleon's new major naval base at Antwerp – and which left Britain to negotiate at a general peace the settlement of her other western and southern European interests at a disadvantage after terms of peace for central and eastern Europe had been agreed.

British objects were saved by Napoleon's repeated refusal to make peace on the terms offered him. The war had to continue and in those circumstances the balance of advantages swung dramatically Britain's way. The longer the war continued the greater chance she had of seizing military control of her particular objects rather than being dependent on the goodwill of her German and Russian allies. The eviction of France from Spain was the first fruit, French abandonment of Holland the second, though the attempt of a small British force to capture Antwerp was checked. The longer the war continued moreover the more need the exhausted European powers had of British material and financial assistance and British ministers took the gamble of throwing their every last penny – and more in paper credit – into this almost miraculous opportunity to snatch the long-sought victory; £26¼ million in money and armaments were provided for the European powers in 1813–15, compared with the £39½ million in the wars hitherto. Armaments from a fully tooled-up British munitions industry were not the least important part of this aid for European mobilisation: over 900,000 muskets were supplied in 1813 alone. All this bore fruit in the Treaty of Chaumont of 1 March 1814 by which the allies agreed to carry on the war to the defeat of Napoleon. Castlereagh pledged Britain in the treaty to provide 150,000 men, equal to the contingent of each of the other three great powers. Since he calculated that British subsidies supported 50,000 men in each of their armies he could maintain that Britain was sustaining half the allied effort – 300,000 men – in the field. With subsidies to lesser allies she also provided 125,000 more. 'What an extraordinary display of power!' he wrote exultantly, 'This, I trust, will put an end to any doubts as to the claim we have to an opinion on continental matters.'[36]

That such an opinion might now be put with effect, however, needed the Foreign Secretary Castlereagh's personal presence with the European leaders in the allied camp to overcome the perpetual long-distance communications obstacle to British diplomatic influence. It also needed three other fortunate circumstances. One was Tsar Alexander's decision at last to act as the liberator of western Europe and to overthrow Napoleon by taking Paris. Another was Metternich's realisation that he could no longer use a strong Napoleonic France to check Russia, so that he needed Britain instead and hence conciliated her over the western European settlement. Lastly, because the war was carried to Paris, the negotiation of the frontiers of a defeated France in western Europe came before an eastern settlement. In a reversal of the disadvantageous 1813 negotiations, the decisions directly affecting Britain were made first, giving Britain a much stronger voice. It was Russia and Britain who got most of what they wanted written into the 1814–15 settlement: Russia because of the sheer size of her army; Britain because of this particular confluence of favourable circumstances.[37]

Napoleon's unexpected total collapse enabled Castlereagh to implement most of the British programme for containing France. The latter was reduced to her 1790 frontiers, surrounded by enlarged buffer states backed by the German powers and a twenty-year Quadruple Alliance of the four great powers established against further French aggression. A second-best solution was, however, adopted for the defence of the Netherlands where the first French break-through had occurred. Neither of the German powers would take over Belgium so that she had to be joined to Holland in a United Kingdom of the Netherlands. Nevertheless with Prussia given adjacent territory, with the British nominee, the Prince of Orange, reinstated in Holland and made the new king, and with proposals of a marriage between his heir and the Princess of Wales, the result was regarded in Europe as a great British triumph and talk was of Britain's 'new Dutch empire'.[38]

The French collapse also meant that Britain no longer had to trade overseas conquests for European advantage and could dictate the maritime settlement. Realising the extent of European jealousy ministers were prepared to return much but felt no need to go so far as Pitt contemplated in 1805. To the acquisitions of 1802 were added French Tobago, St Lucia and Mauritius, the Dutch Cape of Good Hope, and Malta as strategic naval bases, and the Dutch Guiana colonies as economic investments more profitable than all the restored French colonies. Thanks also to a timely peace with the United States in December 1814, which deprived Russia of leverage, Britain further emerged with her regulation of maritime rights unrestrained. While ministers claimed a moderate maritime settlement, Europeans had no doubt of the outcome. The Tsar's adviser, Capodistria, asked where was the European equilibrium (of which British ministers talked) 'when one single power is mistress of all the seas? Is there any other maritime power than England? Can one be created? No, so goodbye equilibrium.'[39]

The Napoleonic collapse was so complete that Britain even obtained her most expendable object: a Bourbon restoration in France. While Metternich preferred Napoleon and the Tsar Crown Prince Bernadotte of Sweden or a junior member of the Bourbon house, it was Castlereagh's advocacy of Louis XVIII at the allied camp and the success of a British trial run of his claims at Bordeaux which won the day. When Napoleon proved unsavable, Metternich preferred the British to the Russian candidate and Alexander I came around at the news from Bordeaux. But it was the Tsar who then carried through the restoration with the aid of Talleyrand and former members of the Napoleonic regime and through them and the Napoleonic Senate even imposed on the Bourbons the constitution which British ministers had puzzled at achieving. The 'Hundred Days' moreover enabled ministers to dispose of the one aspect of the Tsar's settlement they disliked by removing Napoleon from Elba to remote British St Helena where he could disturb neither France nor Europe.

There was, however, a major advance of British diplomacy from her former, blinkered, anti-French vision in Castlereagh's readiness to be involved in the settlement of central and eastern Europe. Having been won over by Metternich to the importance of a satisfactory solution there for the permanence of the western settlement, he broke away from the former policy of Grenville, Pitt, and himself in 1813. Instead of bringing Russia into Europe in alliance with Britain to dictate a settlement against

France, at the end of 1814 he allied with Austria and France to keep Russian influence out of central Europe, his aim being to establish a European equilibrium through 'a union of the two great German powers, supported by Great Britain, and thus combining the minor states of Germany, together with Holland, in an intermediary system between Russia and France.'[40]

How far the final settlement worked as the British intended is matter for debate.[41] Castlereagh's hopes of a continued concert of the great powers were dashed by the early 1820s. The Dutch marriage never took place and the United Netherlands fell apart in 1830. The Bourbons too fell in that year. Castlereagh's equilibrium moreover would have involved continued British support for the weaker German powers against their neighbours, so that it was perhaps fortunate that by 1820 Russia had become dedicated to preserving the European status quo. This, combined with the maritime supremacy now so completely won, enabled Britain to retreat from European affairs towards that outside position, so beloved by public opinion and so infuriating to Europeans, which she had occupied before the wars began.

7. Strategic Problems of the British War Effort

PIERS MACKESY

WHEN war broke out in 1793, Pitt and his colleagues had no reason to doubt that they understood the strategic options which faced them. During the past 54 years, Britain had waged three major wars with France lasting some 23 years; and the lesson of those struggles was that the deployment of the country's military power did not present a clear-cut choice between European and colonial warfare.

I

That dichotomy between continental and blue-water warfare had been the language of parliamentary debate and polemical pamphleteering. Responsible statesmen, however, knew that strategy was not a choice between these opposites but a delicate balance between them. Colonial warfare was the area of Britain's positive interests, with a balance sheet drawn from a list of remote territories gained and lost: the snowy wastes of Canada with their French peasants and their fur-trappers; the fisheries of Newfoundland and the sugar and cotton of the Caribbean; the taxes of India and the trade with China. If wars were fought for wealth, Britain's strategic priority should logically be colonial expansion. Yet the keys to Britain's security lay in Europe.

For Europe could not be ignored. It was true that since the loss of Calais in the sixteenth century Britain had had no realistic territorial ambitions on the continent. But her concern with Europe's fate had not vanished with her forward aims. Her security against invasion, her continental markets, and the containing of her enemies' military resources all demanded that Britain should have allies in Europe and be prepared to aid them with force. By doing so she prevented French expansion, especially into the Low Countries where Britain's vital interests were at stake: these were routes and markets for her exports, and the harbours of the Scheldt which could provide an enemy with invasion bases north of the Straits of Dover. Moreover, Britain's naval superiority rested in large measure on spending more on her fleets than her enemies could do. If France could be forced to maintain great armies on her long continental frontiers, she could not afford the naval expenditure to challenge British predominance at sea.

It was for such reasons that in the days of Louis XIV Britain had fought major campaigns in Europe to prevent a French hegemony which would have controlled the resources of Spain and perhaps of Holland, and could have won for France the control of the Scheldt and Antwerp. So too in the War of the Austrian Succession and the Seven Years War, conflict which had begun in the colonies had soon sucked British armies into the Low Countries and Germany to succour allies and stop French expansion. The American War, when Britain had had no allies and France had consciously avoided European entanglements, had demonstrated that when France reduced her continental commitments she could present a formidable challenge on the oceans.

These lessons from the past were absorbed by the veteran diplomatist, Lord Auckland. 'The security of Europe is essential to the security of the British Empire,' he declared in Parliament in 1799: 'We cannot separate them.'[1] The balance of power – the 'Liberties of Europe' as the English euphemism put it – was the necessary condition of all else: of expansion overseas and trade in Europe; and of security at home, which in the French Revolution included security from subversive doctrines. For Pitt's government in 1793 the continental markets seemed especially threatened. Like the British, the French recognised that wars were won by wealth; and it had long been a French article of faith that the credit system through which Britain largely financed her wars was a balloon inflated with the hot air of confidence. Puncture the balloon, disperse the confidence; and the result would be panic in the City, a run on the banks, and the collapse of the British war effort. By closing the coasts of Europe to Britain's trade France would destroy her. 'The credit of England rests on fictitious wealth,' Kersaint had assured the Convention in January. The attack on that credit had begun with the overrunning of the Austrian Netherlands, an important transit market for British goods; and the next stage would be Holland, where France would also cure her own financial deficit. 'Soon Amsterdam will be your counting house,' Cambon informed the Convention.

It was to save Holland that the British government made its stand in

January 1793 and provoked the Convention to declare war. Unlike preceding wars, which had begun as colonial struggles and imploded into Europe, the French Revolutionary War began in Europe. A scratch British force was rushed into Holland to hold the Maas; and when the tide of war turned against the Revolutionaries, a British army under the Duke of York marched across Belgium with Dutch and Austrian forces to assail the frontiers of France.

Circumstances thus dictated that the first British effort was made in Europe. The Pitt government, however, soon began to recreate the balanced strategy of the Seven Years War. In those days the British army had fought in Germany, defending Hanover, sustaining the Prussian ally, and containing French resources. Behind the cover of these operations, other forces had pursued colonial expansion in Canada, the Caribbean and India; theatres which were isolated from French reinforcement by the British navy's command of the oceans. In 1793 this dual strategy was attempted again, and in the autumn a force of 7000 under General Grey sailed for the West Indies.

There were powerful defensive arguments in favour of colonial operations. In the West Indies lay Britain's largest overseas capital investments; and at least a fifth of her pre-war trade was accounted for by the lucrative triangular commerce in African slaves, West Indian sugar and cotton, and British clothing and victuals. The loss of that commercial empire, now threatened with slave rebellions fomented by French republicans, would have been a national disaster: and not only an economic disaster but a naval one as well, for the colonial trades were nurseries of seamen for manning the Royal Navy. The West Indies, as Pitt's Home Secretary, Henry Dundas, declared, was therefore 'the first point to make perfectly certain'.[2] And in an archipelago like the Caribbean, the only sure means of defence was attack. Static garrisons invited an enterprising enemy to pick them off one by one, whereas the seizure of the French bases would deprive them of their offensive resources. Invitations to intervene from anti-republican French colonists were an added lure.

The operations which were to safeguard Britain's wealth were also expected to deal a death blow to the war potential of France. 'All modern wars are a contention of purse,' Dundas was to tell Pitt in the following year;[3] and it was supposed that if France were deprived of her colonial trade she would be sucked deeper into the bankruptcy which had checked her victory in the American War and toppled her into revolution. The Foreign Secretary, Lord Grenville, subscribed to a similar maxim, in spite of his strong belief in the importance of Europe. 'Whenever we were at war with France,' he told the House of Lords at the end of the war, 'one of our first objects must always be to cripple her marine, which can never be better done than by contracting her commerce by depriving her of her colonial possessions.'[4]

In later years it was to be alleged by Pitt's Evangelical friend, William Wilberforce, that the war of 1793 was caused by Dundas's influence with Pitt and his conviction that the West Indies could be easily conquered. The charge is nonsense, and bears no relation either to the causes of the war, which were concerned with European and domestic security, or to the imperial policy which Britain had pursued since the losses suffered in the American War. That had been a policy of commerce without conquest, except for the naval bases needed to protect the shipping routes. In the minds of Pitt and Dundas Britain's future overseas lay in trade rather than political occupation, in markets which had to be kept open and if necessary opened by force. 'The prosperity of this country knows no bounds,' Dundas was to declare, 'unless...its industry and commercial enterprise shall outrun the extension of its foreign markets.'[5]

It is true that Britain was to occupy almost the whole of the French West Indies in the first eighteen months of the war, but that was a consequence of the war and not a cause. War aims, however, expand with opportunity. To the aim of security was soon added that of indemnity. Dundas, who had been in office in the American War and had subsequently reorganised the government of British India, saw the opportunity to reverse the verdict of the last struggle and end the rivalry with which the French had disturbed the years since the loss of America. To the recurrent *revanchiste* cry in the revolutionary Convention, *delenda est Carthago*, he responded in kind. 'The permanent interests and prosperity of the British Empire' required that the war should be used for the destruction of French naval power and of its foundations. 'This country,' Dundas declared in the summer of 1793, 'having captured the French West India Islands and destroyed their existing fleet, may long rest in peace.' It was a vision to which he recurred; and he yearned to attack the French fleet in Brest and 'give the death blow for half a century to the power of France'. 'If it is in our power we ought to use our best exertions to annihilate their naval power.' And the purpose? To become 'the paramount commercial and naval power of the world'.[6]

This aim placed Britain in an uncomfortable relationship with her allies. Her maritime effort could indeed be defended on strictly strategic grounds: it undermined the enemy's war economy, and sustained the naval power on which Britain's survival as an ally and provider of subsidies depended. But Dundas's wartime memoranda make it clear that for him commercial expansion through war was a national aim which took priority over the common military effort of the successive coalitions. This placed Lord Grenville in an awkward position. As Foreign Secretary he had learned from the First Coalition that the divergent political aims of the continental powers resulted in divergent strategies, with fatal military effects in the operations against France. In structuring the Second Coalition of 1798 he tried to apply the lesson by harmonising the war aims of Prussia, Austria and Russia, so that they would be free to pursue the common goal of defeating France without fear of being stabbed in the back at the peace conference. Yet Britain herself was not to be part of this harmonisation: he refused to allow the future 'maritime peace' to form part of the general discussion.[7]

II

Grenville was capable of wide strategic vision. But strategic concepts evaporate unless there is force to execute them. The lessons of past conflicts showed that the navy was likely, and the army was certain, to be unready for war.

The navy's wartime deployment was complex and extended. Taking as a typical example the situation in January 1809, there were seven naval commands outside Europe (East Indies, Jamaica, Leeward Islands, Nova Scotia, Newfoundland, Brazil, Cape of Good Hope) stretching from Newfoundland to India and absorbing 21 ships of the line (the capital ships of the day), and 176 frigates, sloops and smaller warships. Not one of these 'stationed squadrons', however, was strong enough by itself to face a major enemy force detached from Europe, for it was not possible to be strong everywhere. The hub of British seapower was in Europe, where the enemy's war ports were blockaded to prevent such detachments or pursue them. The coast of Europe south of Finisterre was in the charge of the Mediterranean command, generally with major blockades at Cadiz and Toulon, and detachments and cruisers in the Adriatic, off the Dardanelles, or wherever the protection of convoys or military expeditions and the interception of enemy force might require them. In January 1809 the Mediterranean had 21 sail of the line (as many as the whole world outside Europe) and 51 other warships. The commanders-in-chief included the most resplendent names in the naval history of the wars, St Vincent, Nelson and Collingwood.

But the central pillar supporting the edifice of naval power was the Channel fleet, based on Portsmouth and Plymouth, numbering, in January 1809, 28 sail of the line and 50 other warships, including 10 cruisers on the outstation at Cork. The daily tasks of the Channel fleet were to prevent invasion and cover the vast convoys which carried Britain's overseas trade and military expeditions. These responsibilities it discharged by watching the French main fleet in Brest and cruising to cover convoys. It also provided from time to time blockading squadrons to watch La Rochelle and the Spanish base at Ferrol. The watch on Brest could be maintained either by stationing a pair of frigates off the port while the fleet lay in readiness in the shelter of Torbay; or more rigorously and expensively by stationing the fleet itself off Brest, with an inshore squadron of frigates supported by a capital ship. This 'close blockade' was necessary when invasion was threatened or the enemy were known to be preparing overseas expeditions. But successful blockade could not be guaranteed. Enemy squadrons could escape in fog or easterly winds to trouble overseas theatres, and to meet this situation the Channel fleet had to provide a strategic reserve for the whole world. From the ships of the Channel fleet the Admiralty had to find the force to respond to French irruptions: pursuing the escaped enemy squadron or reinforcing threatened theatres, and guessing from often tenuous evidence what might be the enemy's destination.

Besides the Channel fleet, a second force in home waters covered the North Sea. The squadron was based in the mouth of the Thames, with the functions of watching enemy forces in the Scheldt and at the Texel and protecting the important Baltic convoys. From 1807 a separate force was permanently stationed inside the Baltic to counter the hostility of Russia. In January 1809 the North Sea fleet numbered 15 sail of the line and 20 smaller warships; the Baltic squadron 6 and 25.

Thus, from the outbreak of a war, the navy required large forces in readiness to meet its many responsibilities. But it had always suffered from run-down peacetime strength, and from slow mobilisation of manpower in an emergency. The consequences were severe. In 1756 Minorca had been lost, and Admiral Byng had paid for the failure with his life; and in 1778 the French Mediterranean fleet based in Toulon had sailed unchallenged to the American coast, where it threatened to destroy the British squadron and starve the army. Since then the Pitt ministry had done much to improve the navy's infrastructure. Under the direction of the Comptroller of the Navy, Sir Charles Middleton, the dockyards and storehouses were reformed; new ships of the line were built, and the old ones systematically repaired. The new arrangements had been tested by mobilisation in several recent war scares; and in two respects the enemy was now less formidable as a result of the Revolution. The French navy's officer corps had been undermined; and the Bourbon family compact had been cracked, bringing Spain's naval resources into alliance with Britain's.

Nevertheless some critical weaknesses remained. The shortage of seamen delayed mobilisation and gave the French navy several months of freedom to come and go as it pleased. In spite of a great improvement of health in the navy, there could never be enough British seamen to conduct the nation's trade and man the huge fleet of ships of the line and cruisers needed to meet Britain's many maritime commitments. At the maximum strength in 1810 there were 144,000 seamen and marines in the war fleets, and the wartime expansion caused both naval and merchant crews to be diluted heavily with landsmen and foreigners. More critical was the shortage of warships. At the outset the Royal Navy had 115 ships of the line against 76 French; but the French were larger and more heavily armed, and in weight of firepower the British superiority was only one-sixth. This margin was not enough, for Britain's maritime commitments were greater. And paradoxically, the French squadrons lying in blockaded ports had the initiative and could launch offensives at the moment of their choosing. The British fleets, in a constant state of readiness on their blockading stations, needed reserves of as much as two-thirds of the numbers at sea to cope with the wear and tear of sea service. The shortage of cruisers to scout for the fleets and protect the trade also remained critical, in spite of a huge building programme of frigates and sloops.

In the early years of the war Britain's superiority was sufficient, because the counter-revolutionary rising in Toulon removed 13 sail of the line from the enemy's strength, and the Dutch and Spanish navies were aligned with the British. But the balance changed drastically after 1795, when Spain and Holland changed sides and recreated the hostile maritime coalition which a dozen years earlier had cost Britain her American colonies. The nominal 76 Spanish ships of the line and the 49 Dutch were added to the enemy strength, and the Royal Navy became critically overstretched. One consequence was the British withdrawal from the Mediterranean, which freed Bonaparte's coastal lines of communication in his Italian campaigns against Austria; and when the Austrians made a separate peace at Campo Formio in 1797 they blamed the withdrawal of British naval support for their defeat.

Only victory at sea could restore the naval balance. In 1797 Jervis inflicted heavy losses on the Spanish at Cape St Vincent, and Duncan on the Dutch at Camperdown. This enabled the British government to scrape together a squadron to re-enter the Mediterranean, resulting in Nelson's destruction of the restored Toulon fleet at the battle of the Nile. Barring accidents and surprise, Britain's command of the oceans was now assured till the Peace of Amiens.

The naval crisis returned, however, with the renewal of the war in 1803. Britain's far-flung defensive needs, especially the vulnerability of the British Isles to invasion, enabled France with her central position and her Dutch and Spanish allies to regain the naval initiative. She attempted to win surprise by mounting simultaneous threats on two fronts. In 1798 the French had threatened invasion on the Channel, but struck their blow with their Mediterranean fleet in Egypt. In 1804-5 they maintained a threat to the east, but brought their Mediterranean fleet into the Atlantic and, after threatening the West Indies, attempted an overwhelming naval concentration in the Channel to cover an invasion of the British Isles. The manoeuvre was frustrated by British counter-moves, and in the aftermath a cluster of naval battles, including Trafalgar, destroyed 30 French ships of the line and their bid for naval supremacy.

Thereafter, Napoleon began the slow task of rebuilding his naval strength, aided by his control of the coasts and resources of most of Europe. He shifted his main naval base from Brest to Antwerp, where the rivers Scheldt and Rhine ensured a supply of naval building materials which he could not obtain in Brest. The Royal Navy's task became the slow grind of containing the enemy's remaining squadrons by blockade, while behind the shield of the capital ships the work of exercising the command of the sea was carried out by cruising frigates and sloops which protected trade, and by task forces supporting military operations. Bonaparte's hopes of recreating his naval power were raised by the peace of Tilsit in 1807, which made Russia his ally and secured his hegemony over most of Europe. But a succession of British counter-strokes and the Spanish rising of 1808 deprived him of most of the allied and neutral fleets on which he counted.

III

It is fair to say that through most of these wars the Royal Navy succeeded in fulfilling its strategic roles. It safeguarded the British Isles and colonies, secured the flow of trade, and supported military expeditions. But where were the troops for the expeditions? The state of the army in 1793 was deplorable, in both quality and numbers, and it was to remain short of offensive force throughout the wars.

In peacetime the army's training had always been defective. It lacked training areas and barracks; the units were dispersed in scattered quarters; and the regiments were constantly on the march to control rioting or yield to civilian convenience. These conditions prevented any training but the most basic individual drill from being undertaken for most of the year; and the peacetime establishment reduced the regiments to cadres so weak that few were fit to take the field for war without hasty recruiting. These difficulties were compounded by a deplorable administrative system. In peacetime the administration of the army was normally in the hands of the Secretary at War, a second-rank politician, often venal and invariably immersed in the exercise of political patronage. When a commander-in-chief was appointed, which was usually only in wartime, a succession of mediocre ones – Granby, Amherst and Conway – had done little to remedy the defects. There was no longer a uniform manual of drill and tactics; and the American War, with its loose tactics and small actions, had left a legacy of habits which were unsuited to European campaigns with large cavalry forces. When a new manual was issued in 1792 the reappointment of Lord Amherst as Commander-in-Chief restored a palsied hand to the tiller.[8]

For these reasons, the army at the outbreak of war was unfit to maneouvre in large formations on a continental battlefield. This was not unprecedented. Throughout the century the army's early wartime expeditions had had to train in the field; absorbing their recruits, polishing their battle drill, and practising their brigadiers. The army's initial performance was therefore always shaky unless it was given time to train before it met the enemy in battle: the spectacular victory of the British infantry at Minden in 1759 had been preceded by a year's shaking down and training in the theatre of war. But the armies of revolutionary France allowed no period of grace. The scratch force that Britain had to hurry into the Low Countries in 1793 put up a variable and sometimes embarrassing performance. And the huge and hasty expansion, the poor central direction, and the appalling wastage of men in the West Indies meant that the army took longer than usual to correct its defects. A turning point was the appointment of the Duke of York as Commander-in-Chief in 1795. Firm supervision was introduced; the new drill manual was properly enforced; and light infantry tactics were integrated with the regular order of battle. At last, a full eight years after the first engagements of the war, the army began to perform as it should. In 1801, in Egypt, a force which had been carefully trained by its leader, Sir Ralph Abercromby, proved the effectiveness of the 1792 drill manual in battle with Bonaparte's veterans. In quality the army had turned the corner, and went forward with confidence to its peninsular victories.

Numbers were another matter. In 1793 the army had 39,000 cavalry and infantry, of which only 15,000 were in Great Britain. By 1801, 62,000 men had been lost to the army in the West Indies alone, apart from wastage in other theatres. In spite of these losses, the army was quadrupled by 1801 to 150,000. In 1814, at the end of the Napoleonic Wars, there were 187,000 British regular troops, five times the peacetime establishment. If one adds 51,000 foreign and colonial troops (a term which does not include the East India Company's army), and 26,000 British and foreign artillery, the total of regular troops was more than a quarter of a million.

In spite of these numbers – and with the navy, marines and permanently embodied militia the United Kingdom had a larger proportion of its population under arms than any other major power – there remained an acute shortage of disposable force for offensive operations. After the destruction by disease of the West Indian expedition in 1796-7, the revival of coalition warfare found only 10,000 infantry available for an expedition to Holland in 1799; a number inflated hastily to 24,000 by an Act to allow volunteering from the militia. In part the shortage was caused by constraints on recruiting. There was no conscription for the regular army: conservatives feared, or pretended to fear, a threat to liberty; and keener thinkers followed Adam Smith's doctrine that soldiers, like servants and kings, were labour withdrawn from productive work. Compulsory service by ballot in the militia was more acceptable, and in 1805 a regular army 161,000 strong was backed by 74,000 permanently mobilised militia. But these militia – 31 per cent of the land forces of the nation and 56 per cent of the troops in Great Britain – were exempt from service overseas.

A more fundamental reason, however, for the shortage of men was the breadth of the army's defensive commitments. In the same year 1805, the year of Napoleon's victories over the Austrians and Russians at Ulm and Austerlitz, the British army could find only 16,000 men for a diversionary expedition to north Germany. By then 46 per cent of the army, or 74,000 men, were consigned to defensive tasks overseas: 28,000 of them holding or securing vital naval bases like Gibraltar and Ceylon; and most of the rest either in India, where they did not confront the French, or in the Caribbean islands where their role in this period was essentially defensive. This left 85,000 in the British Isles. But the Irish garrison was largely neutralised by the twin fears of invasion and insurrection: as Wellington observed, 'Ireland, in a view to military operations, must be considered an enemy's country.' Of the 15,000 cavalry in England, few could be sent abroad quickly, for want of horse-transports. One is therefore looking at a nucleus of 42,000 infantry. But from these one must deduct depot troops and recruits, new regiments still being raised, and the skeletons of regiments recently returned from abroad. Some regular forces had to be provided to deal with a possible French counter-stroke across the Channel, and for internal security against riots and disorders in the absence of any police force. It is easy to see how these deductions absorbed 26,000 men, leaving only 10 per cent of the whole British army available for the German expedition.

IV

An historian of our own day has described Pitt as ranking 'with the worst War Ministers in our history'.[9] But the performance of Pitt and his successors must be judged in the context of the constraints within which they were forced to operate, and the dearth of real strategic options. Those options were to become increasingly narrowed after the collapse of the First Coalition, but the lack of troops was with them from the outset.

When Grey's expedition to the West Indies sailed in November 1793 his striking force had been halved by diversions to Brittany and Toulon; and the despatch of the force has often been assailed as a great strategic blunder: a failure to concentrate all possible resources in the decisive European theatre and to eschew colonial 'sideshows'. Even at the time voices were raised against it in government circles, among them Lord Auckland's. In the cabinet the Duke of Richmond pressed for a clear-cut choice between a continental and a maritime effort, 'for to attempt both is to do neither well'.[10]

But the historians' analysis is a crude amalgam of hindsight with doctrines evolved after the wars by the military theorist Karl von Clausewitz from a study of the campaigns of Napoleon. Though Auckland argued that by concentrating on defeating France in Europe Britain might indirectly gain her own ends overseas, the junto at the centre of the war acted on the conviction that France would be rapidly and easily defeated by her continental enemies and her own financial problems. In Europe the Duke of York's army in Flanders, with the usual reinforcement of German auxiliaries, could add some heat to the ring of fire which surrounded revolutionary France on the Rhine, the Alps and the Pyrenees; and the flames of internal insurrection were bursting forth in Brittany and Toulon. And the British ministers placed their trust in the ever-growing French financial crisis. 'If a few months could be tided over', Lord Grenville had written before the outbreak of war, 'the bubble of French finance must I think inevitably burst.'[11] It was the mirror-image of Kersaint's confidence that British credit would collapse. Bubbles and balloons: with such imagery the French and British governments were lured along the path of war.

With these assumptions it was logical to increase the economic squeeze on France by colonial operations on a modest scale, which at the same time furthered Britain's own long-term national goals. What went wrong with the strategy had little to do with the wooden application of so-called principles of war, and everything to do with miscalculation and the unexpected. 'Every fresh account from France', Lord Grenville wrote as the West Indian expedition prepared to sail in November, 'brings decisive proof that the system is drawing to its close.'[12] Yet five days earlier the Austrian commander in Flanders had reported that the initiative was passing to the enemy. The spectacular recovery of the revolutionary armies was utterly unexpected. First at Toulon, and then in Belgium, the allied armies collapsed under French counter-offensives. By the spring of 1795 the allies had been driven from Belgium and Holland, and the British army had been evacuated. The coalition disintegrated. While Austria still fought on, the Prussians pulled out to carve up the last of Poland with the Russians and incorporate north Germany into a neutral zone under their protection. Spain joined the enemy, and Holland became a French puppet.

The collapse of the coalition changed utterly the terms of British strategy, imposing new constraints from which successive governments were never entirely to escape. Britain had lost her bridgeheads into western Europe: Holland and Belgium were in enemy hands, and Hanover was neutralised. Nor were there any longer allied forces in the west to fight alongside the little British army. The auxiliary forces of the German states were cut off, and the Austrians had withdrawn behind the Rhine. In future years British expeditionary forces in Europe would have to operate alone in the heartland of enemy power. Lacking a secure and organised bridgehead, they would have to storm the beaches, organise the resources of the country, and import their own transport and supplies. This was amphibious warfare with all its risks, difficulties and constraints; calling too for an immense tonnage of merchant shipping to transport and supply the army.

The logic became clear: Britain had not the least hope of maintaining a front in Europe unless there was an active eastern front to contain the main French armies, and insurgent support in the invasion area to hamper the enemy's defence. Moreover a major British assault in Europe in these circumstances would require such vast resources, in troops and shipping, as to preclude simultaneous colonial operations. Thus maritime and continental strategies became polarised as they had never been in the past. Instead of parallel efforts in Europe and the colonial world, a cyclical pattern of alternating strategies emerged. A resurgence of warfare by the major continental powers would lead to a British invasion of Europe, followed soon by the military collapse of the allies and a British withdrawal into maritime warfare.

This alternation of temporary lodgments in Europe with colonial operations was later to be interpreted by students of war as a deliberate choice of 'limited warfare', a form of war which was represented as peculiarly suited to an island seapower.[13] It was nothing of the kind, but a second best adopted because the initiative had been lost, the best option closed, and Britain's strategy placed in dependence on the shifting policies of the continental powers. There was no longer a consistent 'right' strategy for a British government to pursue. It could only respond to the changing situation.

The maritime phase of the strategic cycle consisted of two elements: operations to secure naval command, followed by colonial offensives to secure overseas markets and provide bargaining counters for the future peace settlement. Naval command required attacks by the army on enemy fleets in harbour and the occupation of bases overseas. The pattern appeared after the collapse of the First Coalition. The naval keys to the east were secured by seizing the Dutch bases at the Cape of Good Hope and Ceylon; and the largest overseas expedition ever hitherto mounted sailed for the Caribbean.

The Caribbean: always the graveyard of troops and seamen. And now the British forces were caught in a whirlwind of malaria and pandemic yellow fever. General Grey's original small expedition of 1793, after initial successes, had been devastated by disease, and in that condition became involved in a murderous civil war between French royalists and republicans, with black republican levies setting the example of slave insurrection in the British islands. It seemed essential to retrieve this calamitous situation after the disasters of 1794-5 in Europe; to 'counterbalance the French successes in Europe', as Dundas put it. By October 1795 half the regiments in the British army, and the best, were consigned to the West Indies. Their commander, Sir Ralph Abercromby, managed in large measure to restore the situation in the Lesser Antilles and Jamaica; but his force was devastated by disease without securing firm possession of Saint-Domingue. The Spanish island of Trinidad surrendered to Abercromby, giving the British a post from which they hoped to force their way into the trade of the Spanish mainland. But a failure at Puerto Rico spelt the end of the policy of feeding offensives in the Caribbean with fresh units from home. In eight years between the outbreak of war and the peace of Amiens the British army had sent 89,000 officers and men to the Caribbean, and lost 70 per cent of them. The total losses for army, navy and transport crews may have been little short of 100,000.[14]

Such prodigality of life might, if it gained enemy colonies, improve the terms of a compromise peace or mitigate defeat: the West Indian victories certainly strengthened the British economy, the sinews of war. But only coalition warfare in Europe could lead to victory; and whenever the prospect of a coalition appeared Britain was bound to open a military front in Western Europe. The Second Coalition saw an expedition to Holland in 1799 and plans to invade Brittany in 1800; the Third Coalition, expeditions to Hanover (1805) and Stralsund in the Baltic (1807); and the Austrian War of 1809 brought a powerful expedition to Walcheren. All these efforts ended in the same manner. The French fought defensive campaigns in the west with minimal forces – often with military rubbish – and concentrated their resources on the eastern front to defeat the armies of the major military powers. It was the battles at Zurich and Marengo, Ulm and Austerlitz, Jena and Friedland, and at Wagram that made the British bridgeheads in the west untenable. Napoleon was ruthless in exploiting his interior position between the allies by stripping the western front while he struck his decisive blow in the east: more ruthless than the Germans were to be when they attempted a two-front strategy in 1914. For Napoleon knew that the great battle – the *Hauptschlacht* in Clausewitzian terms – would carry the decision everywhere.

The strain on resources and the cyclical polarising of strategy created conflict in Britain's councils. If coalition warfare was the only way to outright victory and the end of French expansion, a major landing was an absolute duty which Britain owed her allies. This was the view of Lord Grenville, who became increasingly opposed to overseas enterprises which would weaken or even preclude a continental invasion when the opportunity came. Britain in his view should nurse her army for a continental war.

Dundas the imperialist took the opposite line. After the failure of the Dutch expedition of 1799 he rejected Grenville's arguments on both operational and political grounds. He no longer believed that a British front could be sustained in Europe, with the limitations imposed by manpower, shipping, and the difficulties of amphibious warfare. Nor did he now believe that victory was possible – or necessary. Britain, he argued, should be laying the foundations for a compromise settlement with the more stable Bonapartist regime in France by expanding overseas. It was now that he gave the boldest formulation to his creed of using the war to establish a worldwide commercial dominion. On news of the Austrian defeat at Marengo in June 1800 he managed, after a bitter conflict in the cabinet which played a part in destroying the ministry, to disengage the army from Europe and embark on a new round of maritime warfare. The first condition of survival was naval predominance. To secure it he launched raids (speculative and unsuccessful) against Spanish naval ports, and reinforced the troops on Malta to end the two-year siege of Valletta. As a step towards renewed colonial offensives he arranged for an army to assemble at Gibraltar. Dundas proposed to use it to attack the Spanish empire, seizing Cuba for bargaining, and acquiring entrepots on the Spanish Main to force open the South American markets. In this he was thwarted, for his colleagues insisted on keeping the army on the European seaboard in case Austria renewed the war. Eventually, however, he was able to send 15,000 men to Egypt, to dislodge the French from this stepping-stone to India before a peace conference began.

The compromise settlement Dundas had foretold was concluded at Amiens in 1801. It failed, and its failure was a blow to the proponents of a purely maritime strategy. For Bonaparte's conduct had confirmed that he was no agent of international stability, but the Corsican plunderer of Lord Grenville's rhetoric. With him no enduring compromise was possible; and nothing short of absolute victory would leave Britain secure. The truth was clear that in the last resort Europe must have absolute priority in British strategy, and the ministries which conducted the

Napoleonic Wars were closer to Grenville's logic than to Dundas's. Continental expeditions were resumed. When continental war blazed up, as it did in the Third Coalition of 1805-7 and in the Austrian War of 1809, the British army re-entered Europe.

The alternating cycle of continental and maritime war continued, however. In the years of isolation, 1803-5, when Britain was threatened with invasion by the Grand Army, the British government held on to Malta even at the risk of alienating the Tsar, and reoccupied the Cape of Good Hope. During the interlude of 1806, after the Third Coalition had been shattered at Ulm and Austerlitz, the short ministry of Grenville and Fox treated the continental war as over, and concentrated on Mediterranean interests while Fox attempted to negotiate with Napoleon. Sicily was occupied to secure the route to the east; and when, Turkey entered the war against Russia a naval expedition was sent to Constantinople, ostensibly to coerce the Turks but perhaps in reality to secure the Turkish fleet. Significantly, instead of sending a military force, from Sicily to support the naval demonstration in the Dardanelles, it was sent to occupy Alexandria for fear that the French alliance with Turkey would renew the threat to Egypt and India.[15]

Prussia's ill-timed intervention in the war was swiftly crushed by Napoleon at Jena (October 1806), and Russia gave up the struggle after the battle of Friedland (June 1807). The consequent Peace of Tilsit produced the most spectacular British swing from a continental to a maritime effort. The Portland ministry, successor to Grenville's, had responded to Russia's demand for direct aid with an expedition to the Baltic of which only the spearhead had landed when Friedland caused its withdrawal. A grave threat now faced Britain. Almost the whole continent was crushed under Napoleon's heel or in alliance with him. The Berlin Decree (November 1807) threatened to close all Europe to British trade, and a vast naval conglomerate would challenge the Royal Navy's command of the sea.

The Portland ministry, with the key offices in the hands of Canning and Castlereagh, reacted with vigour. Like earlier maritime phases, this one began with emergency measures against enemy naval power. The expedition which had been preparing to aid the Russians in the Baltic was diverted to Copenhagen, where it seized the efficient Danish fleet of 16 sail of the line before Marshal Bernadotte could arrive to secure it for Napoleon. A British squadron remained in the Baltic to cover the approaches to Sweden with its 11 sail of the line, and another was despatched to the Tagus where it persuaded the Regent of Portugal to withdraw with his 8 sail of the line hours before Marshal Junot reached Lisbon. Russia's Black Sea fleet, sheltering in the Tagus on its way to the Baltic, was blockaded until it fell into British hands in the following year when Wellesley liberated Portugal. The Turkish navy was blockaded in the Dardanelles; an attack was planned against the Spanish squadron at Minorca; and a small military expedition secured the Portuguese island of Madeira. Thus Napoleon's plan to unite the navies of Europe in a great maritime league was forestalled; and the deathblow to these hopes was delivered in the following year when the revolt of Spain removed the Spanish navy from his control. The Portland ministry followed up these naval measures with plans for colonial expeditions to Spanish America. At that point extraordinary events in the Iberian Peninsula changed the course and pattern of British strategy. The Spaniard rose against French domination, and a British army invaded Portugal.

Between 1808 and the fall of Napoleon nearly six years later, the Peninsular theatre sucked in virtually the whole disposable force of the British army. It is true that numerous colonial expeditions were undertaken during those years for the protection of British trade and territories: in the western hemisphere French Guiana, Martinique, Guadeloupe, and with Spanish help Saint-Domingue; in Africa Senegal; and in the eastern seas Mauritius, Réunion and Java. But all these operations were undertaken by collecting a striking force from local garrisons and not by expeditions sent from home. The British army's striking force became fixed in Portugal, building up to a strength of 47,000. From 1812 much of the Mediterranean garrison was also drawn into Spain.

Can this effort really be justified? The army went into Portugal in 1808 in pursuit of maritime objects: the recovery and defence of Portugal's vital ports and rich colonies, the protection of the Spanish navy, and the denial of Spain's worldwide bases and trade to the enemy. But war in the Peninsula could not decide the fate of Europe. Far out on the periphery of the continent the British army could not loosen Napoleon's hegemony. And it has been argued that when his power was at last shaken by the final coalition which formed after his defeat in Russia, the Peninsular commitment deprived Britain of adequate forces to re-enter the Netherlands and secure her major national interests.

Such arguments fall in with the view which Lord Grenville, now in opposition, continued to assert in the face of Wellington's tenacious defence of Portugal and his sustaining of Spanish resistance. Grenville advocated the hoarding of the British army at home in readiness to support a new coalition just as he had done in 1800 when Dundas was urging the recovery of Egypt. 'Husbanding our resources and acting upon a system of home defence' was his formula. Had this course been followed, it is virtually certain that the Napoleonic regime would have succeeded in pacifying Spain. The consequences for British naval power and the safety of Ireland would have been grave. Britain would indeed have had a powerful army ready to invade the Netherlands in 1813, instead of the 6000 which was all she was able to send. But it would have been an army inexperienced in field operations and without reputation, unfit to compare with the veterans of the eastern allies. And where would those allies have been without the Spanish war? Two hundred thousand good French troops could have been released from the Peninsula. With these in the field in Germany the campaign of 1813 might have taken a different course; and without the authority conferred by Wellington's victory at Vittoria, Castlereagh might not have been able to hold the reluctant German powers together for the final effort.

It was in Portugal that Britain broke loose from the chains which had imprisoned her strategy since 1795. In western Europe the advantage of communications had lain with the French: in the dearth-stricken Peninsula the advantage lay with Britain's seaborne supplies and shorter overland communications. In Spain the British army found the support of an insurgent country which western Europe had not afforded; and in Portugal it had the aid of an auxiliary army of high potential to replace the Germans who had been hired in former wars. And Portugal provided a defensible bridgehead which could be sustained in adversity. Even when the French were not distracted by war in central Europe the British Army could still hold on. And when continental war flared up again in the heart of Europe in 1812, Wellington's war-hardened army was ready to strike. In 1814 British troops were the first of the allies to enter France and protect the white standard of the Bourbons.

8. Public Finance in the Wars with France 1793–1815

P.K. O'BRIEN

I

FROM the Restoration through to the battle of Waterloo Britain's fiscal and financial system functioned to provide successive governments with the indispensable monetary means required to mobilise troops, weapons, ships and sailors to combat the kingdom's foes, particularly the French. For no fewer than 67 of the 155 years between 1660 and 1815 the nation was formally at war with other European powers and the fiscal aftermath of those armed conflicts often persisted for two to four years after the signing of peace treaties. Indeed the objectives, scale and organisation of central government finances can be depicted as being preoccupied with very little else but war and with preparation for the next armed struggle. For example, during periods of conflict the share of public expenditure devoted to the army and navy rose to 60–70 per cent of the state's total income. In interludes of peace when the proportion of taxation allocated to the armed services fell back into the 40 per cent range, a comparable percentage of taxes arriving at the Exchequer was transferred as interest payments to holders of the national debt, which had accumulated as a direct result of money borrowed to finance past wars. Civil administration rarely accounted for more than a fifth of public expenditure.

Long before 1789, the British government's prowess in mobilising money either in the form of taxes or loans was as widely admired (and feared) in Europe as the Royal Navy and perceived to be a more effective offensive and defensive weapon than the army. And the facts show that Britain's long-term fiscal and financial achievement was remarkable. Between 1665 and 1790, a period when the kingdom's population and economic base potentially available for taxation remained relatively small compared to France, Russia, the Habsburg Empire and Spain, the amount of taxes which poured into the Exchequer in London multiplied sevenfold in real terms and increased as a *share* of national income nearly four times.[1] With the possible exception of Holland, the revenue appropriated by the British government (measured on a per capita basis in both absolute and relative terms) was probably far higher than the financial resources that 'despotisms' on the continent managed to expropriate for the service of their dynastic and military ambitions.[2]

Of course the creation of Britain's fiscal and financial system to serve as 'the sinews of war' was not achieved easily or quickly. A framework of law, institutions and a bureaucracy to assess and collect taxes evolved in response to military demands. And that development was not only attended by serious administrative problems but marked from time to time by 'crises', when attempts to extend the boundaries of taxation provoked opposition which appeared to give rise to the possibility of serious riots or revolts. 'Compliance' was largely secured by a prudent choice of the commodities, services, social groups and regions of the country selected to carry the burden of an increasingly expensive and expansive state.[3] For example, the Scots and Welsh almost certainly transferred disproportionately and possibly absurdly low shares of their incomes to Westminster. Despite the exigencies of almost continuous warfare the 'necessities' of the poor remained more or less exempt from indirect as well as direct taxes. Equally, no serious attempts were made to tax directly those with property and higher incomes in terms of equitable and more progressive criteria related to their real capacity to contribute to the needs of the state. The fiscal system manifested the political and administrative compromises and constraints on the government's freedom to operate in this vital area of policy.[4] And after the revolt of the American colonists in 1776 ministers needed no further reminders of real limitations on their powers to tax persons, goods and property nominally under their jurisdiction.[5]

Nevertheless, the steadily increasing range of commodities produced and consumed and above all marketed within the kingdom provided scope for widening and deepening the base available for taxation. Economic development certainly assisted the government to raise ever increasing amounts of taxation, without unduly burdening the poorest classes of the community or arousing serious opposition from the rich and powerful. Taxes became not only more feasible but more acceptable as the economy expanded and diversified from its agrarian base: feasible because the spread of external and internal trade provided successive governments with more opportunities to tax goods and services circulated through established and organised markets. Furthermore, production and commerce became more visible, regular and concentrated in larger scale units for production and distribution, than in other European economies such as France, Prussia and Russia, which continued to be dominated by subsistence and household units of production and consumption. Treasury ministers from Godolphin to Pitt the Younger remained sensitive to connections between the health and evolution of Britain's market economy and their ability to appropriate ever increasing sums of money to fund its navy and army.

Although the country's fiscal base expanded and diversified at a higher rate than the potential base for taxation available to rival states, it would be misleading to suggest that faster economic growth or industrialisation provided the government with really decisive strategic advantages. After all other nations also experienced economic growth from 1660 to 1789, at rates which may not have fallen far short of the rate exhibited by the British economy.[6] What may turn out to be distinctive about the British state was a more radical and sustained improvement in its political and administrative capacity to appropriate and to retain an increasing share of a steadily growing and diversifying national product. That critical proportion grew from 3–4 per cent in the reign of Charles II, to 11–12 per cent of national income during the Seven Years War and the American War of Independence. Perhaps the pronounced upswing in the share of income collected as taxes after the Glorious Revolution of 1688 may simply have brought Britain into line with the autocracies of the continent. Alas, the data are not good enough to rule out that possibility but comparisons with France suggest that it was improbable.[7] Furthermore, contemporary commentators on comparative military strength usually assumed that Britain possessed an outstanding navy and an exceptionally effective fiscal and financial system.[8]

To some extent the financial system did rest upon a particularly favourable economic substructure deeply penetrated by markets for internal and external trade. But the British government also proved particularly adept at forcing a traditionally recalcitrant body of taxpayers to pay for its domestic and foreign policies. By a long process of trial and error the taxes available to central government on the eve of its protracted struggle with revolutionary France included a judicious mixture of more or less unavoidable and acceptable means and instruments for extracting and channelling revenue into the Exchequer.

For example, levies imposed upon the wealth and manifestations of income of the more affluent and politically powerful groups in British society (which provided the government with roughly 20 per cent of total revenue from 1788-92) were grudgingly accepted because they were assessed and administered by country gentlemen. They fell upon stereotyped valuations of their real property, particularly land, and upon manifestations of 'gentry' incomes, such as houses, servants, carriages and riding horses. Direct taxes were administered so that no contact occurred between the upper and middle classes and potentially intrusive officials of the state. Property other than land, houses and mineral wealth escaped lightly and direct taxes on household expenditure could be easily avoided, even by families of substance, who chose not to 'live and spend like gentlemen'.[9] Finally the landed and propertied classes (who in effect taxed themselves) gained substantially from the protection afforded by military expenditures on defence. They after all had most to lose from enemy invasions, unfavourable peace treaties and possible constitutional crises. It was, moreover, their relatives, friends and clients who obtained the rewards from state patronage and who occupied a majority of the best remunerated positions in the civil and military administration.

Even before the eighteenth century British governments had available to them a wide range of taxes associated with a commercial economy. In 1700, however, taxes on land and other immovable types of property (which constitute the only feasible objects for taxation in agrarian economies) financed a mere 35 per cent of peacetime expenditures. Despite extensions to include other types of wealth, dependence on such 'traditional' forms of revenue declined still further so that by 1790 direct taxes (that is levies collected from specified lists of taxpayers) yielded only 18 per cent of total public revenue. Throughout the century taxes fell increasingly and overwhelmingly on people's expenditures. Ministers imposed duties on an ever widening array of goods and services produced or imported into the country. Their officials collected taxes from producers or traders who then passed on excise, customs and stamp duties in the form of higher prices to their customers. From the time of William III onwards an aristocratic Parliament had shifted the *relative* burden of taxation away from real property on to the consumption of families, who purchased domestically produced beer, spirits, salt, soap, candles, coal, glass, leather, bricks, printed cloth and newspapers; also on to the expenditures of those who required the services of lawyers, banks, insurance companies and public transport; and the law compelled people who wished to consume tea, sugar, gin, rum, wine, tobacco, linens, silks, etc. to pay dearly for the privilege of buying such imported 'luxuries'.[10]

The presumption, however, that a tax system dominated by indirect taxes must have been regressive or bore most heavily on the poor needs to be qualified. On the whole basic foodstuffs and other 'necessities' seem to have been exempt or lightly taxed and the weight of taxes on outlay appears to have fallen with proportionate and carefully calibrated severity on the consumption of relatively affluent families. But the incidence of taxes is difficult to locate without recourse to unobtainable information on the expenditure patterns of the various social and income groups included in the taxpaying community. Of course the eighteenth-century fiscal system was not progressive. Equally there can be no presumption that British taxation was relatively more regressive than taxation elsewhere in Europe. And given the absence of tax revolts it cannot be depicted as oppressive or even manifestly unpopular with the majority of taxpayers.[11]

Successive British governments worried less about the inequities of their tax system and far more about its capacity to supply indispensable funds to wage war. Statesmen looked for taxes that were not only acceptable but unavoidable, feasible to administer and which minimised damage to the development of the economy upon which future revenues depended. Unavoidable meant that whenever Chancellors raised the rates of duty (and hence prices on commodities or services selected for taxation) consumers were unable or unwilling to reduce their expenditures to a degree which over time curtailed the quantity taxed and actually reduced total receipts at the Exchequer. There are numerous examples where taxation had been pushed to a point which frustrated the government's search for revenue. Equally by a process of trial and error Chancellors of the day had placed on the statute books a range of taxes (including levies on alcohol and tobacco; tea, sugar and salt; coal and candles; bricks, glass, timber and iron; higher quality cloth and clothing; soap and starch and an array of legal and commercial services) which could be relied upon to respond more or less elastically to the ever increasing demands of the Exchequer.

That capacity to tax had not been built up without a continuous process of legislative innovation and administrative development designed to provide departments responsible for assessing and collecting the king's revenue with the legal powers, the personnel and bureaucratic structures required to implement the intentions of Whitehall.[12] Although by hook and crook governments of the day obtained the revenue needed, the level of achievement in this critical area of policy, from the standpoint of the state, can only be regarded as partial. Despite the small measure of local surveillance exercised by permanent officials of the Treasury over direct taxes, the propertied classes retained almost complete control of their assessment and collection. Furthermore, country gentlemen appointed as Receivers General determined the speed or rather the tardiness it took for 'public money' to reach London.[13] Frauds on the revenue remained pervasive throughout eighteenth-century society, and increased with every elevation of customs, excise and stamp duties. Possibilities for defrauding the king of his income obviously depended upon the particular commodities or services subjected to taxes and varied with the competence of the departments responsible for the assessment and collection of his revenue. Stamp duties, levied upon legal instruments and commercial documents, were not easy to evade. In its department of excise the Hanoverian state possessed, and had carefully nurtured, a body of officials which anticipated many of the features of a modern and diligent civil service.[14] Nothing laudatory could be said about the customs administration which, as several parliamentary committees of the 1780s recognised, manifestly failed to check the well-organised and vigorous efforts of smugglers to run contraband into the kingdom. By the late eighteenth century up to a quarter of dutiable imports sold in Britain may have escaped tariffs despite harsh penalties prescribed by law to check smuggling and Pitt's reforms designed to associate the excise department with the collection of customs dues.[15]

After the American War of Independence the constraints on the government's capacity to raise taxes were obvious to ministers in charge of the country's fiscal system. Shelburne, North and Pitt the Younger took full account of the persistent and entrenched political opposition to proposals for reforms to the scope, principles and administration of direct taxes on income and wealth. They also appreciated how difficult Chancellors of the day found it to manipulate customs duties simply to raise revenue because in their role as 'tariffs' these duties reflected a whole penumbra of policy objectives related to the Navigation Acts, imperial preferences and bilateral treaties with friendly powers. Import duties were not only deeply enmeshed in the complexities of mercantilist policies, but their elevation to raise revenue usually provoked an unmanageable and counter-productive expansion of smuggling as well as increases in administrative costs contingent upon attempts to enforce the letter of the law.[16]

Almost by default stamp and excise duties provided governments of the period with the fiscal instruments necessary to appropriate more and more revenue. Over time these duties did, in fact, supply most of the incremental taxation raised to service an unredeemed national debt which had accumulated from next to nothing at the Restoration to a nominal capital of about £245 million in 1788-92. In the 1660s excises and stamps imposed on goods and services produced and consumed within Britain provided 23 per cent of tax revenue; from 1765 to 1785 their share increased to between 55 and 60 per cent of taxes arriving at the Exchequer.[17]

II

When he became First Lord of the Treasury and Chancellor of the Exchequer some three months after the formal termination of the disastrous attempt to put down rebellion in the Thirteen Colonies, Pitt the Younger set to work to repair the ravages that this expensive conflict had wrought upon the government's finances. Expenditure incurred to prosecute war against the colonists and their allies had cost the country approximately £124 million, a sum greater by roughly a quarter than the entire national income for 1780.[18] During the war, and measured in real terms, taxation had risen by nearly a third, the nominal capital of the national debt had nearly doubled and interest charges had risen from £4.8 million a year before the rebellion against the king to reach £9.5 million at its close.[19] Commentators on post-war politics almost unanimously asserted that taxation had approached politically unacceptable levels, that smuggling and other forms of tax evasion had increased from widespread to rampant, and that the gargantuan scale of national debt seriously impaired the government's credit and its prospects for future borrowing not *if* but *when* the next war broke out. Their pessimistic prognostications alarmed Parliament and prompted the cabinet to investigate ways of cutting expenditures, collecting taxes more effectively and restoring confidence in public credit.[20] Thus, in the immediate aftermath of the American War, Pitt cleared away several millions of navy and other bills by funding operations designed to transform lines of rolling departmental credit into irredeemable or perpetual debt.

These operations bring our attention back to the capacity developed by eighteenth-century governments to borrow both long and short term in order to finance their military operations. Indeed that capability has received far greater publicity from historians than the state's power to tax. So much so that the evolution from 1688 to 1756 of institutions, regularised procedures, negotiable paper assets (bills and bonds) and other features of public borrowing has been accorded the accolade of a 'financial revolution'.[21] And this development manifested in the steady growth of the government's irredeemable (funded) and short-term (unfunded) debt was widely regarded in the eighteenth century and since as the foundation of its military success in conflicts with France and other European states, whose fiscal resources and credit became more rapidly exhausted in the course of protracted armed struggles. There can be no doubt that the reputation enjoyed by the British government as a sound debtor enabled it to borrow considerable sums of money not merely from its own citizens but also from foreigners, particularly the Dutch. Furthermore, the statistical record does at first regard suggest that all five wars engaged in by Britain's army and navy from the Glorious Revolution through to the recognition of the United States in 1783 were basically funded with borrowed money. For example approximately 80 per cent of all *extra* income raised in the course of four conflicts from 1702 to 1783 came from the sale of irredeemable bonds to investors in the national debt; and even in King William's war, from 1689-97, the proportion amounted to 51 per cent.[22] Clearly the credit of the British government was an important weapon which it used sparingly and usually only in wartime. Loans obviated the need for sudden, precipitous and potentially untenable rises in taxes, otherwise required to mobilise and sustain the additional armed force necessary to engage in warfare. Confidence that it alone could quickly and easily borrow large sums of money (and resort to war without unacceptable rises in taxation or even to expropriation) certainly gave Britain's ruling elite strategic leverage over their European rivals in defending and extending national interests.

Nevertheless historians should insist that taxes and not loans were the foundation of the kingdom's finances. As contemporaries recognised, the government's debts had to be properly and regularly serviced otherwise its capacity to raise loans at affordable rates of interest would be seriously impaired. This implied that bills drawn on the Exchequer, the Treasury or the navy had to be paid off at times agreed with departmental suppliers and creditors and, more important, that the government never reneged upon or arbitrarily reduced the interest payments it was legally committed to paying holders of its irredeemable debt. Funds for the redemption of departmental bills could only come from taxation or from the sale of bonds. Interest on its perpetual debt or the redemption of that debt could likewise only originate in tax revenue. Taxes and taxes alone sustained the creation of public debt and the recourse to loans to fund mobilisation for war represented nothing more than deferred taxation.[23]

Furthermore, the access and ease with which eighteenth-century governments borrowed money for military purposes depended on the development of a market for long- and short-term capital. By the 1780s the British government, unlike other European states, could take for granted the existence of financial intermediaries (including the Bank of England, the Stock Exchange, insurance companies, brokers, merchants, banks in the capital, linked to correspondent banks in the provinces) all prepared to deal in public securities and to channel metropolitan and provincial savings into the Exchequer. Outside Holland, no other state could command the services of such an efficient and increasingly integrated network of financial institutions for the placing of public debt. Of course the English system, centred on the metropolis, had developed in part to cater for the needs of the state, but basically financial intermediation had evolved in Britain in order to service the economy. It was, in brief, another product and progenitor of the diffusion of the market. For a profit (often handsome in time of war) the corporations, partnerships and proprietors that made up Britain's relatively advanced financial system stood ready to help their government raise the cash to fund the additional military expenditure required to combat the kingdom's enemies.[24]

But when Pitt took charge of the nation's finances in the unpropitious month of December 1783, he confronted what several of his advisers regarded as a serious 'debt crisis'. Moreover, at that time many of his contemporaries, well informed about public finance, felt British society and its economy had reached the limits of its capacity to bear taxation.[25]

During that brief interregnum between the American and French wars Pitt's attention to detail and growing knowledge of state finance provided him with the reputation and authority necessary to dominate his cabinets and Parliament in this critical area of policy.[26] We should add that members of the House of Commons paid so little attention to the details of tax administration or the management of the national debt that the Prime Minister's authority was virtually unchallenged. Given an opportunity to point to obvious wastage of public money the Opposition used debates on supply simply to embarrass the government. Alternatively Fox and his supporters simply challenged the assumptions upon which the crown's military expenditures were predicated. As budgetary discussions about how taxation and public borrowing might be efficiently managed either in interludes of peace or times of war the parliamentary debates of the eighteenth century exemplify little more than deep ignorance, political animosity and ideological prejudice.

On all matters connected with taxes or the management of the debt (depicted by Wilberforce as 'affairs of a low vulgarising quality') Pitt enjoyed such a reputation that his authority and possible intentions were appealed to by Chancellors of the Exchequer for many years after his death. Before the outbreak of war with France in 1793, as a young First Lord of the Treasury, he had certainly instituted some useful but hardly original or major reforms to the state's finances. With the exception of an excise on bricks, no new and productive sources of revenue appeared on the statute book, and Pitt ran up against intransigent opposition to his proposals to introduce taxes on coal at the pithead, on shopkeepers, printed goods and hops. Although the net for taxation did not widen, several legal and administrative reforms rendered existing taxes more productive of revenue. Undoubtedly the most efficacious of these measures involved the lowering of duties on tea, spirits, coffee, cocoa, wine and muslins in order to undercut incentives to smuggle contraband into the kingdom. The Chancellor complemented this approach by according the customs service greater powers to detain and search ships hovering off the English coasts and associated the Excise Department with the fight against smuggling by taxing imported luxuries at points of distribution as well as at entry into ports.[27] But periodic surveys by excise officers of merchants, shopkeepers and dealers, legally licensed to deal in tea, spirits, wine and tobacco, were not considered to be a particularly effective way to combat frauds on the king's revenue by parliamentary committees who investigated the system in the 1830s. Although they did praise Pitt for consolidating and simplifying the methods of levying dues on imports and for his plan (alas, not implemented) to abolish the payment of fees by merchants to customs officers for services the latter rendered in assessing their precise legal liability for taxation on goods shipped into Britain. Before the war diverted his energies Pitt lent his very considerable support to moves advocated by his advisers to transform the customs service into a more professional and effective arm of government. He also pushed for closer Treasury involvement (through surveyors) in the process of direct taxation.[28] And the amount of money arriving at the Exchequer definitely increased during Pitt's tenure as peacetime Chancellor from around £12 million per annum, 1782–4, to over £16 million, 1790–2; but the share of the increment attributable to his fiscal policy and administrative reforms was almost certainly minor compared with the proportion imputable to growth in the volume of goods and services falling automatically into the net for taxation.[29]

Pitt also turned his attention to that other arm of public finance (the funding system) and in 1786 – a year when interest payments on the national debt absorbed no less than two-thirds of all revenue from taxes – persuaded Parliament to adopt a plan to bring about its redemption or complete repayment over a period of some 35 years. Similar schemes had been tried before during the course of the eighteenth century but they had been abandoned whenever governments of the day found more pressing needs for surplus taxation. But after the American War of Independence political and public concern about the national debt became more intense and widespread. Anxiety about its magnitude rested upon several assumptions: first and foremost that governments would be unable to raise the revenue required year after year to meet their interest obligations without seriously impairing the health of the economy and thereby its tax base; secondly that an interest bill, which absorbed such a huge proportion of peacetime revenues, left central government with far too little income to spend on improving the navy, army and civil administration; thirdly that the scale of debt already outstanding had seriously compromised the government's credit and its capability to borrow, at other than exorbitant rates of interest, when the time came to mobilise military forces to defend the nation's interest against the omnipresent threat of French power and ambitions.

Details of Pitt's plan to deal with these problems owe a great deal to the ideas of Richard Price and are too complicated merely to outline here. But the Chancellor's objectives are reasonably clear. To reassure taxpayers that their burdens would eventually be alleviated and to persuade creditors that their assets would not depreciate in value even when the government began to borrow again in the not improbable event of war, taxes would be imposed and used, not merely as they had under previous administrations, to pay interest on the debt, but also to repay its principal. At some point in the not too distant future British taxpayers, restive under present burdens, could expect relief. Meanwhile, the credit of the state would be reinstated and secured because bondholders would be reassured against an ever increasing and eventually unsustainable accumulation of debt which carried with it the potential danger of a loss of confidence in the government's fiscal capacity to meet its obligations.[30]

Pitt's sinking fund has been misunderstood and misrepresented by generations of historians. In essence it represented a commitment to convert the national debt from an accumulated stock of obligations redeemable only at the option of the government into debt of a defined maturity which would be gradually paid off from, and which had first claim upon, tax revenues. The plan not only came into immediate effect, but Pitt attempted to make the commitment to redeem current as well as future debt inviolable. By a series of legal and administrative expedients he tried to bind his successors at the Treasury not merely to use current budget surpluses to repay debt, but also, whenever the state borrowed long-term, to impose taxes sufficient not only to meet annual obligations for interest but to provide for a flow of tax revenue into a sinking fund which would in the fullness of time rid the government and the country of the incubus of debt.[31]

Pitt's plan was both radical and imaginative. Unfortunately, it depended for the achievement of its aims on the willingness of taxpayers to forego relief from taxes and even to shoulder additional taxes in time of war for the prospect of providing tax relief for generations to come. He assumed that British governments would continue indefinitely to abide by the letter and spirit of legislation passed in 1786 and that future wars would not generate a burden of taxation so unacceptable as to prompt politicians to abandon the sinking fund. Implicitly the plan also embodied a vision of a more peaceful world and to that end it contained an unmentioned but nevertheless positive fiscal restraint on the proclivities of British statesmen to resort to war because they possessed effective fiscal and financial weapons. Finally the sinking fund was coupled with a whole series of diplomatic and commercial initiatives designed to ensure more harmonious relationships between Britain and her European neighbours, including France.[32] Unfortunately for Pitt, his fiscal plans and his country, the French Revolution precipitated Britain's involvement for twenty years in the most costly war in its history.

III

British efforts to defeat the military forces of revolutionary and Napoleonic France cost an enormous amount of money – roughly £1039 million, when added up in current prices. It is very difficult to convey the relative magnitude of the task imposed on the government's fiscal and financial system and the economy at large by the need to mobilise the resources required for more than twenty years of almost continuous warfare. Of course the extra sums committed to support the army and navy varied through time: beginning at £22 million a year from 1793-7, falling back during the peace of Amiens in 1802 and peaking at £84 million in 1815, the year of ultimate sacrifice which culminated in Wellington's victory at Waterloo. The total expenditure corresponds to something like six times the value of pre-war national income, while the incremental sums raised in loans and taxes to prosecute this long struggle amounted in real terms to an annual average of £13.2 million from 1798-1801 and £28.3 million during the war's closing stages. These sums (deflated and expressed in constant prices) can be directly compared with annual expenditures on warfare of £5.2 million in the reign of Queen Anne, £9.5 million during the Seven Years War and £9.9 million during the American War of Independence. There can be no doubt that for most of the years of the quarter century it took to mobilise, sustain and demobilise armed force deemed necessary to secure victory over France, the British government appropriated as taxes and raised as loans revenues unheard of and unimagined by previous generations. And these enormous sums of money consumed by the state amounted at peak years of military expenditure, 1808-15, to something like a quarter of the national income compared to a government share of 6 per cent immediately before the war. Presumably the relative costs (expressed as a share of national income) would have been lower in all previous Anglo-Dutch and Anglo-French conflicts between 1660 and 1793 but were probably well in excess of the shares of national output appropriated by Britain's allies and foes during these years of warfare.[33]

How and how effectively did the government formulate and implement the fiscal and financial strategy which underpinned eventual military success over Napoleon? With difficulty and by resorting to expedients forced upon ministers by the pressures of events is the short answer to this big question. Furthermore, and despite the endless series of military struggles engaged in before 1793, no plan existed to cope with the financial exigencies of protracted warfare. Pitt and his successors simply concocted policies as they went along, from budget to budget. But, although they used and built upon the legacy of fiscal and financial instruments and worked with governmental and private institutions which had carried the state safely through previous mobilisations for war, one major contrast with traditional strategy is marked, namely the far greater recourse to taxes to fund wartime expenditures. That departure flowed from and then fed back to the state's interconnected funding and financial systems.

In the Revolutionary and Napoleonic wars tax revenue financed 58 per cent of all *extra* monies raised for the army and navy between 1793 and 1815; compared to proportions ranging from 19 to 26 per cent in previous eighteenth-century wars. When Wellington's troops fought in the Peninsula, France and Belgium from 1808 to 1815, the government appropriated nearly one-fifth of the nation's income as taxes – a very considerable achievement for that time.

Pitt did not set out to reverse those tried and true fiscal methods of paying for wars by borrowing the money. Indeed, for roughly five years, to 1798, he persisted with the strategy of adding to the national debt and imposed just enough extra taxation to meet interest obligations and to provide revenue for the amortisation of loans instituted in his sinking fund proposals of 1786.

But political and economic conditions as they evolved and affected conditions on the London capital market from 1793–7, persuaded the First Lord of the Treasury and the business community that 'more supplies had to be raised within the year'. For example, grave doubts that the government's irredeemable debt could continue to accumulate without a rather severe depreciation in the prices of its bonds had already emerged in the wake of the enormous quantity of these 'paper promises' sold to finance the American War. Anxiety among both dealers and investors in public securities became widespread as the nominal capital of the funded and unfunded debt increased from £240 million at the beginning of January 1792 to £427 million six years later. Those same years witnessed depreciation in the price of consols from £90 immediately before the war to £50 in 1797–8. In effect both long- and short-term rates of interest just about doubled. Although the king recognised the republican government in France in January 1796, by the closing month of that year peace overtures failed and the Directory had landed troops first in Ireland and then in Wales, just two months later. Anticipations that the forces of revolutionary France would be soon vanquished gave way to contemplation of possible defeat and prediction of a protracted and expensive war. In 1796–7 (which also witnessed naval mutinies off the Nore and Spithead) the security of Britain seemed more threatened than at any time since the 1690s, possibly since the Armada. Stark political facts naturally found their reflection in the prices of public securities and the rates of interest at which the state could borrow money.

Furthermore, the government's difficulties in selling bonds and bills to the capital market were compounded by the gradual breakdown of the 'normal and expected' cooperation between the Bank of England (the government's own bank) and the Treasury. Difficulties first emerged in the spring of 1793, when the Bank (a private and nominally autonomous corporation) refused to act as a lender of last resort and thus exacerbated the commercial crisis which accompanied the beginning of hostilities with France. To contain that downturn in economic activity, the government stepped in and made loans to banks, merchants and other businessmen to help them through early and inevitable liquidity problems, contingent upon reversion to a war economy. On this occasion the directors had responded conservatively to requests for loans and discounts because they were properly concerned about the level of the Bank's bullion reserve in relation to its outstanding notes and overdraft facilities. In the eighteenth century the Bank of England (and through the Bank the entire banking system) regulated what is nowadays called the money supply on a reserve of gold. As and when that reserve declined the directors normally contracted what contemporaries referred to as paper credit, and deflated economic activity. The directors governed the Bank and implicitly regulated national credit, not in terms of any rigidly prescribed rules, but with due regard to: their duties to the government, the circumstances of the moment, their predictions about the immediate future and their legal obligation to redeem on demand the Bank's notes and other outstanding liabilities in gold.[34]

During previous periods of warfare, the directors' pragmatically exercised concern for the Bank's 'treasure' had not prompted them to contract credit either to the government or to the private sector. Indeed Britain fought all except one of its eighteenth-century wars while remaining on a specie standard. The conflict with revolutionary France turned out to be not only different in scope and scale, but coincided with a pronounced upswing in foreign trade and industrial production as well as an extremely bad harvest in 1795.

Pitt's government required support from the Bank to transform bills issued by the Treasury, the Exchequer, the navy and the army into ready cash; and to help contractors and other financial intermediaries meet their instalments on long-term loans floated to fund extra military spending. At the same time, Pitt found contraction of credit to the private sector unwelcome because any deflation of the economy would not only arouse hostility to the war but would diminish tax revenues.

For their part, the directors could not sustain the ever-increasing demands being made upon the Bank by both the government and the economy on a steadily diminishing reserve of bullion. Throughout 1795 and 1796 they repeatedly warned the Chancellor about the state of the reserves, objected strongly to all military expenditures which involved transfers of gold and silver to Europe (or even to Ireland) and constantly pressured Pitt to repay and to restrain the rising amount of credit afforded by the Bank to departments of state.

By improving the mode of estimating future military expenditures, by altering the format of navy bills and through funding operations, the Prime Minister did attempt to contain the volume of short-term debt outstanding, but his cabinet obviously found it irksome to be implicitly advised to reduce military spending commitments in Europe in order to preserve the gold reserve of the Bank of England. Could the Anglo-Austrian alliance, and support for British and mercenary troops on the continent and other theatres of war, be compromised in order to preserve the reserves of a private corporation? Implicitly the directors' advice to the government amounted to a warning that the Bank could collapse, and with it the entire foundations of public and private credit. Meanwhile, in order to protect the gold reserve the directors began to restrict the accommodation normally afforded to the private sector which produced howls of protest and deputations of merchants and bankers waited on the Prime Minister.

The 'crunch' came early in 1797 when demands for the transformation of banknotes and other 'paper' securities into gold intensified to panic proportions, following the landing of French troops in the Celtic reaches of the British Isles. These military threats came at a time when the capital market was already alarmed by an apparently uncontrollable accumulation of public debt. In the weeks preceding the Order in Council of February 1797 (which relieved the Bank of England of its legal obligation to redeem notes and other liabilities in gold) the Bank's reserve drained away rapidly and it fell far below any level consistent with the safety of the Bank.

When the country settled down, with surprising ease, to conduct its economic transactions in a paper currency, not ultimately backed by gold, the government and the private sector could expect support from the banking system for their respective, but interconnected, concerns. With events leading up to the suspension of specie payments fresh in his mind, with the experience of five years of debt accumulation behind him and the prospects of a protracted war before the kingdom, Pitt resolved to finance a far higher proportion of public expenditure from taxes.[35]

Parliament and public opinion readily conceded to the principle. Their Prime Minister's radical departure from the long-established methods used to finance wars was seen as an explicable response to the fiscal and financial experience encountered over the first phase of conflict with revolutionary France when it seemed that public credit and the monetary system might collapse under the strain of expensive and prolonged warfare. Pitt's successors as Chancellor (Addington, Petty, Perceval and Vansittart) persisted with the new strategy, right down to the reversion of peacetime budgetary conditions and the resumption of specie payments by the Bank of England in 1821, because they believed that the financial system should not be subjected to such pressures again. They too recognised that the accumulation of public debt should be contained, not merely to mitigate tax burdens on future generations, but also because competition between the state and businessmen for investible funds would endanger the growth of the economy upon which tax revenue depended. Finally, as statesmen who had observed the effects of contemporary 'hyperinflations' in the United States, France, Spain, Russia and Austria, Britain's rulers were certainly aware that excessive issues of paper securities by central governments and the printing of money by banks under their control could engender a complete loss of confidence in paper money. After Pitt allowed the Bank of England to suspend specie payments, the resort to short- or long-term loans to finance wartime expenditures in the traditional way became fraught with the twin dangers of transforming the Bank into an agency of government and rapid inflation, which could bring about the collapse of public credit.

Over the first five years of this very long war only 11 per cent of the *extra* revenue required for its prosecution emanated from taxes. From 1798 to 1815 that proportion jumped to 64 per cent. Although Pitt experienced few difficulties in persuading his cabinet and Parliament that the military power and ambitions of revolutionary France as well as the conditions on the London capital market demanded a complete overhaul of fiscal strategy, he experienced more problems in translating his new policy into a set of specific and viable proposals for taxation.

Additional tax revenue could come from four sources: innovations to that already impressive range of taxes on the statute book; by raising the rates of duty on commodities and services taxed before the war; through improvements to administration designed to implement the letter of the law and to check evasion; and hopefully through economic growth, which could automatically carry a greater volume of production and income into the net established for taxation. Historians are prone to leave the impression that the Industrial Revolution provided the British government with the resources required to defeat revolutionary France and Napoleon.[36] Not exactly: because revenue statistics show that £47 million or a mere 9 per cent of all the extra revenue collected in the form of taxes from 1793 to 1815 came from additions to the volume or values of goods and services already subjected to taxation before the outbreak of a war which endured for twenty years. Some 36 per cent emanated from new taxes, but the bulk (55 per cent) of that revenue came from pushing up the rates of taxes available to government for a decade before the outbreak of war.

Some part of that 55 per cent represents improvements to revenue administration, but perhaps patriotism also lowered the community's propensity to evade taxes? Nevertheless, it is possible to cite examples of measures designed to raise the efficiency of all the departments concerned with the revenue, especially the customs service. Most of these reforms came, however, late in the war. Their impact, while positive, was almost certainly minor compared with the effective use made of the navy and army to check smuggling.

Economic development was not, however, unimpressive for a war period but the Industrial Revolution did not expand the base for taxation rapidly enough to provide more than a fraction of the extra revenue raised to defeat revolutionary France. Basically that capacity, built up over the century, was already *in situ*. The government simply 'squeezed harder', and depressed the share of national income going to private consumption while restraining, but not halting, productive investment in agriculture, industry and transportation. Furthermore wartime taxes did not fall with undue severity on the economy's leading sectors (textiles, metallurgy, canals and exports). Growth, albeit at a slower pace and possibly at a rate below that anticipated in those optimistic years immediately before the war, made higher taxation more acceptable. For the most part production seems to have been contained but not depressed by the weight of wartime taxation.[37]

Military necessities also produced innovations to the tax base and about 36 per cent of the extra revenue came from some 21 taxes not on the statute book in 1792. Interestingly, no new and productive excise duties appeared, although Pitt and later Petty tried but failed to push iron, clocks, and beer brewed for home consumption into that particular catchment for revenue. Imported tallow, wax, indigo and raw cotton became dutiable – the last at a relatively low rate of 1d. a pound. Merchants enjoying increased protection from the Royal Navy submitted their goods to *ad valorem* convoy duties and to stamp duties on marine insurance. Far and away the most productive and controversial innovation to the armoury of taxation was the income or property tax which passed through Parliament in 1799. That particular tax contributed 28 per cent of the extra money raised for the war and 80 per cent of revenue from all 'new' taxes, imposed between 1793 and 1815. In one sense the income tax represented no departure from principles long accepted by the propertied classes that each citizen should contribute to the needs of the state in accordance with his capacity to pay. That principle was, moreover, in one form or another, already embodied in the land tax, which had been supplying the Exchequer with money for centuries past. But Hanoverian ministers and Parliaments knew that the land tax, based upon stereotyped valuations of real property, had failed to capture not only income from work but also a large share of rents, profits and interest which accrued to the owners of productive wealth other than land. Reform of direct taxation was widely recognised as overdue, but before serious threats to the security of British territory and property emerged from revolutionary France, proposals for a direct tax, properly and equitably assessed on the incomes of the upper and middle classes, were politically untenable. Furthermore, the government's standard recourse to borrowing in order to fund wars and the spread of customs, stamp and above all excise duties, levied on domestically consumed goods and services, meant that the politically contentious and administratively problematical issue of direct taxation of incomes and wealth could be avoided.

In 1795 Pitt told Parliament that 'in a war for the protection of property it was just and equitable that property should bear the burden'.[38] To that end he tightened up the administration of modest and evadable stamp duties upon bequests and legacies. When the House was persuaded that dangers from revolutionary France, together with the possible collapse of public credit and the Bank of England, implied raising more supplies within the year, a reformed system of direct taxation became unavoidable. (As Lord Auckland rightly observed, 'This measure has been accomplished by the union of opinions respecting the nature of French intentions.')[39] Even then, Pitt and the Board of Taxes took two years and a failed experiment (the triple assessment of 1798 which deployed expenditure as a proxy for income) to place the country's first income tax onto the statute book.

Although the 'Act of 1799 for Taxing Income' represents the one big successful fiscal innovation of the war years, it emerged not as a matter of strategy but as an expedient response to a political and financial crisis. It continued throughout the years from 1799 until its repeal in 1816 to carry the hallmarks of legislation designed to conciliate and to reassure that powerful minority among the population liable to pay the tax, namely those whose incomes from property and work exceeded £50–£60 a year.

For example, the rates imposed deliberately and explicitly eschewed progression. As experience with the tax accumulated, loopholes in the law could be tidied up, but its assessment and collection remained under the control of the same amateur administration of country gentlemen who had been responsible for land and other directly assessed taxes long before the war. Through professional inspectors and surveyors, the Treasury pushed, with modest success, to introduce some measure of centralised control over the assessment of income tax, despite Pitt's assurances that the Act sought to avoid 'improper disclosures of circumstances which were repugnant to the manners and customs of the nation'.[40] In effect those liable under the law were taxed by their peers. Despite the intentions of Parliament, the income tax (like its forerunner the land tax) fell with disproportionate weight upon property and upon persons whose incomes came from the ownership of wealth which took the form of visible and immovable assets of calculable and recognised values, namely, land, houses, minerals and government bonds. Incomes assessed under schedule 'D' of the Act (which covered private salaries, professional fees, industrial and commercial profits) provided the government with only about a fifth of the total net revenue from this contentious tax. To all intents and purposes the new income tax was the old property tax writ large, revitalised, and reformed. Owners of government securities came under assessment for the first time and the valuations for purpose of direct taxation of all forms of real estate ceased to be stereotyped and grossly out of line with current market values; but the owners of industrial and commercial assets managed to avoid paying a share that was proportionate to their stake in the wealth of the nation. Meanwhile wages, salaries and fees remained virtually untaxed, except for that small minority of the workforce employed by the government.[41]

Yet major contributions from the income tax underpinned the strategy pursued after 1799 of raising most of the 'supplies' for war within the year. Although the government debt in private hands increased to reach a nominal capital of £921 million by January 1816, its accumulation had been restrained and the Treasury obtained most of this money at an annual cost below the historically high levels of interest which prevailed while Pitt was changing course from 1796–8.

By no means all the flotations or sales of public securities on the London capital market were managed by the Treasury to the best advantage of taxpayers. Examples of inexplicable and inefficient departures from the system of competitive tender can be cited from 1813 to 1814. Errors of judgement connected with the timing of loans are also evident for several flotations. Not enough effort was made to force bonds of denominations higher than 3 per cent consols onto the London capital market, which would have provided the Treasury with more opportunities for conversion operations and reductions in the government's interest bill once the war was over. These 'mistakes' are, however, only detectable in the context of the opportunities open to the Treasury over a given budget year. Blanket condemnation by Victorian economists which refer to the 'extortionate cost' of borrowing during the French wars can be dismissed as an irrelevant hindsight, because governments of the period simply had to pay the current market rate for any money raised in the form of loans. Only at the margin could the Treasury operate to contain the interest bill payable on public securities.[42]

Interest rates on consols certainly rose: from below 3 per cent before the war up to 6 per cent at the peak (1797-8). But for most years from 1793 to 1816 the modal rate of interest hovered around 5.4 per cent which, in retrospect, hardly seems extortionate given the scale of public borrowing and a wartime inflation rate proceeding around 3 per cent a year. The interest rate was also constrained from rising even higher by another strategic innovation, namely the decision to persist throughout the war with the policy inaugurated in 1786 of imposing sufficient taxes to amortise debt over determined periods of time. That decision, criticised and misunderstood once the circumstances surrounding the sale of public securities on the London capital market in wartime had receded beyond memory, augmented confidence in the funding system during several critical years during the long conflict with France. It led investors in government securities to expect that no matter how rapidly debt accumulated, a floor had been set to potential depreciation in the market values of the paper assets they held.[43] Furthermore, the taxes imposed to feed Pitt's sinking fund provided Liverpool's post-war administration with opportunities for granting tax relief during those difficult years of deflation and depression after Waterloo.[44]

Contemporaries had been shocked and remained anxious about the decision to suspend the operation of the gold standard for the duration of the war. For the government the Order in Council of February 1797 created conditions in which urgent and necessary military expenditures either at home or overseas could be financed and not subjected to the restraints of a fully convertible currency. For farmers, industrialists and above all, for merchants engaged in international trade, the flexibility introduced by a non-convertible paper currency implied that after 1797 their transactions remained unhampered by unpredictable contractions of credit by the banking system. Money supplies certainly expanded and the evidence of exchange rate depreciation and price inflation exercised the bullionist critics of the government and the Bank of England from 1799 onwards. In 1809-10, led by David Ricardo, they became excited enough about the dangers of inflation to initiate parliamentary and extra-parliamentary debates which aimed to force the Bank and the government back onto a convertible currency within two years.

Fortunately for the war effort the bullionist attack failed. The government could not have funded Wellington's and allied armies in Europe if the nation's limited gold revenues had been redeployed to ensure full convertibility. Nor could the banking system have provided the credit required by the private sector during several years of crisis (1799-1801, 1803, 1808 and 1810-12) if the Bank of England had been compelled to regulate its note issues on a bullion reserve. In no case were these commercial crises of the period precipitated by 'excessive' issues or extensions of bank credit. The Bank of England and the banking system simply met additional demands for liquidity occasioned by bad harvests or the exigencies of commercial warfare and enemy blockades. Unhampered by the dictates of convertibility, the monetary system was able to respond flexibly to the demands for credit by both the government and the private sector, upon which the government depended for taxes.[45]

No other monetary policy seems feasible in the context of such an expensive war. Unfortunately inflation (modest by twentieth-century standards) did occur and was not restrained by any efforts at the centre to stabilise the growth of the money supply. As usual the real but invisible costs of financial policy fell on those groups (particularly wage-earners) whose incomes lagged behind rising prices. And that same group bore the burden of depression and unemployment which accompanied the deflation of credit when the Bank resumed specie payments at the pre-war parity in 1821.

Four interconnected innovations or departures from tradition marked the government's policies to fund long and expensive wars against France from 1793 to 1815. All four occurred when Pitt the Younger occupied the office of Chancellor of the Exchequer. His successors who took charge of the nation's fiscal and financial policy followed the strategy established by their famous predecessor. Addington, Petty, Perceval and

Vansittart modified here and there, made mistakes or achieved success on points of detail. But on the broad choices of loans versus taxes, stringent or flexible monetary policy, the conduct of debt management, and the selection of taxes, they followed Pitt.

Unlike other conflicts over the preceding century, this war (at least from 1798 onwards) was fought basically with revenue raised from taxes. In turn that money came mainly from pushing up rates of taxes available to the state before the outbreak of war, but supplemented in good measure by Britain's first income tax – another by-product of the French Revolution. That policy contained the accumulation of the national debt and preserved the funding system. Although the government also for the first time waged a major war off gold, and was thereby unhampered by the constraints of convertibility, ministers to a remarkable degree resisted the easy option of turning the Bank of England into an engine of state finance. Inflation remained moderate while the incidence of taxes they introduced and raised to defeat revolutionary France fell broadly on those with most to gain from that victory. By and large the poor were not excessively burdened with regressive levies on items in mass consumption.[46]

Britain's fiscal and financial achievement was no less impressive or important than the famous battles fought by her ships at Trafalgar and troops at Waterloo. Indeed victory over France rested ultimately on the government's success in raising revenue. If the transition from war to peacetime finance was incompetently handled by the Liverpool administration, that should not be blamed on the policies used to provide the indispensable means required to defeat France and to restrain the diffusion of her infamous Revolution.[47]

9. The Impact of the French Wars on the British Economy

FRANÇOIS CROUZET

THE 'unfortunate coincidence' between the French Wars and a vital stage of the Industrial Revolution has been deplored by several historians. The latter expression may be a misnomer, and certainly the rapidity of growth and the extent of technological and structural change in the British economy during the period 1780–1820 must not be over-estimated. Nonetheless, when war broke out in 1793, some developments, which were unprecedented and truly revolutionary, though still limited in scope, had been taking place in some industries (specially the mechanisation of cotton spinning and the emergence of the factory system); other sectors were also on the move (1792 had been the peak of a canal mania), and the growth of population, which had started before mid century, was accelerating.

It is reasonable to assume that the 'twenty-two years war', which was protracted, expensive and fertile in sharp shocks for the British economy, did have some impact (and possibly a strong impact) upon its growth and development. However, any attempt at isolating the respective contributions by the war, by the process of economic change which was on its way, and by the demographic factor, runs into serious difficulties.

When economists want to study the effects of a war, they first define a trend of development during the pre-war period; they assume that the economy would have stayed on the same course if war had not broken out; and they consider any deviations from this trend, during the period of hostilities, as consequences of the war. This approach inevitably involves the resort to counterfactual statements – a reference to what would have happened if peace had been maintained – and one can wonder about the legitimacy and accuracy of defining the trend of growth for a number of years and of extrapolating for the period which follows.

The years from 1783 to 1792 cannot be considered as normal: they are as much a post-war as a pre-war period, during which the British economy – or at least its foreign-orientated branches – vigorously rebounded after the depression which it had suffered during the American War. There can be no certitude that the fast growth, which, for instance, foreign trade had known during those years, would have been maintained if war had not broken out.

One can, of course, observe the changes which took place during the war – especially in the growth rates of production and trade – and try to ascertain how far they were a consequence of the war, or independent from it. One can also attempt to draw balance-sheets of the positive and negative effects of factors which are at work in wartime, such as government finance, recruiting for the forces, blockades, etc. Such will be the approaches in this chapter, but they are impressionistic and greatly rely on guesses. Hopefully, one day sophisticated cliometrics will bring some certitude.[1]

An additional problem is to discriminate between short-run and long-run effects of the wars (one might also say immediate and/or lasting). Many economic disturbances which happen in wartime have no durable consequences; vice versa, booms and slumps occur in peace as well as in wartime. Short-run incidents are not to be overlooked, specially by political historians, in so far as Britain had to survive a succession of economic crises before emerging victorious. On the other hand, economic historians are more interested in long-term consequences, but they are the most difficult to ascertain, to isolate from phenomena which were more or less bound to happen because of trends of long duration in economic and social development.

I

A direct and obvious effect of a great war is the dislocation of international trade. In some respects it was minimised for Britain by her naval supremacy (though many British merchant ships were captured by the enemy), but while relatively safe at sea, British trade was vulnerable to military and political developments on land; it fluctuated with the flow and ebb of French conquest and influence on the Continent. This impact of the military situation was at its apex during the Continental Blockade (1806–13), when Napoleon tried to defeat Britain by closing to her exports the markets of the Continent, while the United States were taking economic sanctions against her, in retaliation for her heavy-handed treatment of neutral trade, and eventually made war on her. In earlier years, however, British trade already had to face serious difficulties on several occasions as when Holland was overrun by the French (1795) or Spain changed from the British to the French side (1796). Eventually, British trade overcame all obstacles; it suffered some major slumps, but it rebounded sharply after each of them. 'Self-blockades' against British exports could not be maintained tightly enough; smuggling was highly profitable and so rampant almost everywhere; Napoleon's allies and also his rapacious marshals and officials disregarded his commands; on the other hand, British traders were flexible and adapted quickly to changing circumstances; they exploited any opportunity, any possible channel of trade, and they succeeded in opening new markets when old ones closed. The kaleidoscopic short-term movements of British trade during the wars merge into broad trends, which are summed up in Table 1.[2]

TABLE 1   Volume of British trade. Mean rates of growth per year (%)

	Exports	Re-exports	Imports
1781–92	6.9	4.7	5.2
1792–1802	5.9	10.9	5.6
1802–14	3.1	2.3	1.2

From the end of the American War up to 1792, British trade had grown very fast; in the early years of the new war, exports fell back, but they increased sharply again from 1798 to 1802, so that their rate of growth from 1792 to 1802 is only one percentage point lower than from 1781 to 1792; this was not a significant slowing down, specially when the high rate of growth of the 1780s is taken into account. As for the rate of growth for re-exports of colonial and foreign goods, it more than doubled from the earlier decade to the next; for imports it increased slightly. On the whole, the war against the French Revolution was a good period for British trade.

On the other hand, after 1802, there was a definite slowing down; volumes of trade drifted downward from 1802 to 1808 and, despite new peak figures in 1809, 1810 and 1814, progress during the later part of the war was far less sharp than around 1800. As for values at current prices, their rate of growth was very low for exports (0.7 per cent per year, between 1802 and 1814); it was better, but modest, for re-exports and imports.

How far was the war responsible for those changes? It is often said that the Napoleonic Wars stimulated British trade, because they crippled England's continental competitors and because, thanks to the Royal Navy, Britain enjoyed a virtual monopoly of relations with non-European countries. Actually these views need to be qualified.

There is no doubt that Revolution and war seriously harmed French industry and trade during the 1790s, but the misfortunes of her chief competitor did not bring many direct benefits to England. The rise of her exports during the 1790s and 1800s was mainly due to the spectacular increase in overseas sales of cotton goods, for which there was no French competition before 1793. True enough, the fall in the export of some French goods which were competitive with British articles – specially silks and linen – must have been helpful for British exports, but only marginally.

As for British ascendancy at sea, it was established gradually, and up to 1807, Britain allowed neutrals – i.e. Americans – to have a substantial share of the carrying trade between Europe and overseas countries. The situation changed with the Orders-in-Council of November 1807 and the American embargo, and henceforth Britain had a quasi-monopoly of trade between the Old and the New World. Sea power contributed to this in another way – by making easy the occupation of many enemy colonies, where new markets were opened to British goods, while their produce had to pass through British ports. This contributed to the increase in Britain's imports and re-exports, though Table 1 shows that it was faster before 1802 than after, despite the full use by Britain, in the later period, of her naval power to become 'the grocer of Europe'. Anyhow, her engrossment of colonial trade was transitory, as France and Holland recovered some of their colonies at the peace. Still, the increase in the carrying trade during the wars strengthened the position of the City as an international supplier of services.

A more durable consequence of the war was the opening to British trade of Brazil and of the Spanish colonies in America which started in 1808; it resulted from the military and political upheavals in the Peninsula and it became definitive when those colonies obtained their independence in the 1820s. This opening was a useful windfall in the difficult circumstances of 1808, but Latin American markets were not as extensive and profitable as many British traders had expected.

The positive effects of the war for British trade appear less significant than it is often thought. And war also had a negative impact. It can be assumed that the slowing down of growth from 1803 was a consequence of the Continental Blockade, which during two periods (late

1807–early 1808, end of 1810–mid 1812) closed most European markets to British goods, and of the conflict with the United States. The impoverishment of the Continent owing to protracted warfare may also have harmed British trade, not only during the wars, but also during the post-war period, when it suffered from protectionism abroad, which was largely a legacy of the war and of the Continental Blockade. This slowing down after 1802 is all the more remarkable as several factors connected with the war were then at work to stimulate British trade: the opening of Latin America, the occupation of enemy colonies, the enforcement of the 1807 Orders-in-Council, and the growing foreign expenditures by government, specially to maintain Wellington's army in the Peninsula. However, the war and the Blockade caused a rise in information, transaction and transport costs, which were tantamount to a tax upon the British economy; this could not but have a damping effect. Both smuggling and the switch to new markets involved higher costs and risks. This helps to explain why the net barter terms of trade moved against Britain after 1802. Moreover the ratio of foreign trade to national product – and of exports to industrial output – which had been increasing during the 1780s and 1790s, declined later.

On the other hand, there were developments in British foreign trade which have no direct or clear connection with the course of the war. The exports boom of 1798–1802 is a case of trade creation, thanks to technological progress in the cotton industry, which made cotton yarn and cloth cheaper relatively to other textiles. As for the upsurge of exports to the United States, which was largely responsible for the increase of total exports during the 1790s and for their keeping up from 1803 to 1807, it resulted mainly from rising demand on the American market, thanks to fast population growth.

The composition of British exports underwent a major change during the wars; as exports of cotton products grew much faster than those of other goods, their share of total exports' values greatly increased: from 6 per cent in 1784–6 to 40 per cent in 1814–16; concomitantly, the share of wool textiles and of metal goods fell back.[3] The main cause was in technology, but the war did help somewhat, in so far as cottons, which were cheap and fashionable, were in a better position to get over barriers against British trade than the products of industries where technology was not improving markedly.

Owing to the slowing down after 1802 (which, true enough, might be part of a long-term cycle), the overall effect of the wars upon the growth of British trade was rather negative. Moreover, as the war dislocated international trade and hampered specialisation, Britain lost some potential gains from trade. True enough her protectionist system was anyhow a major obstacle to specialisation; but there had been, in the 1780s, some signs that a new international economic order, of a less mercantilist hue, might emerge. Actually the protectionist system was strengthened by the war, which, moreover, made Britain's internal terms of trade move in favour of primary production. So the war did delay a reallocation of resources according to comparative advantages.

II

Since the mid eighteenth century, prices had been rising on trend in Britain, but slowly. A major aspect of the war period was an outburst of sharp, though not runaway, inflation: the Gayer index of wholesale prices of domestic and imported commodities rises from 89 in 1790 to a peak of 169 in 1813, that is, by 90 per cent.[4] Agricultural prices rose markedly more than those of manufactured goods and of services; so there was an alteration in internal terms of trade, to the benefit of agriculture, and to the detriment of other sectors, specially industry.[5]

There was much debate at the time about the cause of 'the high price of provisions', and experts are still divided, some stressing the 'real' sources of inflation, others the monetary factor. Prices did not rise continuously, but suffered a number of sharp upward jumps – in 1795, 1799-1800 (in 1800 they were 40 per cent above 1798), 1805, 1808-9, 1812 – which correspond to 'supply shocks', that is harvest failures in Britain and flareups of economic warfare.[6] The vagaries of the British weather are often seen as the dominant factor; owing to bad luck, the number of poor crops was abnormally high during the French Wars; moreover, it happened several times that the harvest failed in two consecutive years – this was the cause of the highest peaks of agricultural prices.

However, supply conditions explain the fluctuations of prices, but not their rising trend in the long run during the wars (after each shock, prices fell back, but remained higher than at the previous trough). There was, of course, an element of cost-push inflation owing to wages claims and rises when food prices were high, but the pressure of a fast increasing population has also to be taken into account: from 1791 to 1811 the population of England and Wales increased by 2,146,000 inhabitants, that is by 28 per cent;[7] these 2 million additional mouths to feed (not to mention the Scots) may have pushed prices upwards, as there is no proof that food production increased by the same ratio. Actually the increase in grain imports (on average they were over twice larger during the wars than in the 1780s) suggests quite the contrary.

Indeed, the growing food deficit resulting from demographic growth could be – and actually was – made good by imports. However, wartime conditions brought about a sharp rise in freight and insurance premiums, which made imported grain more expensive. Though Britain's enemies did not try to starve her (Napoleon actually granted licences to export corn from France to England in 1809 and 1810), it can be argued that Britain would have imported more grain, and at lower prices, under 'normal' conditions.

The war also had more indirect, but significant effects upon prices, through the 'mobilisation'. In rough numbers, at the end of the wars, 500,000 men were with the colours; this was an increase of 400,000 on the pre-war establishment, and it meant a larger drain of manpower, because of losses, which are estimated at 210,000 dead. The forces absorbed at least one-fifth of the increase in the United Kingdom's male population; and in the last years of the war, over 10 per cent of men in the age group 18–45 years was serving in them.

Mobilisation created an additional demand for foodstuffs (and also for horses, fodder, cloth, leather), because recruits were better fed by the army and navy than they had been as civilians. However, the main problem concerns the effect of mobilisation on the labour market. Some writers – with a neo-classical stand – maintain that full employment had prevailed in pre-war Britain; so mobilisation could but create a shortage of labour, which drove money wages upwards and of course reverberated upon costs and prices.[8] On the other hand, neo-Keynesians insist that labour resources were underemployed before 1793; mobilisation created full employment and generated an economic growth which would not have happened but for the war.[9] As a matter of fact, there is no evidence of a widespread shortage of labour during the wars, except in some places and at some moments, for farmworkers and unskilled labourers (the groups from which sailors and soldiers mostly came); and actually their wages increased much more than those of skilled workmen. It is suggested that mobilisation was a factor which limited to some extent the effects of the Malthusian trap which the acceleration in population growth had created in late eighteenth-century Britain.

'Real' factors were also instrumental in Britain's currency problems, which in their turn contributed to inflation. The balance of external payments was precarious and it suffered a number of shocks, because of abnormally high imports (after harvest failures), of blockades which interrupted exports, and above all of government military and political expenditures abroad. Depending upon circumstances, these difficulties resulted either in losses of precious metals or in depreciation of the paper pound (which reached its nadir during the peaks of foreign remittances by government). Depreciation aggravated the deterioration of England's external terms of trade and fuelled internal inflation.

Nonetheless, the bullionist or monetarist explanation of inflation retains its basic validity. Government and the banking system exerted an autonomous pressure upon the price level. True enough, they did not start inflation: from 1793 to 1796, the circulation of Bank notes did not expand and they remained convertible; but later on, and specially from 1808 onwards, their responsibility cannot be doubted (though, after some laxity early in the war, public finances were soundly managed). The generous discount policy which was followed by the Bank of England (which also made liberal advances to the Exchequer) gave to country banks the opportunity to be still more open-handed in their discounts and their notes-issues. Moreover, the Bank had the power to stop or to slow down inflation, through restricting the money supply, but it did not attempt to do so; it was a passive abettor of inflation. The anti-bullionists, followed by many historians, have argued, however, that Britain would not have been able to carry on the war, but for the facilities which resulted from inconvertibility and from some dose of monetary inflation. This is disputable, but the preservation of a stable currency at a time of heavy government expenditure abroad (as in the last years of the war) would no doubt have made necessary a restrictive monetary policy, which would have depressed the economy. Anyhow, monetarists stress the impact of inconvertibility and of the floating exchange rates which prevailed from 1797 to 1821, under which increases in Bank notes issues can have dramatic effects upon prices.[10] From this point of view, war appears as the basic factor of inflation, because inconvertibility would never have been instituted in peacetime. But the 'supply shocks' interpretation also allows a significant role to the war: though harvest failures were at the root of the rise in prices, many circumstances connected with the war helped to aggravate it. It must be stressed, however, that the average rate of inflation (3 per cent per year) was low by modern standards, and the depreciation of the paper pound limited (at the worse, 41 per cent in relation to silver, in 1813); it did not go the way of the *assignats* and confidence in the currency was almost unimpaired.

III

The impact upon production of the disturbances which affected foreign trade and of inflation will now be examined, starting with agriculture, which was responsible for one-third of national product and so was the 'first British industry'. However, for lack of reliable statistical data, it is difficult to be definite (for industrial output, the situation is somewhat better).

Farmers gave a positive answer to the incentive of rising prices, and agricultural output increased faster during the wars than during the two or three preceding decades. Still, it is likely that it did not increase as much as population (as mentioned earlier, Britain's grain deficit rose); this fits with the present view that the performance of British agriculture in the late eighteenth and early nineteenth centuries was not as brilliant as earlier writers had assumed.

This increase in output – by 25 per cent at a rough guess – was achieved thanks both to investment (on a relatively large scale) and to technological progress, to an extension of cultivation and to better farming.

A large share of investment in agriculture was devoted to enclosure operations. Actually the French Wars were the apex of parliamentary enclosures, which had been numerous from 1755 to 1780, but had faltered thereafter; 43 per cent of the Enclosure Acts for England were passed from 1793 to 1815 (with 1811 as the peak year). They authorised the enclosure of 2,900,000 acres, that is 8.9 per cent of England's surface; two-thirds were open fields, but 900,000 acres were commons and waste. Altogether, and including non-parliamentary forms of enclosure, the increase of the cultivated area in England was of the order of 5 per cent (and less in Britain).[11] Historians have argued about the *primus movens* for this outburst of enclosures: was it the rise in grain prices, which promised better returns from land which was turned into arable? Or the fall in *real* interest rates, which made borrowing for improvements cheaper? The former interpretation appears the more valid; the peaks in the number of Enclosure Acts came just after those of grain prices: most of the investment in land improvements was self-financed and in this respect high prices were more influential than low interest rates. The rise in prices, which made profitable the cultivation of mediocre land, triggered off enclosing early in the war and kept it going – and accelerating – up to the peace.

Enclosure ensured significant productivity gains, but as the total increase in the input of land was after all minute, most of the increment in production came from better yields on land which had been enclosed before 1793. But there was nothing new or dramatic; mostly wider diffusion of the 'new' crops, rotations and improved livestock breeds, which are typical of the Agricultural Revolution. The development of farm machinery may have been stimulated by the shortage of labour which has been mentioned, and the use of the scythe and of the threshing machine spread in some areas. However, progress was not universal, for reasons of geography and because of rising wages which made some improvements expensive; for instance, farmers of heavy clay soils – where rootcrops were not a success – kept on the old three-course rotation, which was profitable under high prices of cereals, but ruined them after the war.

The balance between grain cultivation and animal production underwent some alterations; there is no clear trend, over the war period, of the ratio prices of animal products/prices of grains, but sharp short-run fluctuations; so farmers made minor shifts towards cereals or towards fodder and pasture, according to whether wheat or animal products were likely to be the more profitable. However, as prices of animal products rose steadily, an overall shift towards stockraising and an increase in meat consumption per capita are plausible.

According to Deane and Cole, the increase of agricultural production and still more the differential movements of agricultural and non-agricultural prices temporarily halted and even reversed the secular decline in the role of agriculture in the British economy. Its contribution to national income would have risen from 33 per cent in 1801 to 36 per cent in 1811, only to fall back to 26 per cent in 1821; the share of industry changed inversely.[12]

The shift of internal terms of trade in favour of agriculture also brought about a redistribution of income, in which landowners were the big gainers (this can be expected, as they possessed the factor of production with the least elastic supply in relation to prices). During the wars, rents rose on average by 90 per cent, just as much as agricultural prices and more than industrial prices; of course, this average embodies gains resulting from enclosures, and so from investment by landowners. It has been maintained, rather convincingly, that farmers did not do as well as landlords;[13] as for agricultural labourers, they benefited from some increase in real wages, but remained nonetheless very poor.

Undoubtedly the growth of British agriculture would have been slower but for the French Wars. However, this was not all benefit: the extension of arable land, due to high grain prices, became uneconomic when prices fell after 1813 and it contributed to the post-war agricultural depression. On the other hand, war and demographic pressure had forced the lethargic rural sector to move; henceforth, landowners and farmers were shut up in a virtuous circle of innovation, investment, cost reduction; and actually the landed interest reacted to the post-1815 depression not only by imposing protectionism, but also by keeping up investment, and thus preparing further progress.

As for the consequences of developments in agriculture for the rest of the economy, they were altogether negative. Internal terms of trade moved in favour of agriculture at a time when potentialities for economies of scale, technological progress and productivity gains were mostly in industry. The rise of food prices brought about an increase of money wages and therefore a lower return for capital, a decrease of funds available for industrial investment through the ploughing back of profits. Manufactured goods were diverted towards foreign markets, with an increase in incertitude and risk. Hueckel was right in saying that Britain's total product would have been larger if some of the capital which was diverted towards agriculture had been used elsewhere.

Several factors connected with the war were liable to affect the development of British industries. Firstly, of course, in the short run, the fluctuations of exports which resulted from the military and political situation abroad; owing to the slowing down in the growth of exports after 1802, which has been observed earlier, some similar movement can be expected in the manufacturing sector, which exported roughly one-third of its aggregate output. The dislocation of international trade also affected imports of raw materials; their prices rose, and at times (specially in 1808), there were actual shortages and very high prices for flax, timber, raw silk, Spanish wool, raw cotton, etc. However these difficulties were short-lived and had only a minimal influence upon the growth of industry. On the other hand, the combination of increased customs duties upon Swedish and Russian iron with obstacles to imports from those countries around 1800 contributed to the fast growth of Britain's primary iron industry at the time; but this is about the only branch which benefited from the increased protection which war and taxation gave.

War finance is another factor. Heavy customs or excise duties were levied upon various inputs and/or products of industry; the fall in private consumption, which government imposed, reduced demand for manufactured goods; and investment in industry may have been crowded out by heavy government borrowing. On the other hand, many inputs were tax free; fiscal policy was regressive, biased in favour of profits and investment; the suspension of convertibility made trade credit abundant. There were also military orders, for the army and navy; however, their importance must not be anachronistically over-estimated; in the Napoleonic period, unlike in the twentieth century, war did not demand much material – apart from warships; the military consumed much more in the way of foodstuffs, fodder, horses, than of manufactured articles. So government orders benefited only a few branches of industry, for limited periods and not to a large extent; the iron industry (but only 10 per cent of the additional output of its primary branch from 1793 to 1815 was for military purposes), the woollen industry (which made cloth for uniforms) and shoe-making; shipbuilding was the only branch which depended heavily upon government orders. In so far as some new and special capacity was created because of the demand for armaments (i.e. for making small arms), it became useless after the peace.[14]

Obviously, the balance of negative and positive effects of the war was different from one branch of industry to another; indeed there were wide variations in the rates of growth of the main British industries during the wars, as it appears in Table 2, which is based upon calculations by N.F.R. Crafts.[15]

TABLE 2   Output of some industries. Mean rates of growth per year (%)

Industries	1780–90	1790–1811	1811–31
Cotton	12.8	5.6	6.2
Building	3.2	2.0	3.4
Iron	3.8	7.0	3.0
Coal	2.4	2.9	3.2
13 industries	3.7	2.6	2.4

(Weights according to added values of 1801).

Thus, some industries grew more slowly during the wars than before and after them; some others had a faster growth in wartime than during peace. However, one must ascertain how far those changes were a consequence of the war. The slowing down in the growth of the cotton industry resulted mainly from the obstacles which exports of cotton articles met after 1802; but the pace of production had already slackened during the 1790s despite peak rates of growth for exports, a sign that the home market for cottons was not widening as fast as earlier on. This would, actually, have been almost impossible and one wonders whether the very high rates of growth both of exports and of production which had been reached during the 1780s and 1790s could have been maintained, even in peacetime.

The wool textile industry – which was developing anyway much more slowly than cotton – also suffered a sharp fall in its rate of growth, and a real stagnation (specially in the woollen branch) in the last years of the war – as a result of the conflict with the United States. As for the minor textile industries, silk and linen, their growth was very small during the war, but basically because of the competition from cottons.

The Napoleonic Wars, like earlier eighteenth-century wars, had a negative effect upon building (Crafts' calculations tally with Shannon's older bricks index);[16] taxation upon houses, rising prices of materials (specially timber), rising nominal interest rates, diversion of capital towards government loans made for a slowing down in building enterprise, which had unfortunate and lasting consequences for the working classes.

On the other hand, the growth of two major industries – iron and coal – accelerated during the war, the impact of which is obvious on the former. Rising prices for imported bar iron strongly stimulated the substitution of British for foreign iron, and so the making of pig and bar; the industry, which was undergoing a technological mutation (particularly the widespread adoption of puddling in the 1790s), was ready to take advantage of this opportunity. Moreover exports – direct or indirect – took only a modest share of the primary iron industry's output. On the other hand, the small acceleration in the growth of coal output can not be attributed to the war.

As for miscellaneous industries, such as leather (the largest of the group), beer, spirits, soap, candles, paper, they were working mostly for the home market and somewhat immune to export fluctuations, but they were liable to suffer from heavier taxation; actually some of them did grow more slowly during the war than before, some others grew faster. However, they were slow-growing industries, and it would be rash to see any clear influence of the war in the rather minor changes which their rates of growth display.

Altogether, a direct impact of the war on growth is undoubted for only a few industries – cotton, wool, iron, building – but they were the largest in the country, and some effect upon an aggregate and weighted index of industrial output can be expected. Actually such indices are not too reliable for the period under consideration. Table 2 gives rates of growth for one index which has been built up by Crafts, and which, indeed, shows a marked slowing down of industrial growth during the wars; but Crafts has another index, with different weights, according to which the magnitude of the slowing down is quite small! Moreover, both indices show a clear deceleration during the 1790s, followed by a recovery in the rate of growth in the 1800s; but there is some evidence of the reverse, that is the slowest growth being after 1802.[17] Still, there is no doubt that a marked acceleration in the growth of industrial output took place after 1820. A cautious conclusion might be that the growth of British industry suffered some slowing down during the wars, and partly because of the wars;[18] but its progress from 1783 to 1792 had been abnormally fast.

The warning which has been given about aggregates applies, of course, to estimates of national income or product; moreover, they are too crude for measuring changes in rates of growth over short periods, without a risk of serious errors. Suffice it to say therefore that some estimates suggest a relatively fast growth of the economy during the 1790s, followed by deceleration in the 1800s, then recovery in the 1810s and still more in the 1820s; according to other calculations, growth was faster in the 1800s than before, and faltered in the 1810s.[19]

IV

A strategic factor for the long-run development of the British economy was the impact which the wars had upon capital formation. Alas, in this case also answers have to be tentative, because quantitative data on both investment and national product are not fully reliable. According to calculations by C.H. Feinstein, the ratio of *total* investment to gross internal product suffered a 'sharp fall' in the 1800s:[20]

1781–90	13%
1791–1800	14%
1801–10	10%
1811–20	14%

Productive *fixed* capital investment also suffered some slowing down in both the 1790s and 1800s. Still, by using different figures for national product, Crafts has flattened out the fall in the investment ratio.[21]

This fall, however, fits in well with the 'crowding out' hypothesis, which has been vigorously advocated by J.G. Williamson.[22] The enormous loans which the British government issued to finance its war effort absorbed a large share of the nation's savings and deprived the private sector of capital; therefore productive investment was kept below the level it would have reached in peace, economic growth and industrialisation were markedly slowed down. Williamson calculated that but for the war debt the capital formation proportion for 1791-1820 would have been 6.4 per cent higher than it actually was; and that, all effects of the war being combined, the rate of growth of real national income from 1790 to 1815 would have doubled under counterfactual peacetime conditions (the increase being larger for the rate of growth of industrial output).

These views have been criticised by J. Mokyr; after deflating and adjusting the increase in the national debt, he concludes that 'Williamson's estimates of the crowding-out effect tend to be too large by a factor of about 2.5'. There may have been some crowding out of investment (with an upper bound of 3 per cent of national income, 1790-1820), but far below the magnitude proposed by Williamson.[23] As for P.K. O'Brien,[24] he has rightly pointed out that the average ratio of productive investment remained fairly stable during the wars, and that there was no inverse correlation between government borrowing and private investment (they both had peaks in the late 1790s). In his view, government loans were subscribed thanks to an increase in total savings and not at the expense of private investment. First, war expenditure gave a sharp stimulus to an economy which had unemployed resources, national product was increased and to some extent (which must not be over-estimated), the war paid for itself. Secondly, the 'savers', that is roughly the rich, displayed a higher propensity to save and to lend to government; this was a matter both of patriotism and of self-interest, in a war to defend liberty and property against Jacobins and Levellers. However, England under Pitt and Perceval was not the same country as under Churchill, when austerity was gladly accepted: there was a great deal of extravagant and lavish expenditure by the landed classes.[25] Another factor was the fiscal and monetary policy which Pitt adopted in 1797 and which was continued by his successors. It relied more than beforehand on taxation and less on borrowing, so that more funds were available for private investment; but it was also a regressive policy, which transferred income from wage-earners to fundholders, from the poor to the rich, that is from those with a low to those with a high propensity to save. Moreover, thanks to the suspension of convertibility, the banking system was able to grant credit more generously to the private sector. Despite the institution of income tax, profits made in industry and trade escaped lightly, and the ability of industry to self-finance investment was not seriously dented. The suspension also encouraged the extension of the banking system and of financial intermediation generally; the drainage of savings towards the Exchequer was improved.

These criticisms do not, however, completely destroy the crowding out hypothesis. A basic fact remains: for over two decades, very large sums (of the same order of magnitude as total private investment) were borrowed every year by government. Is it possible that such heavy and repeated punctures had no effect upon private investment? That some of the moneys which went into the funds were not diverted from other, more productive uses? Whatever the fragmentation and imperfections in the capital market – or rather markets, as people who bought government securities were not the same as those who invested in business – those compartments were not strictly watertight. On the other hand, there are no signs of serious tension on the capital market, of brutal diversion in financial flows. Interest rates were, on an average for the war period, 20 per cent higher than in peacetime, a 'small' rise, specially *in time of inflation*; government borrowed at over 6 per cent during only a short period in 1797-8. None the less, the investment proportion – even if it did not fall during the war – was rather low; it would likely have been higher but for the war, as a new technology was available for both a widening and a deepening of capital. And more investment would have brought about faster economic growth. In capital formation, as from several other points of view, Britain's performance was better than one could expect in the midst of a major war, but there is no reason to be panglossian. Moreover, the incertitude connected with the war is likely to have deterred some manufacturers from increasing capacity, while the fluctuations of profits – especially after 1802 – lessened their ability to invest through ploughing back.

According to Williamson, Britain did not have enough resources for both industrialising and waging large-scale wars. Actually, she had – or almost. Thanks to a high ratio of *total* savings to national product, the Industrial Revolution went on and the war was won; though the pace of the former faltered, and though for many years much money was squandered with little apparent result.

V

The British economy also managed to preserve the standard of living of the people, despite the pressure of a fast growing population, despite also the increase in consumption by government, which was achieved at the expense of private consumption (on a per capita basis the latter fell by 10 per cent).[26] The course of real wages during the late eighteenth and early nineteenth centuries has been charted recently by several writers. Such studies depend of course upon the representativeness of the cost of living indices which are used; they are besides based upon money wage-rates, and not upon actual earnings by workers (and their families), which were greatly influenced by the level of employment and the number of hours worked per week. Despite these drawbacks and despite some differences between their results, the recent indices of real wages concur to suggest a stability – which, of course, can also be called a stagnation – of real wages during the wars in the medium run, and when averages for several years are used, because there were violent short-run fluctuations, specially serious falls of purchasing power during the years when food prices were very high. The worst crisis, in this respect, was in 1799–1801 (all indices have their lowest figure in 1800); on the other hand, real wages made a strong recovery after these 'subsistence crises' were over. Table 3 illustrates this through an arithmetic average of 7 different indices, for some specified years, and for quinquennial periods; avowedly, this is a very crude kind of measurement.[27]

TABLE 3   An average of 7 indices of real wages (1790 = 100)

		5-year averages	
1795	91	1788–92	101
1797	103	1793–7	96
1800	75	1798–1801	85
1805	96	1803–7	97
1810	96	1808–13	90
1815	109	1814–18	102
		1819–23	119

Both stagnation and fluctuations have connections with the war. The main factor was, of course, the rise of food prices; it has been maintained earlier that it was basically independent from the war, but that the latter aggravated its amplitude and fluctuations; the shift of the terms of trade, both internal and external, to the benefit of primary producers and to the detriment of industry, had also a role, as well as the slowing down in the growth of industry, owing to the obstacles which British exports met. On the other hand, mobilisation, which withdrew from the market a substantial part of the additional male labour force, acted to relieve the pressure of population growth upon wages. Altogether, the war created a pressure downwards upon the standard of living of the working classes, but it is remarkable that the latter did not suffer more and that the purchasing power of labour was roughly maintained, except during a few years of high prices and/or unemployment. As Wrigley and Schofield have suggested, this good performance resulted from the productivity gains which agricultural and industrial change had brought about and which, by the early years of the nineteenth century, had become large enough to increase real wages, despite the pressure both of the war and of rising population. This was an unprecedented breakthrough, an entry into a new era.[28]

A graph of real wages in Britain in the second half of the eighteenth century and the first of the nineteenth is U-shaped; its trough is located during the French Wars, but so is the beginning of the recovery; strangely enough, the latter started while the growth of foreign trade and of industrial production was slowing down.

Recent research has stressed the heterogeneity of the labour market, the complexity of the wages structure, the regional variations in wages. Suffice it to say that the position of skilled workers – including white collar workers – deteriorated during the wars, while there was a significant improvement in real wages for semi-skilled workers and for labourers, including farm labourers. However, none of the indices which have been used embodies a series of the earnings of handloom weavers, which collapsed in real terms during the wars; Lindert and Williamson have pointed out that their aggregate results would have been worse if this numerous and unfortunate group of workpeople had been taken into account.[29] Nonetheless, the consideration of real wages during the French Wars brings some support to the 'optimist' (or rather 'meliorist')[30] view of the consequences of the Industrial Revolution upon the standard of living of the British working classes.

VI

It is possible to draw both a black and a rosy picture of the economic condition of England during the French Wars. On the one hand, the country is stumbling along from crisis into crisis: 1793, 1795, 1797, 1800–1, 1808, 1810–12; there is a massive diversion of resources into a sector with no future, agriculture; a slowing down of industrial growth and of productive investment; altogether, the process of industrialisation is greatly hindered and delayed. Moreover, there is a transfer of income from the 'productive' groups – both working people and entrepreneurs – to the fundholding and *rentier* class, a process which the regressive fiscal and monetary policies of the post-war period did seriously aggravate. Of course, the war strengthened the advantage which Britain had in relation to the Continent and the United States, but this did not make up for the disturbances which her own economy had suffered.

On the other hand, while recognising that the British economy ran several times into serious difficulties, one can stress how it rose to the challenge and victoriously overcame it. Agriculture was indeed greatly improved and it saved the country from starving; despite fluctuations, industrial output went on increasing, technological progress and structural change were not seriously interrupted; even foreign trade surged more strongly after each slump; financial institutions were greatly perfected. So government was able to get the resources which it needed to carry on the war, without killing the goose which laid the golden eggs, that is, jeopardising the sources of wealth creation (specially investment) and its own credit. War can be seen as a catalyst and an accelerator of economic progress.

As a matter of fact, both views are overdramatic; an apocalyptic point of view was frequent among contemporaries: both Pitt in the 1790s and Napoleon during the Continental Blockade were confident that economic collapse would force their enemy into surrender; recent historians have been influenced by the experience of twentieth-century world wars into anachronistic parallels with the Napoleonic period, during which governments made no attempt (except during the brief episode of the Terror in France) fully to mobilise their economies and to subordinate them to the war effort.[31] Indeed, the war effort of Britain, though considerable for a largely traditional economy, with low per capita income, was far less intense than during the twentieth-century world wars.

Undoubtedly there is also a personal and subjective factor in adopting a pessimist or an optimist view of the effects of the wars, plus, sometimes, the influence of the neo-classical or neo-Keynesian stand which writers take. A middle-of-the-road position might be that the economic consequences of the wars were not in the long run as serious as it is often thought. In the matter of enclosures and agriculture generally, was not there much ado about... a quite small percentage of the country's surface being put under the plough? In industry, the deceleration of growth in major branches – cotton, wool, building – is something serious, but the war was not entirely responsible. War was neither a stimulus to, nor a powerful retardative factor of British growth, which, it is now anyway accepted, was 'slow' during most of the Industrial Revolution.

A confirmation can be found in the demographic position. The fast increase in the population of England, which had started before the wars, continued and even accelerated while they were in progress; indeed, some negative aspects can be observed, obviously resulting from economic difficulties and especially from high food prices in some years, but they were minor and short-lived accidents: for instance mortality rose in 1795, in 1801, in 1810; none the less its trend during the wars is downwards, while natality, fertility, reproduction rate, life expectancy at birth are rising. Every indicator points to a healthy demographic situation, on which the wars had little impact. When they came to an end, the rate of growth of English population was three times that of France – a promise that the latter's superiority in numbers over Britain would whittle away and disappear.[32]

There is no need to stress the economic factor in Britain's long resistance to adversity and final victory; she was, before the war, an 'advanced' and 'rich' country; her economic growth, her productivity gains continued during the war; thanks to this, her people displayed an amazing ability both to pay high taxes (from 1803 to 1812), on a per capita basis and in wheat equivalent, the British paid three times more than the French) and to lend to their government; the latter was thus able to hire as mercenaries the armies of East European despots, and its loans, subsidies and arms supplies played a decisive role during the final campaigns of 1813-14. Even then, however, the 'modern' sector of the British economy remained small; of course, the cotton industry was strategic for the rise of British exports during the wars, a rise without which Britain would not have been able to maintain large forces abroad and to finance coalitions. But this was the main contribution of the

Industrial Revolution to the winning of the war. Malthus was mistaken when he wrote in 1820: 'In carrying the late war, we were powerfully assisted by our steam-engines;[33] actually Napoleon was not defeated by steam power, which at the time had a minute impact upon the economy at large.

A last problem concerns the 'economic consequences of the peace'. The Revolutionary and Napoleonic Wars had been the most desperate but the last episode, not only of the Second One Hundred Years War between England and France, but of the mercantilist contests, of the 'wars for trade'. They ended in total victory for Britain; its rivals were destroyed as naval, commercial and colonial powers. Unlike after the Seven Years War, France did not work for revenge and soon fell into decadence. Britain's ascendancy at sea was not to be challenged again before Wilhelm II and Tirpitz. The interval was the rule of *Pax Britannica*, a jingoist expression which, however, well expresses the fact that, during the nineteenth century, Britain was the only superpower, the only world power. At the same time, she was the dominant economy, and the relationship between this position and her naval, political and colonial ascendancy raises a question: was the economic advance and superiority of Britain a product of her victories in the Second One Hundred Years War? Or, to parody Adam Smith's famous dictum, was opulence the reward of successful aggression?

The answer, however, must be negative. The roots of the Industrial Revolution, of Britain's pioneering in new technologies, were in the workshops, mills and factories of Lancashire, the West Riding, the Midlands, not on distant battlefields. True enough, Britain's naval and colonial victories made a contribution, but mostly as far as international services (shipping, insurance, banking) and trade with non-European countries were concerned; but in this field, Britain was already ahead before the Revolutionary and Napoleonic Wars, which only made monopolistic an already dominant position. They destroyed Amsterdam and the City of London remained supreme. But, as far as the 'Revolution of industry' is concerned, it was well on its way when Trafalgar and Waterloo were fought.

10. The Social Impact of the French Wars

CLIVE EMSLEY

ON 1 February 1793 the French National Convention declared war on Great Britain, probably pre-empting a declaration of war against France by Pitt's government. Thus began twenty-two years of war between the two countries punctuated only by the brief respite of the Peace of Amiens and the ten months between Napoleon's first abdication and the beginning of the Hundred Days. While other powers participated, at various times and with varying degrees of intensity, in the Revolutionary and Napoleonic Wars, Britain and France were the principal antagonists; contemporaries drew parallels with the struggle between Rome and Carthage – a parallel especially popular with the French since France, like conquering Rome, was the land power. Nineteenth-century historians described the conflict as 'the Great War'. While Britain and France had fought each other throughout the eighteenth century, the scale of the Revolutionary and Napoleonic Wars was quite different. France achieved, albeit ephemerally, the European hegemony of which Louis XIV had dreamed; Britannia ruled the waves. The wars also, especially in their early phase, had an ideological slant and, while it is probably true that statesmen of the period went to war because they thought that they could win, and win quickly, rather than simply because they hated and feared their opponents' ideas and principles, nevertheless ideas and beliefs about the enemy and about the home nation played a significant role in wartime propaganda.

From the British point of view the conflict falls into two distinct sections given the military opposition and the internal state of the country; the Peace of Amiens provides the break. From 1793 until 1801 Britain faced revolutionary France and, while the internal politics of France shifted significantly in these years, as far as the British government and loyal supporters of Church and King were concerned, the enemy remained an atheistical, levelling power, fully prepared to exploit internal problems in Britain and to foment copy-cat revolutions. From 1803 until 1814, while an element of the earlier concerns continued, the enemy appeared in the rather more traditional light of an imperialist France under an absolutist ruler whose success now threatened Britain's very survival. During the first stage of the wars Britain was riven with internal problems. There were two periods of acute food shortages in 1795-6 and 1799-1801: both shortages provoked widespread rioting. The 1790s saw the growth of Paineite radicalism, some of whose adherents revelled in French phraseology and all of whom bitterly criticised the war; loyalists saw the British Jacobins as traitors and potential insurrectionists. Massive naval mutinies in 1797, and to a lesser extent in 1798, were at least tinged with this radicalism; together with the Irish rebellion of 1798 and rumours of arming and drilling among the British Jacobins, the mutinies exacerbated loyalist fears, not, perhaps, without reason. On three occasions French invasion fleets breached the wooden walls of the Royal Navy: only storms prevented Hoche from landing in Ireland at the end of 1796; Tate's *legion noire* landed in Wales early in 1797 and, while it surrendered in three days, the news was sufficient to prompt a run on the banks as a result of which the Bank of England finally decided to call a halt to payment in specie. Humbert's landing in Ireland was too small and too late to be of much assistance to the rebellion of 1798, but his seasoned troops ran rings around their more numerous opponents. While the Royal Navy achieved some success, the campaigns of the British army in the early phase of the war were generally disastrous; even where the French were beaten climate and weather decimated the British ranks. Military failure, famine, the fear of insurrection joined with the other wartime pressures discussed below to provoke widespread demands for peace particularly in 1797 and at the turn of the century. Internal crises were not so apparent in Britain during the second stage of the conflict. For the two years that Napoleon's army of England sat on the coast around Boulogne there appears to have been a general acceptance, running through all social groups, that the war was now one of national survival. Ireland, unified with the rest of Britain in 1801, was quieter. Food shortages were far less severe. Radical politics could still bring crowds on to the streets; and in 1812, while Luddism flared in northern manufacturing districts, businessmen and leading manufacturers organised on a national scale to call upon the government to change its policy of economic warfare. Luddism, middle-class protest, the assassination of the Prime Minister and war with the United States combined to make 1812 a crisis year, yet the threat of revolution appears less acute in this year than in those immediately before the Peace of Amiens; furthermore if British war policies against France had made an enemy of the United States the news of the campaigns against France was encouraging – by the time that Ned Ludd took up his hammer the Duke of Wellington had already beaten some of Napoleon's most trusted marshals in the Iberian Peninsula.

Wars require money to finance them and men to fight them; the unprecedented scale of the Revolutionary and Napoleonic Wars led to enormous demands both for money and men. Between 1793 and 1815 more than £1,500,000,000 was raised by the British government in loans and taxes to prosecute the war. Most of the money raised by taxation came from increases in the customs and excise duties and from the other traditional practices of eighteenth-century Chancellors of the Exchequer – raising levies on a variety of different possessions and commodities. The demands of war were such, however, that in 1798 Pitt found it necessary to introduce a Bill for a tax on incomes; the tax was abolished with the Peace of Amiens, but revived when war recommenced in 1803. Perhaps the phrase 'the tax that beat Napoleon' makes too great a claim, but income tax raised some 9 per cent of the public expenditure during the war years. Public hostility led to its repeal when the wars ended, nevertheless income tax was a new departure in the British government's fiscal policy, it brought paid officials of the government into involvement with the everyday life and activities of a significant percentage of the population; and while the tax was repealed in 1816, the precedent existed when, in 1842, Peel needed to make up a financial deficit and boost economic recovery.[1]

Even though, before 1793, Britain was regularly at war with France it was the usual practice rapidly to run down the army and navy the moment that peace was signed and to seek to build them up, just as rapidly, the moment that war threatened. Military campaigns overseas were fought by the regular regiments of the army and these were, of necessity, much enlarged in time of war. For home defence there were the county militia regiments of England and Wales; these were augmented in 1797 by the supplementary militia and, in the same year, a Scottish militia was formed. Embodied militia regiments were little different from regular regiments, except that they could not be ordered out of the kingdom. Various Volunteer companies began to be formed in 1793 partly in response to fears of French landings but also because of concern about internal disorder. The Volunteers subsequently grew into an enormous auxiliary force for home defence, though quite how effective they would have been against French invaders remains open to question. Several expedients were tried to improve the efficiency of the Volunteers notably when, in 1808, the government encouraged Volunteer companies to transfer, *en bloc*, into the newly-formed, part-time Local Militia. In February 1794, a year after the war had begun, Parliament voted military estimates for 227,000 regular soldiers and embodied militia and 85,000 seamen; fifteen years later, as the struggle moved towards its climax, Britain was supporting 300,000 regulars and embodied militiamen (excluding colonial troops) and 130,000 seamen and marines. There were in addition, at least on paper, 198,000 local militiamen and 189,000 volunteers. The figures for regulars, embodied militiamen, sailors and marines mean that at least 10 per cent of the male population of military age were serving in the permanently embodied armed forces at the height of the war.[2]

The financial and manpower demands hit unevenly across the social spectrum. In his budget speech for 1797 Pitt expressed regret that his new tax on sugar would hit 'the lower classes of the people' especially; he excused the coarser varieties of tea from increased duties, however, as he understood them 'to be the common beverage of the poorer classes'. The following year George Tierney emphasised how the new income tax would have a different impact on people with different sources of income: he instanced the widow who lived on a pension in contrast to the individual whose capital brought an annual income of the same amount by way of interest.[3] The poor and those people at the bottom end of the middle ranks of society who lived on a fixed income such as a pension or an annuity were hard hit by both the increases in taxes and the wartime inflation. In May 1798 a gentlewoman leasing respectable, but modest, accommodation in London lamented that bankruptcy was staring her in the face and she envied the 'snug habitation' of a friend in Cumberland:

> having three years to wear out the lease we do not know how to help ourselves; there are no hopes of parting with [the house], for you would be frightened to see the number of houses that are to be Lett in this Town. I believe if the war continues, and taxes increase, the grass will grow in London streets.[4]

While farming enjoyed a boom in the war years as Britain became a siege economy, farmers were still ready to complain about taxes and escalating costs:

within the last 7 years iron is advanced 1/3, Labourage, Carpenters and poor rates in the same proportion. You may depend upon it my Lord, it is a matter of serious moment to landed gentlemen.[5]

Besides the demands made by central government there were also financial demands made by local government and these, notably the poor rates, increased as a direct result of the war. As the breadwinners of many poor families disappeared into the armed forces so more wives, children and other dependants were forced to seek assistance. On 9 February 1794 William Rowbottom, an Oldham weaver, noted in his diary that twenty men from his town had enlisted, leaving twenty wives and seventy-nine children on parish relief; two months later the number of wives receiving relief had risen to seventy.[6] The situation was similar in seaports where naval recruiting officers and press gangs swept up all the available seamen to put the navy on a war footing. The romantic, tragic image of the seaman being dragged from weeping wife and children by a heartless press gang is much overdrawn; the majority of seamen appear to have been in their early twenties and unmarried, but the impact of naval recruiting on the poor rates in seaports was, nevertheless, dramatic.[7] Besides the payments to be made to the impoverished families of new recruits under the old Poor Law, legislation of December 1792 required that a weekly dole of one day's labour at the local rate be paid to the wife and each lawful child under ten years of an embodied militiaman; this dole also came out of the local rates. Those areas surrounding military installations or bisected by major roads often found themselves saddled with additional burdens as wives and children, who had come to see husband or father off to war, or discharged and disabled servicemen required assistance returning to their parish of settlement. 'Soldiers wives most excite my compassion', declared the Mayor of Huntingdon in March 1813,

especially when travelling with their children, either to their parishes or to visit their husbands. Many of them appear in such distress that there is no resisting – indeed it wod. be inhuman to resist their petitions for relief permits and for relief, altho by relieving them the parochial rates (already too high in this Borough for the relief of its own poor) are very considerably encreased.[8]

Above all the unprecedented demands for soldiers and sailors affected the lower classes of society. The traditional description of the late-eighteenth- and early nineteenth-century soldier is 'the scum of the earth enlisted for drink' or else a gaolbird recruited from prison; the sailor has a rather more wholesome pedigree, being the unfortunate victim of a press gang. As ever with traditional stereotypes these had some originals but they also grossly oversimplify.

Some men in both the army and the navy were recruited from gaols. But the prison population during the revolutionary and Napoleonic period was far too small to have furnished even a small percentage of the soldiers and sailors required; gaol was only just in the process of being accepted as a key secondary punishment and a high proportion of convicted felons continued to be punished in other ways. More men were recruited from among those simply accused, generally of petty theft, and who were given the opportunity by a magistrate of enlisting rather than spending a lengthy period in gaol awaiting trial; this practice also had advantages for the prosecutor who was consequently saved the time and expense of a prosecution. Throughout the eighteenth century men believed that war brought about a decline in crime by removing dangerous young men and sending them overseas to fight. The corollary was, of course, that peace brought an increase in crime as young men, now skilled in the use of weaponry and hardened and brutalised by the experiences of battle and campaigning, returned to rob and assault respectable inhabitants. Such crime statistics as can be constructed for the century reveal a decline in property crimes during wars, and sharp increases with the return of peace; but the equation is certainly not as simple as many contemporaries conceived. War probably siphoned off those young men who might otherwise have been tempted into theft for a variety of reasons – unemployment, low wages, simple excitement, even the desire to finance peer-group leisure activities. The restructuring of different sectors of the economy necessary with the return of peace, the consequent dislocation of the labour market and the aggravation of this problem by the influx of demobilised servicemen, may account for much of that increase in crime noticeable at the end of wars. There is no evidence that crime was necessarily more brutal in the aftermath of wars and, given the surviving evidence, it would probably be impossible to prove that brutalised ex-servicemen played a disproportionate role in the incidence of crime.[9]

It would be difficult to put a figure on the number of men recruited from the magistrates' parlours, the courts and the gaols; it would be equally difficult to put a precise figure on the numbers recruited into the navy by the press gangs since the regulating captains, responsible for recruiting in the major sea ports, often gave pressed men the opportunity of 'volunteering' after they had been pressed; in this way the man was able to collect his bounty money and he might also choose the ship on which he was to serve. Regulating captains also often preferred negotiation with local seamen's leaders rather than confrontation between their gangs and crowds of angry merchant sailors often backed by local inhabitants.[10] High-handed action by a press gang could provoke serious disorder. According to the local magistrates in December 1803 the press gang in Chester, insisting that it was authorised to seize any and every former seaman, began invading homes and recruiting tradesmen, freemen, apprentices and even farm servants on the way to market, most of whom had never been to sea. The last straw came with the seizure of Daniel Jackson, a private in the Royal Chester Volunteers. Jackson was a former sailor, but his comrades resolved to rescue him and, as the deputy mayor pointed out, the Chester Volunteers contained 'above one *fifth* of the males of all ages within this city'. Angry Volunteers broke into the gang's rendezvous house and then marched on to the gaol and liberated Jackson. The only native of Chester in the press gang promptly deserted; and subsequently the Home Secretary, insistent that the ringleaders of the rescue be prosecuted, perceived 'a determination to screen these rioters'.[11] Trouble was especially likely when warship commanders sent their own gangs ashore to pick up men for their crews; the gangs in such instances did not have to worry about continuing to live in the community after their actions. In October 1793 a frigate commander ignored the advice of the local regulating captain and sent a gang ashore in Liverpool – a port which had a tradition of making life difficult for press gangs. During the resulting fracas a midshipman from the frigate killed the master of a merchant ship. The population of Liverpool, unimpeded by the local authorities, turned on the regulating captain and his men and destroyed both recruiting houses in the port.[12] Warships also pressed men from merchant ships on the high seas; while this could not lead to the same kind of disorder as in seaports it did not help Anglo-American relations since many of the men taken from merchant ships claimed American citizenship.

Pressing was not confined to the navy. In the early years of the war crimps provided men for the army, and some employed methods little short of kidnapping. In the summer of 1794 the death of a young man seeking to escape from a crimping house at Charing Cross occasioned the destruction of this house by an angry crowd, and widespread attacks on other recruiting houses in London. More crimp riots followed in

January and July 1795 before the worst excesses appear to have been checked.[13]

But pressure from agents of the law and coercion by press gangs and crimps were not the only means by which the ranks were filled. Some recruiting sergeants were unscrupulous and tricked young men into taking the king's shilling; other recruits seem cheerfully to have got drunk with the recruiters or to have spent their bounty money on getting drunk. The bounty money paid to recruits proved a considerable attraction, especially in times of economic hardship. The metal trades of Birmingham had enjoyed a brisk trade with France which came to an abrupt end with the declaration of war; in February 1794 Samuel Garbett, one of the town's leading businessmen, lamented to Lord Lansdowne:

> The Gentlemen in administration who exalt upon the success of raising soldiers should know that it was the consequence of manufacturers being so much distressed that thousands were thrown out of employ, many in this town have been, and more will be, under the necessity of going into the army for Bread. I know of one instance where a man left every shilling of the Bounty Money in his Wife's cupboard which was the only notice she had of his having left town as a soldier.[14]

Military bounty money provided a significant income to the poor tenant farmers in the Highlands of Scotland during the Revolutionary and Napoleonic Wars, as it had done during earlier conflicts. The poor Highlanders could also find themselves pressured into receiving the bounty as clan chiefs and landlords expected them to volunteer in person, or else send sons to favoured regiments, in return for improved leases, new holdings or simply to avoid eviction.[15] The regular army found the militia a useful source of recruits, especially as embodied militiamen grew accustomed to military life, though pressure might also be exerted to encourage such a transfer. Joseph Mayett of the Royal Buckinghamshire Militia recalled one instance of volunteering for the regulars 'during which time we that did not volunteer was very Sharply disciplined for they Continually marched us about from place to place and made us do all the duty'.[16] Mayett himself had volunteered for the militia shortly before the rupture of the Peace of Amiens. He was a young agricultural labourer and was much attracted by the sight of soldiers and the sound of a military band: 'this was congenial with my Carnal nature and a great opening for Satan to draw me away from all thoughts about religion'.[17] Such attractions, together with the pull of patriotism which was especially strong in the early stages of the Napoleonic War, should not be under-estimated as encouragements to recruitment.

Patriotism, and a desire to preserve the country from Jacobinism of both the French and the British varieties, provided one of the principal incentives for men to join the Volunteer corps; but there were others. The yeomanry cavalry regiments became the pinnacles of county society and many gentlemen probably enrolled as much for this reason as for any other. The poor urban infantry Volunteer may also have volunteered because of patriotism and the splendour of the uniform. It was during the Revolutionary and Napoleonic Wars that military pomp in Britain became an increasingly apparent aspect of patriotism and earlier concerns about a standing army and the soldiery in general began to be nudged into the background. But the poor urban infantry Volunteer may also have found it prudent to 'volunteer' because his employer was the local corps commander, because the pay for his weekly training was a valuable addition to the family income, and/or because in the early years of the wars membership of a Volunteer company was a means of avoiding the militia ballot. In the famine years of 1799 to 1801 many of the Volunteer corps, especially in large urban areas, became distinctly unreliable as the high cost of provisions severely cut their living standards; worse still, some of these corps actively participated in food riots thus exacerbating the fears of many propertied gentlemen.[18]

In 1795 some militia regiments proved unreliable during the famine and participated in food riots. Every county had its own militia regiment recruited by ballot, theoretically of all men aged between 18 and 45 in the county, though in practice there were many exemptions. In peace time two-thirds of a regiment trained for two weeks each year, but little effort had been made to keep the militia either up to strength or adequately trained in the decade between the end of the American War of Independence and the embodiment of the militia shortly before the National Convention's declaration of war. The early years of the war, in consequence, witnessed frantic efforts in training and in filling up the ranks of the militia; the lack of discipline probably contributed to militia involvement in the riots of 1795. A man balloted for his county's regiment could serve in person; alternatively he could pay a fine or, better still, find a substitute to serve in his place – the substitute was the best option because, as long as the substitute was serving in the ranks, the man who had hired him was exempt from the ballot. The supplementary militia, and the Army of Reserve established in 1803, were also recruited by ballot. Loyal or not, many men had no desire to be balloted into any of these corps. The ballot fine or the hiring of a substitute brought considerable financial hardship to many; subscription clubs were set up in many areas to provide the money, or part of the money, necessary for a club member to avoid such military service. Sometimes poor but respectable labourers could rely on their employers or other members of local gentry to provide financial assistance.[19] Hostility to the ballots also manifested itself in riots; the creation of the supplementary militia brought widespread disorder as crowds set out to destroy the lists from which the ballots were to be made or else to prevent the ballot from proceeding.[20] The creation of the Scottish militia, according to one gentleman, led to the country going 'stark mad as if it had been bit by Corsica'. More people were killed by the cavalry in the anti-militia riot in Tranent in August 1797 than died at Peterloo.[21]

Scattered references give glimpses of the way in which the war affected plebeian families. In September 1795 Rowbottom drew a fancy heading 'British Heroeism' in his diary under which he wrote about his neighbours, the Buckly family: James Buckly was in the 93rd Foot bound for the West Indies and of his six sons, two were serving in cavalry regiments, a third was in the navy, while the other three were still too young for war.[22] It was not until 1797 that the Duke of York, as commander-in-chief, ordered commanding officers to list their dead by name, but even after this the chances of a plebeian family receiving notification of a husband or son being killed or wounded, or dying of disease, were slim and depended more upon the report of a man's comrades than any notification from his regiment, his ship, or the state. Some men uprooted themselves to evade the recruiters. Thomas Carter, a tailor, left home to avoid a militia ballot.[23] John Nicol was pressed during the Revolutionary War; on the outbreak of the Napoleonic War he sold his cooper's stock and most of his furniture and left Edinburgh for the countryside – even then he did not rest easy at night.[24] It was reported to the Home Office in the summer of 1803 that there were seamen, avoiding the press gangs by working in the Kingswood colliery near Bristol, sufficient to man a 74 gun battle-ship.[25] Yet the impact of war was not always negative. Some men profited from their time in the services. The regimental schools established by the Duke of York taught some soldiers basic literacy and numeracy, and the more capable were given the opportunity of developing these and administrative skills in the non-commissioned ranks. Perhaps more important, as will be argued below, the demands of war gave some soldiers and sailors a greater awareness of their value

industrialisation
vage.

in society and a feeling that their sacrifice for 'their' country should be reciprocated.

Societies are never static and, as it became embroiled in the Revolutionary and Napoleonic Wars, British society was in the midst of those colossal changes which, in the span of a century, transformed it from being largely rural and agrarian to being largely urban and industrialised. Whether or not the paramountcy of class conflict in history is acknowledged, it is clear that tensions existed between different social groups in eighteenth-century Britain. These tensions were often local in their immediate origin, but they were none the less real for that. The war exacerbated some of these tensions and, in some instances, gave them a national complexion.

The war highlighted the division between old and new capitalist elites. The City of London was the centre of the old commercial elite which clung to the vestiges of mercantilist and imperialist ideologies, which dominated trade with the Indies and which was happy to see French colonies gobbled up. The City, furthermore, had long possessed a large and influential parliamentary lobby. The war fostered pacifist tendencies among some provincial businessmen and merchants; more importantly it fostered ideas of free trade among them and encouraged national organisation among the new elite to influence parliamentary behaviour. The most significant demonstration of the organisational strength of the provincial manufacturing and business interests came with the massive campaign of 1812 directed against the East India Company's monopoly of trade with the orient and against the Orders-in-Council by which the government had responded to Napoleon's declaration of economic warfare with similar declarations of their own; unfortunately, economic warfare against Napoleon's Europe led to American embargoes on British goods and contributed to the causes of the War of 1812. Castlereagh, and his fellow ministers, regretted that the government was 'forced to give way to our manufacturers',[26] but the petitioning campaigns were successful in bringing about both a relaxation of the Orders-in-Council and, subsequently, a revision of the East India Company's charter.

During the 1790s much of the most articulate opposition to the war came from middle-class Dissenters, men who, although wealthy, educated and influential, were debarred from participating in local politics by Tory-Anglican oligarchies, and debarred from national politics, unless they became occasional communicants of the Church of England, by the Test Acts. As the cost of the Revolutionary War mounted these men insisted that the country was spending beyond its means. Pessimistically they pointed to what they believed to be a declining population and, worse still, to a declining economic performance. The census of 1801, Britain's ability to keep fighting and to keep financing coalitions undermined their economic arguments; the unlikelihood of being able to conclude a meaningful and lasting peace with Napoleon undermined their arguments about the continuation of the war. As a result, during the second stage of the conflict, the anti-war arguments shifted to what were perceived as being the social consequences of the war. The anti-war party pointed to a small group of contractors, financiers and placemen who were profiting from the war and their close links with the government, while the mass of the population, in particular the small businessman and the professional man, suffered as a result of the war taxation and inflation. Such ideas contributed to, and fostered, the increasing self-awareness and self-confidence of the provincial middle class and helped to develop both their hostility to the wealth and power of the metropolis and their criticism of the luxury and self-indulgence among wealthy members of the old elite.[27]

But members of the new middle class were not only to be found among critics of the war. Many among the middle class were immensely patriotic, organising and contributing to patriotic funds, establishing and officering Volunteer corps. Such activities may have been in support of the status quo, but they also contributed to middle-class assertiveness, giving those who participated the opportunity to assert parity with, even on occasions superiority to, the established landed elite.[28]

Wartime financial demands on the middle classes were not only made by central government; local poor rates, already increased as a result of war, were increased still more in the famine years of 1795 to 1796 and 1799 to 1801, and in those periods of economic dislocation brought about in the manufacturing districts by the economic warfare and by the American embargo. The Reverend Thomas Malthus published the first edition of his *Essay on the Principle of Population* in 1798, hard on the heels of the first of the great wartime dearths; the second, much larger edition of the *Essay*, appeared in 1803, hard on the heels of the more serious famine. While many of his readers probably contributed liberally to subscriptions for the hungry poor and for temporarily impoverished manufacturing operatives, the messages of the *Essay* − that there were rigid laws of population growth and food supply (emphasised in the first edition) and that the poor could help themselves by greater moral restraint (emphasised in the second edition) − struck a chord with men who felt themselves increasingly impoverished by wartime taxes and soaring poor rates expended, apparently, on those who were bound to fall victim to famine and war, and who did little or nothing to help themselves.

In the same way that wartime events and pressures helped sections of the emerging middle class to identify themselves as a distinct social group with distinct attributes and values, so the war years contributed to similar self-identification among activists within the emerging working class. Wartime demands gave increased industrial muscle to the workforce in certain key industries; and the men were not slow to recognise this. Workers in the royal dockyards provide probably the clearest example. Towards the end of 1793 the ropemakers at Plymouth Dockyard went on strike to save a workmate from the press gang; given the absolute necessity of the dockyards working at full stretch fitting out and repairing warships, the navy could not allow any prolonged interruption of work and the dockyard authorities capitulated to the ropemakers after only three days.[29] By the turn of the century the workforces in the five major yards – Deptford, Woolwich, Chatham, Portsmouth and Plymouth – had combined and were sending delegates to press concessions from the Navy Board; these negotiations between representatives of the workforce and the employers were almost contemporaneous with the passage of the first Combination Act. Ironworkers and miners profited from the demands for their skills. The seamen of the Tyne and Wear who were able to escape the press gangs were also able to push up their pay rates. The shortage of men to bring in the harvest meant that, on occasions, women and soldiers had to be employed; in the spring of 1805 farmers in Northumberland complained of having to offer 15s. or 18s. a week to farm labourers on hiring day, and even then men were refusing employment until they had investigated the market.[30] Many of those who were able to profit in wartime, however, faced wage cuts or under-employment when peace meant a reorganisation of their trade, and a labour market swollen by demobilised servicemen. For some, especially those who organised their workmates, peace meant the sack. The Navy Board grasped the chance offered by the Amiens interlude to get rid of those men who were perceived as being the ringleaders of industrial action (though many had to be reinstated when hostilities resumed). Employers in the coal trade seized the opportunity given by the return of hundreds of seamen in 1815 to cut wages, but to insist on maintaining the skeleton crews accepted by sailors on their colliers in wartime because of the shortage of men; the resulting strike paralysed the east coast during the summer of Waterloo.[31]

Problems created by the war, worsened by the war, or at least believed to have been worsened by the war, provoked mass demonstrations and petitioning among the plebeian classes. In 1795 the London Corresponding Society was able to bring hundreds, perhaps thousands to meetings and demonstrations in the metropolis calling for bread, peace and reform. Mass clandestine meetings assembled in the manufacturing districts at the turn of the century; possibly there was also serious revolutionary intent in some of these meetings, but bread and peace were unquestionably high on the agenda.[32] The successive crises which hit the manufacturing districts during the Napoleonic War also led to mass organisation and petitioning. In Birmingham the workforce joined with the employers in the campaign against the Orders-in-Council; in Lancashire, where the pattern of industrial production was centred on larger units with a greater gulf between employer and employee, the workforce turned to Luddism and linked up with men in Yorkshire and the industrial Midlands who were threatened by the imposition of new work practices.

The war years witnessed a succession of patriotic festivals designed to foster and to cement loyalty to king and constitution; military or naval victories provided the occasion for such celebrations, as did George III's jubilee.[33] Fear of French invasion, coupled with fear of British Jacobinism, was a powerful spur to the organisation of such festivals. It was also a spur to loyalist pamphleteers to urge the unity of all social groups against the common enemy. A key element in the propaganda for home consumption during the 1790s was the insistence that, in his own humble way, the poor Briton had as much to lose as his wealthy, social superior should the French invade or should Jacobin-style revolution occur. When, in 1798, the classical scholar Gilbert Wakefield had the audacity to suggest the opposite, the Attorney General descended on him with the rarely used *ex officio* information which ensured that, even had Wakefield been found innocent on the charge of seditious libel, he would have faced considerable costs.[34] Loyalist propaganda urged the unity of social groups again in the dark days of 1803 to 1805. In August 1803, for example, a correspondent of *The Loyalist* explained that the war:

> is for the defence of everything that is dear to us, there cannot be the least *distinction* of interest – we must *all* conquer, or we must *all* fall together. It is not the cause of the rich and the great alone.... Is not the *cottage* of the peasant as valuable to its owner as the proudest *palace* of the prince is to its more exalted occupier? I know you have not

all of you great fortunes to lose; but you live by the fruits of your labour or the amount of your independent income. Be it which it will, and small as it may be, you live upon it: it keeps you and your family; and I will only ask whether you could live without it?[35]

Others suggested that additional benefits should, or could, accrue to the poor man as a result of his loyal participation in the struggle. William Burdon of Hartford House, Northumberland, for example, advised 'the lower ranks of society' that by:

coming forward to aid, not to defend your richer superiors, they will contract a debt of gratitude which, after the contest is over, they will not fail to repay: by being brought nearer to each other, they will be better acquainted with your wants, your virtues, and your condition; and by thus becoming more familiar the distance between you will be lessened, and they will treat you with more humanity and respect, if you conduct yourselves firmly, honestly, and soberly.[36]

Yet in spite of such propaganda and such promises, as the war continued questions began to be asked by working men about what they were getting out of it; and it was not lost upon them which social group provided the bulk of the soldiers and the sailors, and which social group was first to suffer from trade dislocation. In July 1811 Samuel Whitbread received a letter from one of a committee of textile workers in Bolton which had organised a petition to Parliament for relief; the war, in James Nisbet's analysis, was crippling trade and leading to wage cuts. 'Surely, sir, the wisdom of the legislature can devise some means to help us. We will do our duty, as Loyal, as peaceable subjects, but grant us existence otherwise who shall fight the Battles of our country.' He went on to note that '[m]ost of our youth are serving their country'.[37] The question of what the poor men had fought for in the war was put more stridently after Waterloo and appears significantly in the ballad literature of the period:

Come all you thoughtless young men, a warning take by me
And never leave your happy homes to sail the raging sea
For I have ploughed the raging main this twenty years or more,
But now I'm turned adrift to starve upon my native shore.
When war at first assail'd us I quickly left my trade,
Our country was in danger, I flew to lend my aid.

And in my country's service, long, long fatigues I bore,
But now I'm turned adrift to starve upon my native shore.[38]

Economic and political demonstrations and disorders in the immediate post-war years commonly had a leavening of ex-sailors and ex-soldiers; disillusion and bitterness about the rewards for their efforts doubtless contributed to their involvement.

Of course not every soldier or sailor returning from the wars became bitter and disillusioned and was transformed by such sentiments into a radical or a rioter. The majority probably regarded their war service as an interruption to 'normal' life; their service became something to be cashed in when in need of a job, or when in trouble. A few veterans, certainly a higher proportion than those who returned from any previous conflict, decided to write up their adventures, and printers were prepared to publish them – both of which illustrate a different angle of the growing self-awareness and self-confidence among members of the working classes: the ex-soldiers and ex-sailors who wrote memoirs believed that their stories were worth telling, and the printers recognised that there was a market for the adventures of such humble men. When George Wood published his recollections of the war as a young officer in 1825 he referred to the large number of accounts by ordinary soldiers and declared that one of his principal objects was 'to correct the too general misapprehension, that the sufferings and hardships of war are almost exclusively the lot of the private soldier'.[39]

An influential sociological hypothesis has posited that there is a direct correlation between military participation and economic, social and/or political advancement: the search for support in war brings a corresponding extension of social levelling and political and economic equality.[40] The experience of the Revolutionary and Napoleonic Wars, however, would seem to negate the neat equation of the 'military participation ratio' in both Britain and France. The men who fought the battles, on a completely different scale to previous eighteenth-century conflicts, who kept ships at sea, who made uniforms and munitions, were not noticeably better off as a result of their involvement in the wars.[41] Yet if the participants, as individuals, experienced little in the way of material benefit, the wars did play a significant role in the development of certain social groups in Britain. Both the provincial middle class centred in the new industrial Britain and the emergent working class broadened their confidence and their self-awareness by both their patriotism and as a result of their involvement in campaigns against the war or against aspects of war policies. Some of these campaigns remained local, but significantly others were national; the national campaign against the Orders-in-Council provided a model, as well as some of the key personnel for the national campaign for parliamentary reform launched by the Birmingham Political Union at the end of the 1820s. But while the experience of the wars had contributed to the development of new social groupings it also strengthened the existing ruling elite. The wars had been won without sweeping changes in government or administration (the union with Ireland was the most significant exception here). Wartime governments might take up the demands of the provincial middle classes for economy and for weeding out corruption; but they would not touch any fundamentals in government or constitution and the eventual victory appeared to justify their stance. Success in war boosted the mixture of distrust, fear and pity with which the 'free-born Englishman' of the eighteenth century viewed his continental neighbours. The course of the French Revolution, the elevation of Napoleon, and his final defeat by British-financed coalitions, and by an army commanded by a British general, confirmed the superiority of Britain with its organic constitution. This constitution, eulogised by Burke, now stood triumphant in contrast to the absolutist regimes of both Napoleon and those states so frequently beaten by France, as well as in contrast to the revolutionary attempts to build a new political and social system from scratch.

11. 'Things As They Are': The Literary Response to the French Revolution 1789–1815

IAIN ROBERTSON SCOTT

THINGS As They Are was the original title of the most celebrated English Jacobin novel of the 1790s, *Caleb Williams* (1794) by William Godwin. Godwin exposed the evils of contemporary society and demonstrated how it might be ordered in a more rational fashion, in accordance with man's natural state of freedom and equality. This critical concern for the state of 'things as they are' was a theme which preoccupied all the major literary figures of the revolutionary period.[1] Between the 1790s and the 1810s, however, this initial enthusiasm for rational philosophy and radical change gradually evolved into a greater acceptance of the existing social and political system. In all but a few cases, the influence of Rousseau, Paine and Godwin himself was supplanted by a more conservative philosophy which owed most to the ideas of Edmund Burke.

This essay is concerned with those authors who reached maturity in the 1790s when the debate on the French Revolution was most intense. The worlds of politics and of literature were unusually close during this period. Political commentators such as Godwin and John Thelwall also wrote novels and verse; poets such as William Wordsworth, S.T. Coleridge and Robert Southey wrote political pamphlets and journalism. Even writers such as Jane Austen, who are not normally associated with political disputes, were still influenced by the political arguments of the day. The political thinking of these authors reflected current ideas, but also developed, pragmatically, in response to the great events of the Revolutionary and Napoleonic era. Each writer believed he or she could make a positive contribution to the political and moral education of society.

Contemporary criticism of those poets, such as Wordsworth, Coleridge and Southey, who lost their faith in radical politics, has coloured all subsequent evaluations. In the 1790s they were attacked by government writers on *The Anti-Jacobin* journal for being dangerous revolutionaries and enemies of the country. By the 1810s they were being criticised by Whiggish journals such as the *Edinburgh Review* for betraying radical principles and becoming ministry toadies. These extreme views of their careers were a consequence of the heated, partisan debates of the period, rather than accurate reflections of their political development. In more recent years, critics have argued that there was no sudden shift to conservative views, but a genuine reassessment of their previous convictions in the disillusioned aftermath of the French Revolution. Nevertheless, even in this subtler revision of their political careers, there is still a tendency to accept the general shift between the two polar extremes of Jacobinical youth and Tory middle age.

In fact, it will be argued here that none of the writers ever subscribed to full-blooded French Jacobinism, nor did those who later became conservative ever wholly accept a Tory stance in the 1810s. Three distinct, but interlocking, stages can be discerned in their political development. The high-water mark of the radicalism of these writers was reached between 1789 and 1794 when they subscribed to republican principles, but without showing much enthusiasm for revolutionary methods. After 1795 the authors became disillusioned with France and with rational philosophy. There was a subsequent attempt to find a new philosophical basis for republicanism which took greater account of the practicalities of existing society. Finally, when war resumed in 1803, most of these writers, with the exception of Blake, Godwin and William Hazlitt, began to recognise worth in the British nation state, and in its constitution, which had withstood the despotism of Napoleon and was now the sole beacon of liberty in Europe. Nevertheless, they still found much to criticise in the state's handling of Britain's developing industrial society. The philosophy they developed, in response, was a more liberal, humanitarian type of conservatism than that of the Tory ministry.

In literary terms this ideological journey marks a departure from the rational, neo-classical style which rejected artificial elaboration in favour of natural simplicity and which, in Britain, was associated with the radical writing of the 1790s. The style which then emerged, in so far as it can be satisfactorily categorised, was 'Romanticism' which was associated, initially, with the forces of the counter-revolution. Romanticism marked a turning away from universal values to the private and domestic; it gloried in spontaneity rather than the rationally planned; and, instead of rejecting the past, it stressed the organic nature of man and the traditional society of which he was a part.

I

1789–1794

Many authors reacted to the outbreak of the French Revolution with all the passion and idealism of youth. William Blake welcomed the inauguration of a new age of liberty, equality and fraternity for all of mankind, in his poem *The French Revolution* (1791). He was a fervent supporter of the Revolution and is said to have worn its emblem, the white cockade, in the streets of London. Wordsworth witnessed events at first hand by embarking on a walking tour of France in 1790, and he was deeply impressed with the sense of joy and liberty he encountered everywhere.[2] Years later, in *The Prelude* (1805), he recalled, in famous lines, this sense of exhilaration which he shared with fellow republicans everywhere:

> Bliss was it in that dawn to be alive
> But to be young was very heaven![3]

Robert Southey similarly recollected how 'Old things seemed passing away, and nothing was dreamt of but the regeneration of the human race'.[4] Man's potential for progress now seemed limitless.

In its initial, fairly bloodless phase, the Revolution was in fact welcomed by a wide section of British society for its overthrow of royal absolutism and for its apparent inauguration of a constitutional monarchy on the British model. Enthusiasm for the early Revolution, however, did not necessarily imply a Jacobinical desire to turn the world upside down by extreme or violent methods. In fact the writers' republican sympathies were rooted as much in the pacific English Dissenting tradition as in the rational school of the French *philosophes*.

Nearly all the literary figures under discussion came either from a Dissenting background (including Blake, Godwin, Mary Wollstonecraft and Hazlitt) or mixed in Dissenting circles in the early 1790s (for example, Wordsworth, Coleridge, Maria Edgeworth and Robert Bage). This tradition of Dissent, which dated back to the seventeenth-century republicans and Commonwealthmen, was individualistic, levelling,

critical of government and stressed pacific constitutional change (as
exemplified in the 1689 Revolution Settlement) rather than the need for
armed revolt. William Blake's radical views were derived from his urban
Dissenting background and from the circle of Dissenting intellectuals who
met at the house of the printer, Joseph Johnson. Blake's writings of
1790-4 share in the millenarian vision that the old world was coming
to an end; and poems such as *The Marriage of Heaven and Hell*
(1790-3) and *The Visions of the Daughters of Albion* (1793) are pacifist
works which oppose all symbols of authority. Blake appealed to an ancient
Anglo-Saxon past of freedom and fraternity, rather than to a Rousseauist
state of nature. Men were then unencumbered by the domination of
aristocracies, governments and established religion. While not sharing
Blake's millenarian vision, Godwin, who had once been a Dissenting
minister, also stressed the value of pacific, educational means of change
in *Political Justice* (1793) and in his early novels. These works were
to have a major influence on many other writers.

Although it is still common practice to refer to these writers as 'Jacobin'
they were, in fact, much closer ideologically to the more moderate
Girondin group who were supplanted in power by the Jacobins in 1793.
During his visit to France, Wordsworth mixed in Girondin circles and
The Prelude records his discussions with his Girondin friend, Michel
Beaupuy, who helped to shape Wordsworth's early political
philosophy.[5] Other British writers also mainly identified themselves
with the moderate, middle-class, intellectual wing of radicalism. They
did not participate in popular radical activity nor did they join radical
societies. Like Godwin, they professed deep suspicion of any form of
political association and they all valued their independent positions.

Although these writers shrank from revolutionary methods, they were
undoubtedly republican theorists. They may have approached radicalism
through Dissent, but they were also influenced by the rational philosophy
of the French Enlightenment. The thinking of Rousseau is evident in
Wordsworth's *Descriptive Sketches* (1793), where there is an appeal to an
original, unrestrained state of nature in which each man was equal and
free to exercise his own reason.[6] In this simple state, untrammelled
by the vices of civilised society, rational man would, of necessity, become
more moral and benevolent. This regard for an earlier, innocent state
of man was a feature of the neo-classical cult of primitivism which
particularly interested the radical novelists. In works such as Robert
Bage's *Hermsprong* (1796) and Mrs Inchbald's *Nature and Art* (1794/96),
the current state of urban society was castigated for its hypocritical

language, its empty mannerisms and its social conventions which smothered the true, candid thoughts and feelings still associated with country folk. Wordsworth's 'Preface' to the *Lyrical Ballads* (1800) is a late, but definitive, exposition of this theme.

These writers argued that political power should be based on reason, rather than on money, rank, influence or physical strength, and that this would, of necessity, lead to better government. This emphasis on reason and necessitarian logic informed both the content and the style of contemporary novels. This is perhaps most evident in Holcroft's *Anna St. Ives* (1792), in which radical themes determine the entire structure of the novel so that nothing extraneous to the rational argument is included. The novel is, in fact, a contest between the forces of rational philosophy and the prejudices and vices of artificial society. For these writers there was no such thing as original sin; merely bad habits or errors produced by adverse social circumstances which repressed or distorted man's rational faculties. If people were educated to obey their reason, rather than their passions, evil would wither away. This concept of error explains why all the literary figures of the 1790s were so interested in crime and punishment. Godwin's novel, *Caleb Williams*, demonstrated how conventional forms of punishment were pointless because crimes were the result of repressive social circumstances and, until the state itself was reformed, crime would still persist.

This appeal to reason led many authors to claim rights for men which were universal, inalienable and individual. The two abstract rights which they stressed most were liberty and equality. Godwin was initially disposed against any type of formal government because of its tendency to oppress individual liberties, but most of the writers argued that government was necessary to protect and promote the freedoms of the citizen. In his *Letter to the Bishop of Llandaff* (1793), Wordsworth followed Paineite thinking in praising liberty as an individual right, unrestrained except by rational laws which had been approved by the rest of society under a democratic constitution. Blake, however, was much more pessimistic than other writers about the possibility of man ever being able to break free of the physical and spiritual prisons imposed by society. The tragedy which Blake perceived was that man had largely connived at his own imprisonment. He believed that even the French Revolution, which had initially renounced oppression, had become transformed, by 1794, into an increasingly tyrannical struggle for power. People still clung fearfully to the old despotic forms and accepted authoritarianism as a necessary price for security. In *The Book of Urizen*

(1794), the figure of Urizen represents a false, repressive god whom the people worshipped rather than God Himself. The establishment of church and state merely perpetuated Urizen's rule. Blake therefore pleaded for a new, clearer vision which would penetrate this narrow, fearful view of life and its falsely comforting certainties. Only then could a more liberal, godly society be formed and the corruptions of the past be swept away.

Although many writers recognised the basic equality of all men in the sight of God and nature, they also acknowledged ineradicable differences between men, in respect of intelligence, strength and talent. These would always prevent an absolute levelling of society. Like most contemporary radicals, these writers wished only to ensure a fairer distribution of society's rewards and material comforts, apportioned according to merit. An exception was Coleridge who, along with Southey, planned to set up an ideal community or 'pantisocracy', where all land and wealth would be communally owned. Coleridge argued that communal ownership was the only practical basis for establishing a truly egalitarian system. In advocating this, he challenged the traditional defence of private property which even Paine supported. After the scheme had been abandoned, Coleridge continued to argue that there had to be a prior equalisation in the material condition of the people before they could be guaranteed equal rights in any meaningful sense.[7]

The egalitarian ideals of these writers conditioned their views on the upper classes and the common people. In radical literature the aristocracy were invariably portrayed as parasitic, dissipated tyrants whose inordinate power and wealth rested on hereditary property rights rather than on any real moral worth or usefulness. Wordsworth argued that their unearned luxury upset all sense of moral value and undermined the work ethic of the rest of the people.[8] Coleridge attacked all forms of materialism in every class and, like Burns, he argued that the hallmark of a great man was his deeds and not his title or riches.[9] The novelist Robert Bage attacked the aristocracy's political and judicial influence, and their irresponsible attitude to their tenants in *Man As He Is*. Although few of the writers wished to level society, they did advocate a more meritocratic system, less differentiation between classes and a more caring, responsible society.

The section of society with which these authors were most in sympathy was the common people. The literature of the period showed an unprecedented concern for the political and economic condition of the people as worthy citizens in their own right and not merely as objects of upper-class benevolence. Poets such as Wordsworth and Burns found, in country folk, a simpler, innately moral existence which convinced them that, when man was free to live a natural life, he could attain a more perfect state of society. Common people were no longer regarded as marginalised figures but, by being closer to nature, they were nearer to those universal moral truths from which the rest of society might benefit; Wordsworth found in them the true aristrocracy.[10]

These writers translated their radical views on society into political and constitutional terms in a variety of ways. The most extreme plan was Coleridge's and Southey's scheme to set up a pantisocracy in America where a small band of unmarried men and women would enjoy religious toleration, a communal sharing of all tasks and an equal say in their own government. This plan would have subverted all the traditional institutions and principles of the existing British constitution, but, by 1795, the scheme had fallen apart through lack of finance and sufficiently enthusiastic volunteers. Thereafter, Coleridge and Southey turned to the more conventional democratic reforms favoured by the other writers. These authors regarded all monarchical systems of government as greater or lesser species of tyranny and they therefore wished to create a republican state. None the less, their sympathy for the common man did not necessarily imply that they were willing to accord the poor full political rights at once. Even more extreme radicals, such as John Thelwall, recognised the need for the uneducated lower orders to be guided by the superior rationality of the higher classes, until they were sufficiently informed to exercise responsible, independent political judgement. Wordsworth, in his *Letter to the Bishop of Llandaff*, went further than most in arguing that the people could be entrusted to vote, but he added that only the small landed proprietors had the experience to govern responsibly. Many writers also attacked the corruption prevalent in the existing system. They believed that only a republican system, fully accountable to the people and based on merit, would be free of this corruption.

Although most of these authors envisaged the eventual granting of adult male suffrage, few, not excluding Mary Wollstonecraft, were willing to grant female suffrage because women were regarded as dependent creatures incapable of exercising independent judgement. None the less the writers of the 1790s, a significant proportion of whom were women, argued that it was oppressive circumstances, rather than intrinsic flaws, which rendered women weak and dependent. In poems on Joan of Arc and Charlotte Corday, Robert Southey demonstrated how women could display spirit, intelligence and determination in equal proportion to men. Mary Wollstonecraft, in her novels and in her *Vindication of the Rights of Women* (1792), argued that women should be granted more equal rights as rational human beings and she questioned the need for the repressive bond of marriage. Elizabeth Inchbald, in *A Simple Story*, showed how important education could be in raising women's status in society. These women writers were ideally placed to highlight the injustices of all oppressed people, not just of their own sex. Their oppressed state, however, rendered them powerless to alter this condition in any direct way. Fiction writing thus became a potent tool for revising current prejudices and awakening other women to the injustice of their social position. For women, literature was perhaps their only practical means of political expression and influence.

Between 1789 and 1794 radical literary figures responded enthusiastically to the French Revolution and its republican ideals, but they cannot be described as Jacobins. They were intellectual, Dissenting republicans of the middling orders of society who wished to raise the common people to their natural, inalienable rights, but who preferred non-violent methods of reforming the political system. Their own poems and novels were designed, in part, to educate society and so hasten the day of change.

II

1795–1802

The year 1794 attained the high-water mark of literary radicalism. In the seven years which followed, the faith of many writers in republicanism remained firm, but there were significant changes in their rationalist argument against the state of 'things as they are'. Two factors were instrumental in effecting these changes.

First, the climate of political opinion in Britain turned decisively against the Revolution when war was declared in 1793. The writers now found themselves rejected by the common people themselves, in whom they had placed such trust and hope. It became clear that the faith of these authors in the rationality of man had been too sanguine and that the people were more fickle than they had realised. In the fervid counter-revolutionary atmosphere of 1794 many writers were frightened into political silence.[11] They were also attacked by the popular anti-Jacobin circle of writers who branded even the most moderate reformers, such as Charles Lamb, as Jacobinical enemies of the state. In Canning's celebrated poem, *The New Morality* (1798), he satirised the radicals' misguided faith in the perfectibility of man. Robert Bisset's *Douglas, or the Highlander* (1800) attacked Fox and Sheridan and all those 'who would annihilate government, order, property and morals'.[12] These and other such anti-Jacobin fictions are important because they contained truths which impelled more radical writers to re-examine, more critically, their own rational philosophy. As will be seen, elements of this counter-revolutionary critique were to be absorbed into their political thinking in the later 1790s.

This process of re-evaluation was quickened by a second, more important factor – the writers' own disillusionment with the aggressive and despotic course of the French Revolution. The declaration of war presented the authors with the dilemma of whether to remain faithful to republican principles, which were now associated with their country's enemy, or follow their patriotic feelings and end their support of France. Out of this dilemma was born a less rational, more pragmatic, political philosophy; one which sought to reconcile republican ideals with the more complex realities of the everyday world, which they now perceived. At first most of the writers argued that France had been forced into a defensive war by her aggressive neighbours. Coleridge likened her to an ox which had been maddened and had burst from its own fields to rampage across the countryside.[13] Wordsworth argued that since war set man against man it could never be a force for universal, libertarian and fraternal principles.[14] Blake, already sickened by the September Massacres, wrote poems such as *America*, *Europe* and *The Book of Thel* which had strongly pacifist themes. He profoundly regretted that the French Revolution, which had promised to enlighten the world, had disintegrated into another European war. After 1795, Blake turned away from practical politics into a much more private, visionary world, less accessible to the general public. Robert Burns died in 1796, but poems such as *Does Haughty Gaul Invasion Threat?* (1795) show that he had lost faith in France and now supported Britain in the war. He believed that although democratic reforms were still required, they could only be effectively accomplished by Britain herself. Most other writers, however, did not rally to Britain's side, but tended to regard both sides as deeply flawed. The French invasion of free, republican Switzerland in 1798 offered the final proof that France could no longer be trusted as the guardian of libertarian principles. Thereafter, only a few writers, such as Godwin, Coleridge and William Hazlitt, continued to believe that France might yet regain her democratic ideals under new leadership.

As a result of these wartime experiences, writers began to investigate why democratic policies had not established a firmer hold on the minds of the French people, but had been supplanted by violence and war. They searched for ways in which republicanism could be established more securely. Instead of basing their political beliefs on the abstract appeal to man's unfettered rational faculties, which had meant little to ordinary people, these writers now appealed to the whole of man's nature; to his feelings, domestic attachments, habits and traditions, as well as to his reason. This was the start of a more Romantic, counter-revolutionary outlook. Democratic change was now to be effected more slowly, not in direct opposition to 'things as they are', but using the existing social state as the context, or home, from which republicanism could grow.

William Blake had always rejected abstract rational systematisation. For him, rationalism was not the end of all thought, but rather its beginning. In *The First Book of Urizen*, he argued that there had to be a revitalisation of the heart, because only then could man use his reason imaginatively and creatively. After 1794, even William Godwin, himself, recognised that he had not sufficiently emphasised the importance of feeling, domestic affections and civic virtue. In *St Leon* (1799) and *Fleetwood, or the New Man of Feeling* (1805), Godwin acknowledged that the appeal to individual, rational rights merely created a selfish society, which, far from subduing man's darker passions, actually unleashed them without any social restraints, as the Reign of Terror had proved. In Holcroft's *Hugh Trevor* (1794-7), the necessitarian logic of *Anna St. Ives* was now jettisoned for a more picaresque form which acknowledged that life did not always run on rational lines, but was much more complex and variable than had previously been supposed. The very act of writing narrative fiction forced Godwin, Holcroft and other authors to consider the practicality of their political theories for the characters they created. This modification of abstract ideology to accord with everyday life was to be one of the major contributions made to political debate by the Romantic writers.

The most original and complex critique of rational philosophy was made by Wordsworth and Coleridge. They renounced their appeal to a Rousseauist state of nature and began to accept the Burkean idea that, for most people, the traditional state of society, with all its customs, institutions and moral duties, was in fact the only 'natural' state. In his *Essay on Morals* (1798), Wordsworth stressed the need for an appeal to habitual feelings and moral responsibility and not merely to individual reason. Thus, when Wordsworth appealed to nature in the *Lyrical Ballads*

(1798 and 1800), he meant a force which not only enlivened man's reason, but also his feelings and moral sense. In *Tintern Abbey* (1798) he described how he found in nature, the 'anchor of my purest thoughts' and the 'soul/Of all my moral being'.[15] This was not the unrestrained Rousseauist state of nature, but a power which chastened and subdued, and which led him to consider other people, and not just the selfish rights of the individual. This was a dutiful, rather than a licentious, state of nature. These feelings were most readily aroused in the countryside where communion with nature was an habitual source of benevolence and inspiration. In this simple, traditional society was to be found the best model for society as a whole. Although Wordsworth still advocated a democratic system of government, he now envisaged it growing from, and embodying, the customs and moral values of rural life.[16]

At first it would seem that this identification of Burkean themes in the *Lyrical Ballads* is contradicted by Wordsworth's own 'Preface' to the 1800 edition, which is often cited as evidence of his continued radicalism. In fact, the 'Preface' contains both radical and conservative elements which are typical of this transitional period in political thought. Wordsworth was being radical in placing ordinary people at the centre of his poetic art and in trying to use their unaffected speech to convey the moral truths he found in common rustic life. Moreover, publishing the 'Preface' in 1800, at the height of counter-revolutionary opinion and directed at a mass readership, was also a radical act. Nevertheless, he stressed that the simple language of the people arose 'out of repeated experience and regular feelings';[17] it had habitual roots, and drew its truth and strength from stable customs and domestic affections. In the 'Preface', as in the poems themselves, Wordsworth was appealing to man as an habitual, moral, social being. He no longer based his politics on a universal state of man, but on man living in a particular, traditional, rural community with time-honoured values: specifically the English countryside of his own Lake District.

In the later 1790s Coleridge also based his politics on an appeal to the whole of man's nature, and not merely his reason: 'We approve not of that proud philosophy, which addressed itself to men as to beings of pure intellect, and would destroy their passions and their affections. It is unsuited to our nature, and must therefore be false and dangerous.'[18] Unlike Wordsworth, however, Coleridge did not appeal to nature itself, but to God who had created nature and whose habitual, moral laws had to inform all social relationships and political systems. This moral order could not be violated with impunity as is shown in *The Rime of the Ancient*

Mariner (1798), when the albatross, 'a Christian soul'[19] is shot by the mariner. This disruptive act of the individual, self-governing will brings retribution, and salvation is only to be found in the Kirk where all together pray. Thus, Coleridge warned of the consequences of French rationalist teaching which seemed to elevate the individual will and reason above both moral responsibilities and the guidance of state religion. Whereas Wordsworth's politics were based on an appeal to the natural state of man in rural society, Coleridge appealed to man's natural state as part of a godly community to be found in towns and countryside.

As the radical authors began to shift the basis of their political beliefs away from a Rousseauist state of nature to the 'natural' state of social man, there was a corresponding change in their interpretation of the rights which people might expect. Instead of personal, inalienable rights, there was a much greater stress on rights which had been limited by moral duties. Instead of the absolute, abstract freedoms, which had led to licence and anarchy in France, there was an emphasis on moral rights, pragmatically conditioned by social circumstance. The violent course of the Revolution had proved that men were infinitely fallible and were not all equally capable of rational perfection.

In the verse of Blake and the Lake poets, and in the later novels of Holcroft and Godwin, the early optimistic, visionary faith in the perfectibility of man began to diminish. All the authors showed a much greater awareness of the practical obstacles to reform and of the need for the common people to be educated before they could be expected to act responsibly. Nevertheless the lower orders were still at the centre of the writers' concerns. Southey's poems, such as *The Pauper's Funeral*, *The Soldier's Wife* and his *Botany Bay Eclogues*, sympathetically portray the poverty and suffering of the ordinary people who are the victims of circumstances beyond their control. In all the writers, moreover, there is the sense of poverty and oppression being more intractable than had previously been supposed. Although they still wished to see differentials narrowed, in poems such as Wordsworth's *The Female Vagrant* (1798), the essential spiritual equality of all men is more passively regarded as some consolation for their present lack of material equality. Generally, the writers now recognised that the ordinary people's progress to a more equal social and political role in the community would be long and faltering.

Between 1795 and 1802 many writers still supported the idea of a democratic state, but there was a much greater awareness that significant changes would have to be effected in the minds and hearts of the people before this could be established. A new republican system would have to develop gradually from the existing state of society so that it would be pragmatically attuned to the people's traditional habits, feelings and attachments. The rights which it guaranteed could not be individual or absolute, but must be social and moral. The whole basis of their political philosophy now rested on an appeal to the state of social man, rather than on rational man. Nevertheless, this attempt to combine republican ends with more conservative means necessarily involved accepting some of the values associated with the existing system, which were antithetical to democracy itself. The tension between these contradictory forces was to be heightened by the events of the Napoleonic era that caused these writers to choose between a predominantly radical or conservative approach to politics.

III

1803–1815

During the Napoleonic era most of the writers (with the exceptions of Godwin, Blake and Hazlitt) abandoned their attempts to find a more stable basis, or home, for their republican beliefs, and instead embraced the security of home itself – the constitution of their own nation state. None the less, while Burkean philosophy became ever more pertinent, none of the writers merely accepted the status quo; they retained some of their former humanitarian, popular, concerns in a philosophy which attempted to blend liberal instincts with Tory sentiments.

The political sympathies of the poets, Wordsworth, Coleridge and Southey, changed most during this period, and the actions of Napoleon were important in promoting this change. These three writers had hoped that peace would provide the stable conditions in which the democratic ideals of the early Revolution could grow again more securely. During the Peace of Amiens, even Blake believed that France and Britain could now grow together as one peaceful, libertarian whole.[20] These high hopes were crushed by the conduct of Napoleon who, far from restoring more democratic government as Coleridge had expected, merely used the Peace to regroup his forces for even more ambitious plans of European domination. The independence of Switzerland was again subverted, a French army remained in the Netherlands, and designs were made on Egypt, Syria, the Greek Islands and Malta. By 1803, the Lake poets were convinced that Britain was now justified in renewing the war. When Napoleon was crowned Emperor in 1804, it merely confirmed that France was now governed by a despot worse than those of the ancien regime. As the course of the Revolution came full circle, Wordsworth described it as 'a dog/Returning to his vomit'.[21] The absolute tyranny of Napoleon, and the idolatry of the French people, seemed to indicate that not only was France beyond redemption, but that republicanism itself was innately flawed. No longer could the authors blame adverse wartime circumstances for the crushing of republican instincts. Even in peace, republicanism had failed to withstand the forces of despotism. The writers now looked to Britain for a more dependable constitutional system which had held firm for centuries against the forces of both tyranny and anarchy.

Napoleon was the outstanding political figure of the age and his character had a peculiar fascination for creative writers. His actions helped them determine the moral nature of the war. Once Coleridge's initial admiration had passed, he became convinced that Napoleon was not just a despotic ruler, but Evil Incarnate; the universal enemy of civilisation, freedom and moral values. In his articles for *The Courier* he argued that Napoleon actively promoted evil like the Devil himself.[22] Similarly, Southey wrote in *The Curse of Kehama* (1810) about an ambitious ruler who sought dominion not only on earth, but also in Heaven and Hell. Neither writer, however, wished to suggest that Napoleon was invincible and so, in Southey's poem, Kehama's pretensions to superhuman powers end in failure as he becomes the slave, rather than the lord, of evil. This view of Napoleon, as a demonic force, polarised the writers' concept of the war as a conflict between absolute evil and absolute good. In this scenario, Britain was now clothed in the mantle of virtue: she had become the instrument of God on earth.

Britain was not suddenly transformed into a moral force after 1803 because she now opposed a tyrannical foe. Although Wordsworth, Coleridge and Southey supported Britain in the war, they did not claim that she had become a consciously positive force for good until she joined in the Portuguese and Spanish campaign for freedom after 1808. Even then, all three writers were alarmed by the Convention of Cintra which seemed a betrayal of Portuguese interests in favour of the French. Robert Southey, in particular, remained highly critical of the government's policies until 1810.[23] None the less, the three poets believed that the war against Napoleon did eventually transform Britain into a nation truly committed to spreading liberty and morality throughout Europe.

Coleridge concluded that the war had its golden side since 'as the war tended to moralise the Nation, so did the Nation succeed finally in moralising the War'.[24] The conflict had become a moral crusade led by Britain. The Whigs and radicals who continued to call for a peace treaty were regarded as the enemies of the Christian spirit of the British nation and its constitution. The writers' identification with the government's position was reinforced by the upsurge in radical activity in the 1810s. Southey was to describe the English army as 'the single plank between us and the red sea of an English Jacquerie'.[25] The views of the authors had finally become polarised. The tensions in their political ideology between the philosophy of idealism and the experience of practical reality, between libertarianism and patriotism, had been resolved. On the one side stood the forces of evil – Napoleon, the Whigs, radical reform and republicanism itself – on the other stood the forces of morality – the Tory government, the existing national constitution and the established church.

Not all the writers changed their political allegiances after 1803. The conduct of Napoleon sustained, rather than challenged, the radical beliefs of William Hazlitt. Hazlitt had been too young to be directly influenced by the Revolution itself, but he admired its libertarian, egalitarian spirit. In *An Essay on the Principles of Human Action* (1805) and, more extensively, in his *Life of Napoleon* (1828), Hazlitt revealed his continued faith in radical politics. He portrayed Napoleon as a great, if occasionally flawed, genius whose finer ideals had been crushed by the combined weight of lesser enemies. Although Hazlitt had never subscribed to the strict systematisation and rationalism of the early radical writers, he retained his liberal, reforming outlook during the war years. He realised that the French had introduced change too rapidly and irresponsibly, but he regarded this as a failure of application rather than an intrinsic flaw in republicanism itself. Thus, like the Lake poets prior to 1802, Hazlitt continued to support gradual democratic reform, learning from the experience, rather than rejecting it altogether.[26]

William Blake also retained his radical convictions throughout the war years, but not because of any admiration for Napoleon. In his prophetic books, *Milton* (1804–8) and *Jerusalem* (1804–20) he still revered the early French Revolution, but as a vision or a symbol of the struggle against oppression, rather than as an event to be emulated. Blake now placed his faith in more inward, spiritual means of change, rather than direct political reform. He still believed, however, that society was fundamentally divided between rich and poor, and that there had to be a more Christian sharing of the produce and riches of the kingdom.[27] Blake argued that if the poor sometimes appeared a sinister mob, this was only because the state denied them their share of its benefits, and oppressed them. Society thwarted man's capacity for good and, although one could never wholly disengage from society, man had to extract what was best from it to create a freer self. Man, rather than society, had to become the master. The spiritual dedication which Blake now advocated was based on the visions of the Biblical prophets and of Jesus, who found true freedom in the inner condition of man, in a state of retreat from contemporary society. Blake's later writings were framed in a much more obscure, millenarian style which precluded the more popular, and genuinely radical, appeal of his earlier work.

Whereas Hazlitt, Blake and also Godwin, still hoped to reform society and government, the other major writers turned to a more conservative defence of the existing state and constitution. The Burkean elements, which were already inherent in much of their thinking before 1802, now became dominant. Instead of promoting the idea of political change, Wordsworth, Coleridge and Southey appealed to pragmatism and tradition. The British constitution, unlike French republicanism, had stood the test of time and so its laws and institutions had a prescriptive right to survive. The habitual feelings and domestic affections of the people were not now regarded as a basis from which republicanism could grow, but were recognised as the very core of the constitution and the source of its constancy. Republicanism had proved to be a short-lived disruptive system because it rejected national traditions and thereby destroyed the moral values which linked one generation with the next. Wordsworth argued that there had to be, 'an humble reliance on the wisdom of our Forefathers, and a sedate yielding to the pressure of existing things'.[28] Coleridge advocated a reliance, not merely on national traditions, but on the ever-constant moral truths to be found in the Bible, which were to be discovered in all laws and institutions which had survived the test of experience.

The constitutional system which these writers now supported was that based on the Revolution Settlement of 1689, which Burke argued had merely recovered and confirmed the more ancient principles of the nation, against the despotic designs of James II. Like Burke, they regarded the Revolution Settlement as an established framework, perfectly suited to British society and requiring only a few minor adjustments when changing circumstance demanded them. The writers defended the mixed character of the constitution and believed that its three balanced elements of monarchy, aristocracy and democracy ensured that the views of all the people were taken into account, even if not everyone was actually represented. The system of influence and patronage, which the writers had once condemned, was now applauded as a means of oiling the machinery of the state and ensuring that there was stable, responsible government. When radicalism revived in the 1810s, the writers increasingly regarded the existing constitution of church and state as the only firm rock in a sea of troubles. They now argued that the only rights which could be meaningfully and safely enjoyed were civil rights, such as the right to possess property, which were limited by the nation's laws.

Within this more conservative political outlook, the attitudes of Wordsworth, Coleridge and Southey towards the social classes also began to change. They now perceived more flaws in ordinary, uneducated people. Wordsworth and Coleridge argued that popular feelings could be relied upon only when they were channelled into a moral cause by participation in some great national event, like the war.[29] They still believed that each class was entitled to a comfortable, happy life, but only within the bounds of their existing class. The time-honoured, expedient differentiations between the social orders had to be respected. Any attempt to raise the lower classes out of their useful role would only disrupt the social fabric of the nation. While not losing their concern for the social welfare of the poor, the whole emphasis of their political philosophy shifted towards the middle and upper classes, who had a greater material stake in the nation and were, therefore, its natural rulers. Coleridge greatly admired the middle classes and believed that their contribution to commerce was 'a principal source of Civilisation'.[30] Wordsworth revered the small tenant farmers, but increasingly he also mixed in aristocratic circles. He believed that these great families were a repository for the accumulated wisdom of the past. Byron subsequently attacked him as an apostate in *Don Juan*, noting, 'the converted Jacobin having long subsided into the clownish sycophant of the worst prejudices of the aristocracy'.[31] None the less, these writers always stressed that, in return for their privileges, the aristocracy also had to respect the community of interest which linked all of society and which placed upon them social duties to perform. They only held power in trusteeship for the rest of the nation. Wordsworth, Coleridge, and Southey all admired the upper classes, but they also recognised that they neglected those social responsibilities that sustained the interdependent fabric of the state. In pursuing this idea, these authors departed from an unquestioning Tory support of the status quo. In the *Lay Sermons* (1816–17), Coleridge argued that in the 1810s the upper classes had become infected by the selfish materialism of the new industrial, capitalist age, and were beginning to forget their traditional duties. Even in the works of the more conservative Jane Austen there is apprehension over the behaviour of the gentry class and their neglect of social responsibilities. Like Wordsworth, she had a deep reverence for the agrarian communities and she always upheld the centrality of the family and the importance of its domestic affections. Although she barely mentions the great events of her time, her novels are deeply imbued with conservative political thinking.[32]

It is clear that those authors who adopted a more conservative philosophy after 1803 did not adopt an uncritical viewpoint. By strengthening, rather than destroying the existing constitution, they hoped to help the people. There were two areas in which Wordsworth, Coleridge and Southey in particular, felt the current political system was not usefully serving the people as it should. First, there had to be a greater concern for the welfare of the people and, since the upper classes were neglectful of their duties, state intervention was necessary to reform social conditions. Second, these authors advocated the intellectual and moral education of all the people in order to counteract the moral laxity of the time and mitigate the spiritually deadening effect of the new factory system. The result of this thinking was a new humanitarian brand of conservatism which went beyond the more limited Burkean conception of the state as the preserver of the nation's independence and the upholder of law and order.

In the 1810s, most conservative writers blamed the improvidence and vice of the poor themselves for their distress. In contrast, Wordsworth, Coleridge and Southey, who wrote most extensively on the problem, were convinced that much of the distress and the low moral standards emanated from the new economic system established on the principles of Adam Smith. In the pursuit of wealth, rather than welfare, employers had set up factories which used workers as anonymous parts of a great industrial machine. Southey's *Letters from England* (1807), Wordsworth's *The Excursion* (1814) and Coleridge's *Lay Sermons* (1816–17), all described how factory toil imperilled the health of the workers, how traditional local attachments were lost and how the people's moral spirit was broken. The machines themselves were not evil, but instead of serving the people, they had been used only for the profit of a few irresponsible employers. Wordsworth wanted the new industries to be curtailed as much as possible, so that man could revert to his former state, as part of an interlinked rural community. Southey wanted factory conditions improved, especially for children, and favoured a return to small farming communities. Public works and emigration schemes were to ease the problem of unemployment and poverty. Although both these writers had a genuine desire to help the poor, they also advocated reform so that the people would become more satisfied with the existing state. As Southey said, 'I wish for reform, because I cannot but see that all things are tending towards revolution, and nothing but reform can by any possibility prevent it.'[33]

Coleridge held a more organic vision of industrial change and its relationship to the state. He accepted the new industrial world as an indisputable part of natural society and did not wish to see any curtailment of its activity. He advocated factory reforms to improve conditions and was employed in 1818 by Sir Robert Peel to write pamphlets in support of his Factory Bill. Coleridge believed that, if industrial practice was reformed by the state, not only would the people benefit, but the whole economy would prosper for having a willing workforce: 'I feel assured that the Spirit of Commerce is itself capable of being at once counteracted and enlightened by the Spirit of the State, to the advantage of both.'[34] Thus, Coleridge had a wider, organic vision of the future which envisaged social and industrial change being embraced by the state, so enlarging the role of government. Change was not to be retarded, or reluctantly conceded, as in the more Burkean attitude of Southey and Wordsworth, but it was to be welcomed as a condition of life itself. Coleridge was not interested in preserving the social structures of the past so much as adapting their constant Christian values to changing circumstance.

These conservative authors argued that educational provision had also been neglected by the existing political system. They no longer favoured the rationalist educational schemes of their youth but, instead, argued for a national system which not only instructed the people intellectually, but also taught them respect for the traditions, institutions and moral values of their society. Although their aims were conservative, they were still more progressive than those of most Tories who feared that any extension of education would merely lead to frustration and popular unrest. Wordsworth, Coleridge and Southey favoured the 'Madras' system of Andrew Bell which was grounded in the teaching of the Church of England. Since they now believed the established church to be a vital bulwark of the constitution, educational provision, based on its principles, would not only disseminate moral values, but would also bind people more closely to the nation state and distance them from the revolutionary beliefs associated with Dissent. Southey's pamphlet, *The Origin, Nature and Object of the New System of Education* (1812), and Book IX of Wordsworth's *The Excursion* both argued that it was the parental duty of the state to set up Bell's system on a national scale.

Coleridge developed these educational theories in a more radical way. He argued that the upper classes had become so selfish that they themselves needed to be re-educated in moral values. In *The Statesman's Manual* (1816), he recommended the formation of a 'clerisy' composed of the most learned people in each profession who would initiate the moral education of their peers. Thereafter Bell's scheme could be effectively introduced for the rest of society. Although Coleridge did not wish to see the lower orders raised out of their class, he did believe that, through education, they would inevitably gain a more important, responsible role in the state. The body politic, like the human body, was a living entity composed of distinct but interdependent organs, each with different levels of importance. Education would enable the lower orders, as a class, to grow in stature within this political and social organism. Coleridge looked forward to the day when education 'will render it impossible for him, when a Man, to be treated or governed as a child'.[35] Coleridge's much more dynamic idea of the state, as a continually changing organism, meant that his conservative philosophy was not just humanitarian, but thoroughly liberalised and far ahead of Tory thinking.

It is clear, therefore, that those authors who embraced conservative ideas after 1803 did not merely accept the state of things as they are. In advocating state intervention, social welfare and national education, they retained some of the liberal instincts and popular concerns which were a hallmark of the preceding decade. Undoubtedly they had travelled far from their early radical position, as can be seen in the extreme discomfiture of Southey when his youthful radical play, *Wat Tyler*, was printed in 1817 when he was Poet Laureate. Despite the charges of apostasy which were heaped on these writers by the younger Romantic generation of Byron and Shelley, none of them was an absolute convert to Tory philosophy. Their ideological position was more subtle and sophisticated. Robert Browning later referred to Wordsworth as 'the lost leader'[36] who had betrayed his radical principles, but perhaps a more appropriate image was employed by the traveller, Louis Simond, who visited Southey in 1810 and described his host's political stance thus: 'When the metamorphosis takes place, it happens frequently that the new insect, fresh out of his old skin, drags still some fragments of it after him, – just enough to indicate what he was before.'[37] Even this does scant justice to the original organic synthesis of Coleridge's liberal-conservative philosophy which had such a seminal influence on British political theory. After 1820 it was perhaps the more humanitarian brand of conservatism of these writers which was to have a greater impact on Victorian politics than the modified radicalism which Hazlitt, Blake and Godwin exemplified.

All the poets and novelists of the Revolutionary and Napoleonic era had been involved in national political issues to an unprecedented degree and had responded in ways which were original, imaginative and compassionate. They sustained the debate on political ideas into a new century of change and reflected its differing problems. They probably addressed a wider popular readership than political theorists, and the political philosophy which emerged was less abstract and more pragmatic, reflecting their literary interest in the everyday life and thought of the people. Thus, their political work is important in its own right and it presents, perhaps, the best means for understanding how the radical movement in Britain came to terms with the death of revolutionary idealism. In their varying, distinctive ways these writers attempted to rescue what they considered to be the most valuable liberal principles of the 1790s and to ensure that they would grow within, rather than confront, the state of 'things as they are'.

List of Abbreviations

Add.MSS	Additional Manuscripts
BL	British Library
CRO	County Record Office
EHR	*English Historical Review*
EcHR	*Economic History Review*
FO	Foreign Office Papers
HJ	*Historical Journal*
HMC	Historical Manuscripts Commission Reports
HO	Home Office Papers
IHS	*Irish Historical Studies*
Internat.Rev.Soc.Hist	*International Review of Social History*
ISPO	Irish State Papers Office
JBS	*Journal of British Studies*
JMH	*Journal of Modern History*
Jn.Roy.Soc.Antiq.Ire	*Journal of the Royal Society of Antiquaries of Ireland*
North Hist	*Northern History*
P & P	*Past & Present*
Parl Hist	William Cobbett's *Parliamentary History of England*
PRO	Public Record Office
PRONI	Public Record Office of Northern Ireland
SCH	*Studies in Church History*
SHR	*Scottish Historical Review*
Soc Hist	*Social History*

Bibliography

The place of publication of books is London, except where otherwise stated or for the publications of learned societies.

1. PITT AND THE 'TORY' REACTION TO THE FRENCH REVOLUTION 1789–1815

The magisterial volumes of John Ehrman's biography of *The Younger Pitt* [*The Years of Acclaim* (1969), *The Reluctant Transition* (1983)] have reached 1796. Students and readers wishing to investigate matters discussed in the above essay should consult this wonderful introduction to the world which the French Revolution at one time looked like turning upside down. Further discussion of that world, stressing the elements of strength and cohesion, is Ian R. Christie's *Stress and Stability in Late Eighteenth Century Britain* (1984). A straightforward summary of the British experience during the revolutionary period may be found in Clive Emsley's *British Society and the French Wars, 1793–1815* (1979). Valuable material is contained in the less well-known *Britain and Revolutionary France:Conflict,Subversion and Propaganda* ed. Colin Jones (Exeter Studies in History, no. 5, 1983). Robert R. Dozier, *For King, Constitution and Country: The English Loyalists and the French Revolution* (University of Kentucky Press, 1983), is the first detailed and scholarly study of the English loyalists. It replaces the controversial account in E.C.Black, *The Association* (Harvard University Press, 1963). Interactions between loyalism and radicalism may be followed in Albert Goodwin's *The Friends of Liberty: The English Democratic Movement in the Age of the French Revolution* (1979). The electoral dimension to politics in the age of the French Revolution is contained in the five volumes of *The House of Commons, 1790–1820*, ed. Roland G. Thorne (1986). The emergence of a Tory Party during the revolutionary period, as well as the development of party politics in general, are discussed in Frank O'Gorman, *The Emergence of the British Two-Party System, 1760–1832* (1982). Older discussions of the Toryism of the period may be found in A.S.Foord, *His Majesty's Opposition, 1714–1832* (Oxford University Press, 1964); H.W.C. Davis, *The Age of Grey and Peel* (Oxford University Press, 1924); and Keith Feiling, *The Second Tory Party* (Oxford University Press, 1924). The fourth and sixth chapters of J.C.D. Clark's study of *English Society, 1688–1832* (Cambridge University Press, 1985) are required reading although the arguments contained therein have not commanded universal acceptance.

2. THE OPPOSITION WHIGS AND THE FRENCH REVOLUTION 1789–1815

Two books are essential reading for a detailed treatment of the Whig Party during the 1790s: Frank O'Gorman, *The Whig Party and the French Revolution* (1967) and L.G. Mitchell, *Charles James Fox and the Disintegration of the Whig Party* (Oxford, 1971). L.G. Mitchell, *Holland House* (1980) deals with Foxite attitudes and the creation and perpetuation of the Foxite legend. The structure of the party on the eve of the French Revolution is analysed in Donald Ginter, *Whig Organisation in the General Election of 1790* (Berkeley and Los Angeles, 1967). Michael Roberts, *The Whig Party 1807–12* (1939) remains a magisterial study. Several biographies place leading personalities in their political context, notably, J.W. Derry, *Charles James Fox* (1972); Roger Fulford, *Samuel Whitbread* (1967); E.A. Smith, *Whig Principles and Party Politics, Earl Fitzwilliam and the Whig Party* (Manchester, 1975); and P.J. Jupp, *Lord Grenville* (Oxford, 1985). There is stimulating comment in A.D. Harvey, *Britain in the Early Nineteenth Century* (1978) and in the same author's 'The Ministry of All the Talents: the Whigs in Office', *HJ*, xv

(1972). J.J. Sack, *The Grenvillites* (Chicago, 1979) and his article, 'The Memory of Burke and the Memory of Pitt: English Conservatism Confronts Its Past', *HJ*, xxx (1987) correct too great a concentration on Fox. Frank O'Gorman, *Edmund Burke: His Political Philosophy* (1973) is especially useful, R. Willis, 'Fox, Grenville and the Recovery of the Opposition', *JBS*, xi (1972) redresses too narrow a concern with the earlier period. A shrewd survey of Fox's reputation with reformers and radicals, J.R. Dinwiddy, 'Charles James Fox and the People', *History*, lv (1970) balances more reverential accounts. The relevant chapters of A.S. Foord, *His Majesty's Opposition* (Oxford, 1964), J.A. Cannon, *Parliamentary Reform* (Cambridge, 1973) and H.W.C. Davis, *The Age of Grey and Peel* (Oxford, 1929) contain valuable material. The 1806 peace negotiations are dealt with in Herbert Butterfield, *Charles James Fox and Napoleon* (1962), while the same author's, 'Charles James Fox and the Whig Opposition in 1792', *Cambridge Historical Journal*, ix (1949) is an important pioneering work.

3. POPULAR RADICALISM AND POPULAR PROTEST 1789–1815

H.T. Dickinson, *British Radicalism and the French Revolution, 1789–1815* (Oxford, 1985) offers a succinct introduction to recent debates, while both John Cannon, *Parliamentary Reform in England, 1640–1832* (Cambridge, 1973) and Edward Royle and James Walvin, *British Radicals and Reformers, 1760–1848* (Brighton, 1982) place this period in the context of the longer-term development of radicalism. There is no substitute for reading E.P. Thompson, *The Making of the English Working Class* (1963: paperback rev. edn, 1968) for the flavour of his revision of established accounts of the period. Albert Goodwin, *The Friends of Liberty* (London, 1979) offers a detailed and masterly study of the popular radicalism of the 1790s. Shorter and more accessible is G.A. Williams, *Artisans and Sansculottes: Popular Movements in France and England during the French Revolution* (1968). Ian R. Christie, *Stress and Stability in Late Eighteenth Century Britain* (Oxford, 1984) and Roger Wells, *Insurrection: the British Experience, 1795–1803* (Gloucester, 1983) represent opposed interpretations of the degree of threat to the established order after 1789. Finally J.R. Dinwiddy, *From Luddism to the First Reform Bill* (Oxford, 1986) is a judicious appraisal of the later period and the connection with post-war radicalism.

4. IRELAND AND THE FRENCH REVOLUTION

Much of the foregoing essay is based upon Marianne Elliott, *Partners in Revolution. The United Irishmen and France* (London and New Haven, 1982; pbk 1988); *Watchmen in Sion. The Protestant Idea of Liberty* (Field Day Pamphlet No 8, Derry, 1985) and 'The origins and transformation of early Irish republicanism', *Internat. Rev. Soc. Hist.*, xxiii (1978) 405–28. However, to understand the dramatic events of the 1790s in Ireland some background knowledge is advisable. The best general accounts are: David Dickson, *New Foundations: Ireland 1660–1800* (Dublin, 1987); T.W. Moody and W.E. Vaughan (eds), *A New History of Ireland*, Vol. iv, *Eighteenth-century Ireland, 1691–1800* (Oxford, 1986); R.F. Foster, *Modern Ireland, 1600–1972* (1988); R.B. McDowell, *Ireland in the Age of Imperialism and Revolution, 1760–1801* (Oxford, 1979); Edith Mary Johnston, *Ireland in the Eighteenth Century* (Dublin, 1974); Gearóld Ó Tuathaigh, *Ireland before the Famine, 1798–1848* (Dublin, 1972); J.C. Beckett, *The Making of Modern Ireland, 1603–1923* (1966). A different kind of general work, L.M. Cullen's interpretive, *The Emergence of Modern Ireland, 1600–1923* (Dublin, 1983), throws new light on the 1790s. The best book on public opinion in the period is still R.B. McDowell, *Irish Public Opinion, 1750–1800* (1944). The fullest account of the 1798 rebellion is Thomas Pakenham, *The Year of Liberty* (1969; pbk, 1972). A new interdisciplinary journal, *Eighteenth-Century Ireland*, has been appearing annually since 1986 and *Irish Economic and Social History* publishes an annual bibliography of new publications.

Useful collections of essays are: Patrick J. Corish (ed.), *Radicals, Rebels and*

Establishments, Historical Studies, XI (Belfast, 1985); Thomas Bartlett and D.W. Hayton (eds), *Penal Era and Golden Age. Essays in Irish History, 1690–1800* (Belfast, 1979); Samuel Clark and James S. Donnelly, Jr. (eds), *Irish Peasants, Violence and Political Unrest, 1780–1914* Wisconsin, 1983; Manchester, 1983); L.M. Cullen and François Furet (eds), *Ireland and France 17th–20th centuries: towards a comparative study of rural history* (Paris, 1980); C.H.E. Philpin (ed.), *Nationalism and Popular Protest in Ireland* (Cambridge, 1987); Peter Roebuck (ed.), *Plantation to Partition : Essays in Ulster History in Honour of J.L. McCracken* (Belfast, 1981); and, placing Ireland in the European context, Otto Dann and J.R. Dinwiddy (eds), *Nationalism in Europe in the Age of the French Revolution* (1988). W.H. Crawford and B. Trainor (eds), *Aspects of Irish Social History, 1750–1800* (Belfast, 1969), is an excellent collection of documents, introduced by J.C. Beckett.

On the United Irishmen see also: James S. Donnelly, Jr, 'Propagating the Cause of the United Irishmen', *Studies*, LXIX (1980) 5–23; Nancy J. Curtin, 'The Transformation of the Society of United Irishmen into a revolutionary mass organisation, 1792–4, *IHS*, XXIV (1984–5) 469–70; M. Wall, 'The United Irish Movement', in *Historical Studies*, V, ed. J.L. McCracken (1965) pp. 122–40. On the immediate impact of the Revolution the articles of John Hall Stewart still capture some of the early euphoria: 'The fall of the Bastille on the Dublin Stage', *Jn.Roy.Soc.Antiq.Ire.*, LXXXIV (1959) 78–91: 'The French Revolution on the Dublin Stage, 1790–1794', ibid., XCI (1959) 183–92.

5. POPULAR CONSERVATISM AND MILITANT LOYALISM 1789–1815

For conservative ideology, see J.C.D. Clark, *English Society 1688–1832* (Cambridge, 1985) pp. 199–276; H.T. Dickinson, *Liberty and Property* (1977) ch.7; J.A.W. Gunn, *Beyond Liberty and Property* (Kingston and Montreal, 1983) ch.4; Thomas Philip Schofield, 'Conservative Political Thought in Britain in Response to the French Revolution', *HJ*, XXIX (1986) 601–22; and Robert Hole, 'British counter-revolutionary popular propaganda in the 1790s', in *Britain and Revolutionary France: Conflict, Subversion and Propaganda*, ed. Colin Jones (Exeter, 1983) pp.53–69. On popular loyalism, see Austin Mitchell, 'The Association Movement of 1792–3', *HJ*, IV (1961) 56–77; Donald E. Ginter, 'The Loyalist Association Movement of 1792–93 and British Public Opinion', *HJ*, IX (1966) 179–90; E.C. Black, *The Association* (Cambridge, Mass., 1963) ch.7; Robert R. Dozier, *For King, Constitution, and Country: The English Loyalists and the French Revolution* (Lexington, 1983); H.T. Dickinson, 'Popular Loyalism in Britain in the 1790s', forthcoming in *The Transformation of Political Culture in Late Eighteenth Century England and Germany*, eds A.M. Birke and Eckhart Hellmuth (Oxford); Alan Booth, 'Popular Loyalism and public violence in the north-west of England 1790–1800', *Soc Hist*, VIII (1983) 295–313; H.T. Dickinson, *British Radicalism and the French Revolution 1789–1815* (Oxford, 1985) ch.2; J.R. Western, 'The Volunteer Movement as an Anti-Revolutionary Force, 1793–1802', *EHR*, LXXI (1956) 603–14; R.B. Rose, 'The Priestley Riots of 1791', *P & P*, 18 (1960) 68–88; and Linda Colley, 'The Apotheosis of George III: Loyalty, Royalty and the British Nation 1760–1820', *P & P*, 102 (1984) 94–129. On the religious and cultural background, see Deryck Lovegrove, 'English Evangelical Dissent and the European Conflict 1789–1815', *SCH*, XX (1983) 263–76; W. Stafford, 'Religion and the Doctrine of Nationalism in England at the time of the French Revolution and Napoleonic Wars', in *Religion and National Identity*, ed. S. Mews (Oxford, 1982), pp. 381–95; Nancy Uhlar Murray, 'The Influence of the French Revolution on the Church of England and its Rivals, 1789–1802', unpublished D.Phil.thesis (Oxford University, 1975); Betty T. Bennett, *British War Poetry in the Age of Romanticism 1793–1815* (New York, 1974); John Ashton, *English Caricature and Satire on Napoleon I* (New York, 1888); and Herbert M. Atherton, 'The British Defend their Constitution in Political Cartoons and Literature', in *Studies in Eighteenth Century Culture*, vol.II, ed. Harry C. Payne

(Madison, 1982) pp.3–31. On the political and social context, see Ian R. Christie, *Stress and Stability in Late Eighteenth-Century Britain* (Oxford, 1984).

6. BRITISH DIPLOMACY AND THE FRENCH WARS 1789–1815

Although now looking rather dated the standard outline is still A.W. Ward and G.P. Gooch (eds), *Cambridge History of British Foreign Policy*, I (Cambridge, 1919). J.M. Sherwig, *Guineas and Gunpowder. British foreign aid in the wars with France 1793–1815* (Cambridge, Mass., 1969) is a valuable supplement stressing an important dimension. John Ehrman, *The Younger Pitt*, I, *The Years of Acclaim* (1969; pbk edn, 1984) and II, *The Reluctant Transition* (1983; pbk edn, 1985) provides a solid coverage of British diplomacy between 1789 and 1796 which is supplemented by Peter Jupp's biography of Pitt's Foreign Secretary, *Lord Grenville 1759–1834* (Oxford, 1985), while T.C.W. Blanning, *The Origins of the French Revolutionary Wars* (London and New York, 1986) provides a useful summary in the context of the wider involvement of the European powers in the first and second coalitions. Earlier examinations of aspects of Britain's relations with the French Royalists – Harvey Mitchell, *The Underground War against Revolutionary France: The Missions of William Wickham 1794–1800* (Oxford, 1965) and W.R. Fryer, *Republic or Restoration in France?* (Manchester, 1965) – have been massively reinforced by Maurice Hutt, *Chouannerie and Counter-Revolution. Puisaye, the Princes and the British Government in the 1790s*, 2 vols (Cambridge, 1983). Britain's relations with other powers in the War of the Second Coalition (1799–1801) form part of Piers Mackesy's major studies, *Statesmen at War. The Strategy of Overthrow 1798–1799* (London and New York, 1974) and *War without Victory. The Downfall of Pitt, 1799–1802* (Oxford, 1984), though an alternative critical view is presented by P.W. Schroeder, 'The Collapse of the Second Coalition', *JMH*, LIX (1987) 244–90. Another critical view of British diplomacy is presented by E.E. Roach, 'Anglo-Russian Relations from Austerlitz to Tilsit', *International History Review*, V (1983) 181–200. A more general view of European hostility can be seen in A.D. Harvey, 'European attitudes to Britain during the French Revolutionary and Napoleonic era', *History*, LXIII (1978) 356–65. There is great need for a re-examination of British diplomacy in the Napoleonic Wars (1803–15) and particularly of Britain's part in the final coalition. C.K. Webster, *The Foreign Policy of Castlereagh 1812–1815. Britain and the Reconstruction of Europe* (1931), magisterial in its day, now seems too hagiographic and blinkered while his useful documentary collection, *British Diplomacy 1813–1815* (1921), is inevitably selective, and there is nothing focused on British statesmen to compare with the penetrating insights of E. Kraehe's *Metternich's German Policy*, I: *The Contest with Napoleon, 1799–1814* (Princeton, 1963) and II *The Congress of Vienna, 1814–1815* (Princeton, 1983) which place Castlereagh's efforts in a wider perspective.

7. STRATEGIC PROBLEMS OF THE BRITISH WAR EFFORT

On naval and military administration, see Sir Herbert Richmond, *Statesmen and Seapower* (Oxford, 1946); J.A. Houlding, *Fit for Service: The Training of the British Army, 1715–1795* (Oxford, 1981); Richard Glover, *Peninsular Preparation: The Reform of the British Army, 1795–1809* (Cambridge, 1963); and Christopher Lloyd, *The Nation and the Navy: A History of Naval Life and Policy* (1961). On campaigns and operations, see Sir Henry Bunbury, *Narratives of Some Passages in the Great War with France (1799–1810)* (1854; new edn, 1927); David Geggus, *Slavery, War and Revolution: The British Occupation of Saint Domingue, 1793–1798* (Oxford, 1982); Michael Duffy, *Soldiers, Sugar and Seapower: The British Expeditions to the West Indies and the War against Revolutionary France* (Oxford, 1987); Sir John Fortescue, *History of the British Army*, IV–X (1899–1920); David Gates, *The Spanish Ulcer: A History of the Peninsular*

War (1986); Richard Glover, *Britain at Bay: Defence against Bonaparte, 1803-14* (1973); Piers Mackesy, *The War in the Mediterranean, 1803-1810* (1957); Sir William Napier, *History of the War in the Peninsula and South of France, 1807-1814* (1828-40; abridged edn, ed. C.H. Stuart Chicago, 1979); Sir Charles Oman, *A History of the Peninsular War,* 6 vols (Oxford, 1902-30); and S.G.P. Ward, *Wellington's Headquarters: A Study of the Administrative Problems in the Peninsula 1809-14* (Oxford, 1957). On strategy and higher direction of the war, see John Ehrman, *The Younger Pitt: The Reluctant Transition* (1983); Michael Howard, *The British Way in Warfare: a Reappraisal,* Neale Lecture, 1974 (1975); Piers Mackesy, *Statesmen at War: The Strategy of Overthrow, 1803-1810* (1974); and Piers Mackesy, *War without Victory: The Downfall of Pitt, 1799-1802* (Oxford, 1984).

8. PUBLIC FINANCE IN THE WARS WITH FRANCE 1793-1815

In order to evaluate the impact of the Revolutionary and Napoleonic Wars on British public finance, it is necessary to comprehend how the system evolved and the way it functioned for several decades before the French Revolution imposed herculean tasks upon it from 1793 to 1815. Unfortunately, there is no single study that sets the scene for the wars with France. But the following books provide good background reading: J.E.D. Binney, *British Finance and Administration 1774-94* (Oxford, 1958); C.D. Chandaman, *English Public Revenue, 1660-88* (Oxford, 1975); P.M.G. Dickson, *The Financial Revolution in England: A Study in the Development of Public Credit 1688-1756* (1967); S. Dowell, *A History of Taxation and Taxes in England,* 4 vols (1888, reprinted 1965); E.L. Hargreaves, *The National Debt* (1930); W. Kennedy, *English Taxation 1640-1799: An Essay on Policy and Opinion* (1913); P.K. O'Brien, *War and Public Finance in Britain 1793-1815,* Part I, (forthcoming Oxford); and P.K. O'Brien, 'The Political Economy of British Taxation, 1660-1815', *EcHR,* XLI (1988). For the history of public finance in the years immediately preceding the outbreak of the Revolutionary War in 1793, there are several excellent studies including: Ian R. Christie, *Wars and Revolution, Britain 1760-1815* (1982); John Ehrman, *The Younger Pitt: The Years of Acclaim* (1969); and J. Holland Rose, *William Pitt and the National Revival* (1911). Although there are plenty of older histories which deal with war finance, modern studies on the taxation, monetary and debt management policies pursued from 1793 to 1815 are few, but begin to appear: Phyllis Deane, 'War and Industrialization' in J.M. Winter (ed.), *War and Economic Development* (Cambridge, 1975); John Ehrman, *The Younger Pitt: The Reluctant Transition* (1983); Denis Gray, *Spencer Perceval: The Evangelical Prime Minister, 1762-1812* (Manchester, 1963); J. Holland Rose, *William Pitt and the Great War* (1911); A. Hope-Jones, *Income Tax in the Napoleonic Wars* (Cambridge, 1939); P.K. O'Brien, *War and Public Finance in Britain 1793-1815* Oxford, Part II; J.M. Sherwig, *Guineas and Gunpowder. British Foreign Aid in the Wars with France, 1793-1815* (Cambridge, Mass., 1969); and M. Turner (ed.), *Malthus and his Times* (1986). The clean-up or reconstruction of state finances in the aftermath of the wars with France is covered in: A.W. Acworth, *Financial Reconstruction in England, 1815-22* (1925); Boyd Hilton, *Corn Cash and Commerce: The Economic Policies of the Tory Governments 1815-30* (Oxford, 1977); and B. Gordon, *Political Economy in Parliament, 1819-23* (1976).

9. THE IMPACT OF THE FRENCH WARS ON THE BRITISH ECONOMY

This is a short and selective list, mostly of recent works, though it includes some 'classics': N.F.R. Crafts, *British Economic Growth during the Industrial Revolution* (Oxford, 1985); François Crouzet, *L'Economie britannique et le Blocus Continental (1806-1813),* 2 vols (Paris, 1958; 2nd ed, Paris, 1987); François Crouzet, 'Bilan de l'économie britannique pendant les guerres de la Revolution et de l'Empire', *Revue Historique,* 475 (1965)

71-110; Ralph Davis, *The Industrial Revolution and British Overseas Trade* (Leicester, 1979); Phyllis Deane, 'War and Industrialization', in J.M. Winter (ed.), *War and Economic Development. Essays in Memory of David Joslin* (Cambridge, 1975) pp. 91-102; M.M. Edwards, *The Growth of the British Cotton Trade, 1780-1815* (Manchester, 1967); Clive Emsley, *British Society and the French Wars 1793-1815* (1979); J.A. Frankel, 'The 1807-1809 Embargo Against Great Britain', *Journal of Economic History*, XLII (1982) 291-308; W.F. Galpin, *The Grain Supply of England during the Napoleonic Period* (New York, 1925); A.D. Gayer, W.W. Rostow and A.J. Schwartz, *The Growth and Fluctuation of the British Economy, 1790-1850*, 2 vols (Oxford, 1953; 2nd edn, New York, 1975); E.F. Heckscher, *The Continental System. An Economic Interpretation* (Oxford, 1922); G. Hueckel, 'War and the British Economy, 1793-1815: A General Equilibrium Analysis', *Explorations in Economic History*, X (1973) 365-96; G. Hueckel, 'Relative Prices and Supply Response in English Agriculture during the Napoleonic Wars', *EcHr*, XXIX (1976) 401-14; A.H. John, 'Farming in Wartime : 1793-1815', in E.L. Jones and G.E. Mingay (eds), *Land, Labour and Population in the Industrial Revolution* (1967); P. Mathias and P.K. O'Brien, 'Taxation in Britain and France, 1715-1810. A Comparison of the Social and Economic Incidence of Taxes Collected for the Central Governments', *Journal of European Economic History*, V (1976) 601-50; J. Mokyr and N.E. Savin, 'Stagflation in Historical Perspective: the Napoleonic Wars Revisited', *Research in Economic History*, I (1976) 198-259; P.K. O'Brien, 'Government Revenue, 1793-1815. A Study in Fiscal and Financial Policy in the Wars against France', unpublished D.Phil. dissertation (Oxford University, 1967); M. Olson Jr, *The Economics of the Wartime Shortage. A History of British Food Supplies in the Napoleonic Wars and in World Wars I and II* (Durham, N.C., 1963); C.N. Parkinson (ed.), *The Trade Winds. A Study of British Overseas Trade during the French Wars 1793-1815* (1948); and J.M. Sherwig, *Guineas and Gunpowder. British Foreign Aid in the Wars with France, 1793-1815* (Cambridge, Mass., 1969).

10.   THE SOCIAL IMPACT OF THE FRENCH WARS

For a general overview of the social impact of the wars see Clive Emsley, *British Society and the French Wars 1793-1815* (1979). Richard Glover, *Britain at Bay: Defence against Napoleon 1803-1814* (1973) is also useful though its primary concerns are the military preparations to meet the expected invasion. There are two interesting and useful regional studies of the war's impact and of local military preparations, both of which are published by county record offices: M.Y. Ashcroft, *To Escape the Monster's Clutches* (North Yorkshire Publications No. 15, 1977) and R.G.E. Wood, *Essex and the French Wars* (SEAX Teaching Portfolio: Essex CRO Publications No. 70, 1977). The social impact of recruitment is best followed up, for the army, in J.R. Western, 'The Recruitment of the Land Forces in Great Britain 1793-1797', unpublished Ph.D. thesis (Edinburgh, 1953), for the militia, in J.R. Western, *The English Militia in the Eighteenth Century* (1965) and for the navy, in Michael Lewis, *A Social History of the Navy 1793-1815* (1960). The latter should be supplemented by Clive Emsley, *North Riding Naval Recruits: The Quota Acts and the Quota Men 1795-1797* (North Yorkshire CRO No. 18, 1978) and, more importantly, N.A.M. Rodger, *The Wooden World: An Anatomy of the Georgian Navy* (1986) which, while it deals principally with the mid-eighteenth-century navy, challenges the popular and traditional picture of naval recruitment and sea life. Wartime propaganda can be followed up in Robert Hole, 'British Counter-revolutionary Popular Propaganda in the 1790's', in Colin Jones (ed.) *Britain and Revolutionary France: Conflict, Subversion and Propaganda* (Exeter Studies in History No. 5, University of Exeter, 1983) and in the documentary collection F.J. Klingberg and S.B. Hustredt (eds), *The Warning Drum: The British Home Front Faces Napoleon. Broadsides of 1803* (Berkeley and Los Angeles, 1944). Also important in this respect, and for the development of attitudes to the monarchy and the nation, are two articles by Linda Colley, 'The Apotheosis of George III: Loyalty, Royalty and the British Nation 1760-1820', *P & P*, 102 (1984) and 'Whose Nation? Class and National Consciousness in Britain 1750-1830', *P & P*, 113 (1986). The impact of the war on the lower classes and on labour has tended to be subsumed in studies of the impact of industrialisation, of Luddism and of the 'making' of the working class. Roger Morriss, *The Royal Dockyards during the Revolutionary and Napoleonic Wars* (Leicester, 1983) has some valuable comment on a workforce directly involved in the war effort. J.E. Cookson's work has emphasised the importance of the war in developing middle-class consciousness, *The Friends of Peace: Anti-war Liberalism in England 1793-1815* (Cambridge, 1982) and 'Political arithmetic and war in Britain 1793-1815', *War and Society*, 1 (1983).

11. 'THINGS AS THEY ARE': THE LITERARY RESPONSE TO THE FRENCH REVOLUTION 1789-1815

There is a whole library of books concerned with the idea of Romanticism. M.H. Abrams, *The Mirror and the Lamp* (Oxford, 1953) and H.G. Schenk, *The Mind of the European Romantics* (Oxford, 1979) are two seminal works on Romantic theory. Hugh Honour, *Romanticism* (1979) deals with the art of the period. Boris Ford (ed.), *From Blake to Byron*, in *The New Pelican Guide to English Literature*, v (1982) is a useful guide to the literary figures and trends of the times.

There are a number of general books which deal with the relationship between Romantic literature and political ideas. First and foremost is the invaluable study by Marilyn Butler, *Romantics, Rebels and Revolutionaries* (Oxford, 1981). Olivia Smith, *The Politics of Language, 1791-1819* (Oxford, 1984), and D. Aers, J. Cook and D. Punter (eds), *Romanticism and Ideology* (1981) both contain stimulating essays on the major writers of the period. Roger Sales, *English Literature in History: 1780-1830, Pastoral and Politics* (1983) discusses the political ideas of poets interested in rural society. Older studies, which are still useful, include Crane Brinton, *The Political Ideas of the English Romanticists* (Oxford, 1926) and Amanda Ellis, *Rebels and Conservatives* (Bloomington, 1967). Alfred Cobban, *Edmund Burke and the Revolt Against the Eighteenth Century* (1962) explores the writers' indebtedness to Burkean philosophy.

The best work on the radical novelists of the 1790s is Gary Kelly, *The English Jacobin Novel, 1780-1805* (Oxford, 1976). The best study of Mary Wollstonecraft's life and fiction is Claire Tomalin, *The Life and Death of Mary Wollstonecraft* (1974). Hazlitt's literary and political criticism is examined in detail by David Bromwich, *The Mind of a Critic* (Oxford, 1983). For Jane Austen's politics, see Alistair M. Duckworth, *The Improvement of the Estate* (Baltimore and London, 1971); Marilyn Butler, *Jane Austen and the War of Ideas* (Oxford, 1975); Warren Roberts, *Jane Austen and the French Revolution* (1979); and Mary Evans, *Jane Austen and the State* (1987).

The political ideas of the Romantic poets have received greatest attention. There is an interesting collection of the political work of minor poets contained in Betty T. Bennett, *British War Poetry in the Age of Romanticism, 1793-1815* (New York, 1976). The best studies of Blake's political philosophy are Jacob Bronowski, *William Blake and the Age of Revolution* (1972); David V. Erdman, *Blake: Prophet Against Empire* (Princeton, 1969); John Beer, *William Blake, 1757-1827* (Windsor, 1982). The most comprehensive study of Southey's political career is to be found in Geoffrey Carnall, *Robert Southey and His Age* (1960). The politics of Wordsworth and Coleridge has generated the most interest and controversy, although attention has mainly centred on their early radical phase. Their joint political careers are examined in A.S. Byatt, *Wordsworth, Coleridge and Their Time* (1970). Articles which examine the extent of their revolutionary commitment include G. Watson, 'The Revolutionary Youth of Wordsworth and Coleridge', *Critical Quarterly*, xviii (1976) 49-66 and J. Beer, 'The "Revolutionary Youth" of Wordsworth and Coleridge: another view', *Critical Quarterly*, xix (1977) 79-87. N.H. Roe,

'Wordsworth, Coleridge and the French Revolution, 1789–95', unpublished D.Phil thesis (Oxford, 1985) discusses their early radicalism. Iain R. Scott, 'From Radicalism to Conservatism: the Politics of Wordsworth and Coleridge, 1797–1818', unpublished Ph.D. thesis (Edinburgh, 1987) argues for their transition to a liberal conservative ideology. Mary Moorman, *William Wordsworth: The Early Years* (Oxford, 1957) and *The Later Years* (Oxford, 1965) is still the standard introduction to the poet and his politics. F.M. Todd, *Politics and the Poet* (1957) is a general account of Wordsworth's political activities. J.K. Chandler, *Wordsworth's Second Nature* (Chicago, 1984) is a magnificent study of the influence of Burke on the poet. The best biographies of Coleridge, which examine his political ideas, include W.J. Bate, *Coleridge* (1968); J. Colmer, *Coleridge, Critic of Society* (Oxford, 1959); J. Cornwell, *Coleridge: Poet and Revolutionary, 1772–1804* (1973); Katharine Cooke, *Coleridge* (1979). The best examinations of Coleridge's political theory are Carl Woodring, *Coleridge and the Idea of the Modern State* (New Haven and London, 1966); and the magisterial introduction to *Essays On His Times*, 3 vols, ed. David V. Erdman, in *The Collected Works of Samuel Taylor Coleridge* (London and Princeton, 1978).

Notes and References

INTRODUCTION: THE IMPACT ON BRITAIN OF THE FRENCH REVOLUTION AND THE FRENCH WARS
1789–1815 H.T. Dickinson

1. On conservative ideology see H.T. Dickinson, Liberty and Property (1977) pp.270–318; J.A.W. Gunn, Beyond Liberty and Property (Kingston and Montreal, 1983) pp.164–93; J.C.D. Clark, English Society 1688–1832 (Cambridge, 1985) pp.199–276; and Thomas Philip Schofield, 'Conservative Political Thought in Britain in Response to the French Revolution', HJ, XXIX (1986) 601–22.

2. On the re-emergence of parties see B.W. Hill, British Parliamentary Parties 1742–1832 (1985); Frank O'Gorman, The Emergence of the British Two Party System 1760–1832 (1982); and Austin Mitchell, The Whigs in Opposition 1815–1830 (Oxford, 1967).

3. The parliamentary politics of the early nineteenth century is a very neglected subject. The best introduction is A.D. Harvey, Britain in the Early Nineteenth Century (1978).

4. Radicals and revolutionaries are treated in detail in the essays by John Stevenson and Marianne Elliott in this volume. For a discussion of the innovations made by the radicals of the 1790s see also H.T. Dickinson, Liberty and Property, ch. 7 and H.T. Dickinson, British Radicalism and the French Revolution 1789–1815 (Oxford, 1985) chs. 1 and 3.

5. On this subject see J.E. Cookson, The Friends of Peace (Cambridge, 1982).

6. On the Jacobin novelists see Gary Kelly, The English Jacobin Novel 1780–1805 (Oxford, 1976); on the minor poets see Betty T. Bennett, British War Poetry in the Age of Romanticism 1793–1815 (New York, 1976); on the caricatures see M. Dorothy George, English Political Caricature 1793–1832 (Oxford, 1959) and John Ashton, English Caricature and Satire on Napoleon I (New York, 1888); and on Jane Austen, see Warren Roberts, Jane Austen and the French Revolution (1979).

7. On religious developments see, in particular, Nancy Uhlar Murray, 'The Influence of the French Revolution on the Church of England and its Rivals, 1789–1802', unpublished D.Phil dissertation (Oxford, 1975); W.R. Ward, Religion and Society in England 1790–1850 (1972) chs 2–4; David Hempton, Methodism and Politics in British Society 1750–1850 (1984); and John Walsh, 'Methodism at the end of the eighteenth century', in R. Davies and G. Rupp (eds), A History of the Methodist Church in Great Britain, I (1965) 277–315.

1. PITT AND THE 'TORY' REACTION TO THE FRENCH REVOLUTION 1789–1815 Frank O'Gorman

1. John Cannon, Aristocratic Century: the Peerage of Eighteenth-Century England (Cambridge, 1984) pp.115–16.

2. English Historical Documents, 1783–1832, eds A. Aspinall and E.A. Smith (1971) pp.253–4.

3. R.G. Thorne, The House of Commons, 1790–1820, 5 vols (1986) I, pp. 126, 149, 165, 235.

4. John Cannon, The Fox–North Coalition: the Crisis of the Constitution (Cambridge, 1969) pp. 235–6.

5. See, below, the essay by John Derry.

6. Frank O'Gorman, The Whig Party and the French Revolution (1967) pp.209–18.

7. A.S. Foord, *His Majesty's Opposition, 1714-1830* (Oxford, 1964) pp.445-9.

8. See, for example, *The Examiner*, no.58 (5 February 1809);no.68 (16 April 1809); *Blackwoods*, iii, 294-8 ('Thoughts on Public Feeling').

9. Cannon, *Aristocratic Century*, p.153.

10. *The War Speeches of William Pitt*, ed. R. Coupland (Oxford, 1940) p.21.

11. A point which Pitt frequently emphasised. See, for example, his speech of 7 June 1799, *The War Speeches of William Pitt*, pp. 244-5.

12. J.C.D. Clark, *English Society, 1688-1832* (Cambridge, 1985) pp.263-7.

13. See, for example, M. Weinzerl, 'John Reeves and the Controversy over the Constitutional Role of Parliament during the French Revolution', *Parliaments, Estates and Representation*, v (1985) pp.71-7.

14. On the development of a loyalist movement and the activities of the Reeves Societies see, below, the essay by H.T. Dickinson.

15. John Ehrman, *The Younger Pitt: The Reluctant Transition* (1983) pp.42-6.

16. John Stevenson, *Popular Disturbances in England, 1700-1870* (1979) pp.151-5.

17. Albert Goodwin, *The Friends of Liberty: The English Democratic Movement in the age of the French Revolution* (1979) p.288.

18. Lord Grenville to the Duke of Buckingham, 7 November 1792, *Memoirs of the Courts and Cabinets of George III*, ed. Duke of Buckingham and Chandos, 4 vols (1853-5) II, p.224.

19. Lord Grenville to the Duke of Buckingham, 14 November 1792, ibid., 286-8.

20. See, below, the essays by John Stevenson and H.T. Dickinson.

2. THE OPPOSITION WHIGS AND THE FRENCH REVOLUTION 1789-1815 *John Derry*

1. For the conduct of the Whigs see J.W. Derry, *The Regency Crisis and the Whigs 1788-9* (Cambridge, 1963) chs. II-IV, and L.G. Mitchell, *Charles James Fox and the Disintegration of the Whig Party 1782-94* (Oxford, 1971) ch. IV.

2. For Fox and the French Revolution see J.W. Derry, *Charles James Fox* (1972) ch. 7.

3. 30 July 1789, in *Memorials and Correspondence of Charles James Fox*, ed. Lord John Russell (1853-7) II, P.361.

4. For a critique of Burke see Frank O'Gorman, *Edmund Burke: His Political Philosophy* (1973) ch. VI. For Price see Peter Brown, *The Chathamites* (1967) ch. 8. A convenient edition of Burke's *Reflections* is that published by Penguin Books with an introduction by Conor Cruise O'Brien.

5. For tensions in the Whig Party see Frank O'Gorman, *The Whig Party and the French Revolution* (1967) chs 2-3 and Mitchell, *Charles James Fox*, chs V-VI. For the great debate, see *Parliamentary History*, XXIX, 364-401.

6. In addition to O'Gorman and Mitchell, Herbert Butterfield, 'Charles James Fox and the Whig Opposition in 1792', in *Cambridge Historical Journal*, IX (1949) is essential reading.

7. For Fox's changing relationship with the radicals see J.R. Dinwiddy, 'Charles James Fox and the People', *History*, LV (1970).

8. For Fox and the war, see Derry, *Charles James Fox*, ch. 8. A selection of Fox's speeches was published in the Everyman Library (1924).

9. See Peter Jupp, *Lord Grenville* (Oxford, 1985) Part 3, and also A.D. Harvey, 'The Ministry of All the Talents: the Whigs in Office', *HJ* (1972).

10. For the Whigs and the war, see Michael Roberts, *The Whig Party* (1939) ch. II.

3. POPULAR RADICALISM AND POPULAR PROTEST *1789-1815* *John Stevenson*

1. E.P. Thompson, *The Making of the English Working Class* (1963; pbk rev. edn, 1968) pp.171-2.

2. Ibid., p.199.

3. Ibid., p.194.

4. Ibid., p.195.

5. G.A. Williams, *Artisans and Sans-Culottes: Popular Movements in France and England during the French Revolution* (1968).

6. G.A. Williams, *Madoc: The Making of a Myth* (1979) pp. 89–117.

7. Albert Goodwin, *The Friends of Liberty: The English Democratic Movement in the Age of the French Revolution* (1979).

8. George Rudé, *Wilkes and Liberty: A Social Study of 1763 to 1774* (Oxford, 1962); George Rudé, *The Crowd in History: A Study of Popular Disturbances in France and England, 1730–1848* (New York, 1964) pp.33–65.

9. E.J. Hobsbawm, 'The machine breakers', in E.J. Hobsbawm (ed.), *Labouring Men: Studies in the History of Labour* (1964) pp.5–22.

10. Thompson, *The Making*, p.64.

11. E.P. Thompson, 'The Moral Economy of the English Crowd in the Eighteenth Century', *P & P*, 50 (1971) 76–136.

12. Thompson, *The Making*, pp.76–83.

13. Hobsbawm, *Labouring Men*, pp.5–22, 34–63.

14. C.R. Dobson, *Masters and Journeymen: a prehistory of industrial relations, 1717–1800* (1980).

15. For the range of tactics used by workmen see John Rule, *The Experience of Labour in Eighteenth-Century Industry* (1981) ch.4.

16. Dobson, *Masters and Journeymen*, pp.20–9.

17. John Stevenson, *Popular Disturbances in England, 1700–1870* (1979) pp. 127–34.

18. M. Thale (ed.), *The Autobiography of Francis Place* (Cambridge, 1972) pp.112–13.

19. Goodwin, *The Friends of Liberty*, pp.65–99.

20. R.B. Rose, 'The Priestly Riots of 1791', *P & P*, 18 (1960) 68–88.

21. A. Prentice, *Historical Sketches and Personal Recollections of Manchester* (Manchester, 1851; new edn, 1970) pp.2–3.

22. Cited in K.J. Logue, *Popular Disturbances in Seotland, 1780–1815* (Edinburgh, 1979) p.149.

23. John Money, *Experience and Identity, Birmingham and the West Midlands, 1760–1800* (Manchester, 1977); H.T. Dickinson, *Radical Politics in the North-East of England in the later Eighteenth Century* (Durham County Local History Society, 1979).

24. H.T. Dickinson, *Liberty and Property: Political Ideology in Eighteenth-Century Britain* (1977) pp.195–269.

25. Thale, *Autobiography of Francis Place*, p.197.

26. G.A. Williams, 'Locating a Welsh Working Class: the Frontier Years' in D. Smith (ed.), *A People and a Proletariat: Essays in the History of Wales, 1780–1980* (1980) p.35.

27. Logue, *Popular Disturbances in Scotland*, p.154.

28. See John Bohstedt, *Riots and Community Politics in England and Wales, 1790–1810* (Cambridge, Mass., 1983) and A. Charlesworth, *An Atlas of Rural Protest in Britain, 1548–1900* (1982) pp. 97–103, 116–18.

29. Marianne Elliott, 'The "Despard Conspiracy" Reconsidered', *P & P*, 75 (1977) 46–61.

30. Roger Wells, *Insurrection: the British Experience, 1795–1803* (Gloucester, 1983).

31. J.L. Baxter and F.K. Donnelly, 'Sheffield and the English revolutionary tradition, 1790–1820', *International Review of Social History*, xxv (1975) 398–423; and for the 'Black Lamp' see J.R. Dinwiddy, 'The "Black Lamp" in Yorkshire, 1801–1802' and J.L. Baxter and F.K. Donnelly, 'The Revolutionary "Underground" in the West Riding: Myth or Reality?', *p&p*, 64 (1974) 113–35.

264   BRITAIN AND THE FRENCH REVOLUTION 1789-1815

32. See J. Anne Hone, *For the Cause of Truth: Radicalism in London 1796-1821* (Oxford, 1982).

33. I. Prothero, *Artisans and Politics in early nineteenth century London: John Gast and His Times* (1979).

34. Ibid., pp.40-6.

35. For a brief summary of views see John Stevenson, *Popular Disturbances in England, 1700-1870* (1979) pp.155-162; and J.R. Dinwiddy, 'Luddism and Politics in the Northern Counties', *Soc Hist*, 4 (1979) 33-51.

4. IRELAND AND THE FRENCH REVOLUTION *Marianne Elliott*

*I wish to thank Dr Sean Connolly for some helpful criticisms of this article and Graeme Kirkham for allowing me to read his unpublished paper 'Literacy in North-West Ulster, 1680-1860'.

1. For the Dutch parallel see Wayne P. Te Brake, 'Popular politics and the Dutch patriot revolution', *Theory and Society*, 14 (1985) 199-222; Henk Reitsma, 'Netherlands', in Otto Dann and John Dinwiddy (eds), *Nationalism in Europe in the Age of the French Revolution* (1988).

2. A.P.W. Malcomson, ' "The parliamentary traffic of this country" ', in Thomas Bartlett and D.W. Hayton (eds), *Penal Era and Golden Age, Essays in Irish History, 1690-1800* (Belfast, 1979) pp.137-61.

3. A.P.W. Malcomson, *John Foster, The Politics of the Anglo-Irish Ascendancy* (Oxford, 1978); W.J. McCormack, *Ascendancy and tradition in Anglo-Irish Literary History, 1789-1939* (Oxford, 1985) pp. 61-96.

4. Patrick J. Corish, *The Catholic Community in the Seventeenth and Eighteenth Centuries* (Dublin, 1981); M. Wall, *The Penal Laws* (Dublin, 1961); Louis Cullen, 'Catholics under the Penal Laws', *Eighteenth-Century Ireland*, I (1986) 23-36; and S.J. Connolly, 'Religion and History', *Ir.Econ.and Soc. Hist.* x (1983) 66-80.

5. T. Dunne, 'The Gaelic response to conquest and colonisation: the evidence of the poetry', *Studia Hibernica*, 20 (1980) 7-30.

6. Marianne Elliott, *Watchmen in Sion. The Protestant Idea of Liberty* (Field Day Pamphlet No 8, Derry, 1985); David W. Miller, *Queens Rebels, Ulster Loyalism in Historical Perspective* (Dublin, 1978): idem. 'Presbyterianism and "Modernization" in Ulster', *P & P*, 80 (1978) 66-90.

7. ISPO: (Irish State Papers Office), Westmorland Corr., 11, ff. 22, 29 and 30, correspondence between Whitehall and Dublin Castle, Oct.-Dec. 1791.

8. W.H. Drummond (ed.), *The Autobiography of Archibald Hamilton Rowan* (Irish University Press reprint, 1972) pp.126-133.

9. *Freeman's Journal*, 18 Mar. 1794; PRONI, T.2541/1B1/4/12, George Knox to Abercorn, 14 Feb. 1793.

10. Kent CRO, U.840/0.143/3 and 0.144/10, secret information of April 1795; Trinity College Dublin, Ms 873 fo. 70, Mary Ann McCracken describing the widespread circulation of Paine in Ulster; Ray B. Browne, 'The Paine-Burke controversy in eighteenth-century Irish popular songs', in R.B. Browne, W.J. Roscelli and R. Loftus (eds), *The Celtic Cross* (Perdue, 1964) 80-97.

11. Accounts of proceedings of the Dublin United Irish Society are in ISPO, 620/19-21 and 53. Most of these papers are published in R.B. McDowell (ed.), 'Proceedings of the Dublin Society of United Irishmen', *Analecta Hibernica*, 17 (1949) 1-143.

12. Marianne Elliott, 'Irish republicanism in England: the first, 1797-9', in Bartlett and Hayton, *Penal Era*, pp. 204-21; idem, *Partners in Revolution*, pp. 173-89, 282-90; H.T. Dickinson, *British Radicalism and the French Revolution* (Oxford, 1985) pp.49-54.

13. The fullest account of the classical republican tradition is still J.G.A. Pocock, *The Machiavellian Moment: Florentine Political Thought and the Atlantic Republican Tradition* (Princeton, 1975).

14. These addresses are printed in the *Northern Star*, 1 and 15 Dec. 1792 and 20 Mar. 1793.

15. Marianne Elliott, 'Ireland', in Dann and Dinwiddy, (eds) *Nationalism in Europe*.

16. The United Irish reform plan and discussion documents are in ISPO, 620/20/1 and PRO, HO 100/51/100. Further documentation, plus a full discussion, can be found in R.B. McDowell, 'United Irish plans of parliamentary reform, 1793', *IHS*, 111, no. 9 (Mar. 1942) 39–59.

17. David Dickson, 'Taxation and disaffection in late eighteenth-century Ireland', in Samuel Clark and James S. Donnelly, *Irish Peasants Violence and Political Unrest, 1780–1914* (Wisconsin, 1983) pp. 37–63.

18. Lynn Hunt, *Politics, Culture, and Class in the French Revolution* (Berkeley, 1984; London pbk, 1986); François Furet, *Interpreting the French Revolution* (Cambridge pbk, 1985).

19. I gratefully acknowledge help by Laura Mason of Princeton University on this point.

20. ISPO, 620/20–21 for UIS attendance figures.

21. Kent CRO, U840/0.143/3, information of Francis Higgins, 13 Apr. 1795; also Nancy J. Curtin, 'The transformation of the Society of United Irishmen into a revolutionary mass organisation, 1792–4; *IHS*, XXIV (1984–5) 469–70.

22. Robert Darnton, *The Literary Underground of the Old Regime* (Cambridge, Mass., 1982) pp. 1–40; Hunt, *Politics, Culture and Class*, p. 205 and ch. 6 generally.

23. Elliott, *Partners in Revolution*, pp. 59–61; Archives Nationales, AF IV 1671/1/99–105 and Archives de la Guerre (Paris), MR 1420 fo. 28.

24. PRO, HO 100/46/154–6, John Keogh, the leading figure of the Catholic Committee explains in detail reasons for Catholic alienation.

25. PRONI, D.607/C/56, (McNally) to Lord Downshire, 8 Dec. 1794.

26. Elliott, *Partners in Revolution*, p.42.

27. A.J. Fitzpatrick, 'The economic effects of the French Revolutionary and Napoleonic Wars on Ireland', unpublished Ph.D. thesis (Manchester, 1973).

28. David W. Miller, 'The Armagh Troubles, 1784–95', in Clark and Donnelly, *Irish Peasants*, pp. 155–91.

29. Pitt's policy towards Ireland can be traced through the series HO 100 and PRO 30/8 in the Public Record Office, London. A good analysis can be found in John Ehrman, *The Younger Pitt. The Reluctant Transition* (1983).

30. *Parl Hist*, XXXIII, pp. 208–505.

31. Fitzpatrick, 'The economic effects...', pp. 30–2; Malcolmson, *John Foster*, p.372.

32. Thomas Bartlett, 'An end to the moral economy: the Irish Militia disturbances of 1793', *P & P*, 99 (1983) 41–64.

33. L.M. Cullen, *The Emergence of Modern Ireland, 1600–1900* (Dublin, 1983) pp. 23, 131–2, 236–8. Graeme Kirkham in his unpublished paper 'Literacy in North-West Ulster, 1680–1860' presents a statistical analysis of this claim and while he largely endorses it, his findings reveal marked differences between Catholic and Protestant, rural and urban inhabitants, with a higher level of literacy found in the latter of both groupings.

34. See for example Defender trials in T.B. and T.J. Howell (eds), *A Complete Collection of State Trials* (1809–28), XXV, 757 and 767; also T. Bartlett, 'Defenders and Defenderism in 1795', *IHS*, XXIV (1984–5) 373–94.

35. *Life of Theobald Wolfe Tone*, ed. by his son W.T.W. Tone, 2 vols (Washington, 1826) I, pp.170–1; PRONI, T.2905/11/1–9, transcripts of Portland Mss from Nottingham Univ. Lib.; *Northern Star*, 10–13 Oct. 1792.

36. Marianne Elliott, 'The United Irishmen as Diplomat', in Patrick J. Corish (ed.), *Radicals, Rebels and Establishments, Historical Studies*, XI (Belfast, 1985), pp.69–89.

37. L.M. Cullen, 'The 1798 rebellion in its eighteenth-century context', in Corish, *Radicals, Rebels and Establishments*, pp.91–113.

38. Marianne Elliott, 'The "Despard Conspiracy" Reconsidered', *P & P*, 75 (1977) 46–61.

5.   POPULAR CONSERVATISM AND MILITANT LOYALISM 1789–1815 *H.T. Dickinson*

1. Clive Emsley, 'An Aspect of Pitt's Terror: prosecutions for sedition during the 1790s', *Soc Hist*, VI (1981) 155–84; idem, 'Repression, "terror" and the rule of law in England during the decade of the French Revolution', *EHR*, C (1985) 801–25; and H.T. Dickinson, *British Radicalism and the French Revolution 1789–1815* (Oxford, 1985) ch.1.

2. Austin Mitchell, 'The Association Movement of 1792–3', *HJ*, IV (1961) 56–77; Donald E. Ginter, 'The Loyalist Association Movement of 1792–93 and British Public Opinion', *HJ*, IX (1966) 179–90; E.C. Black, *The Association* (Cambridge, Mass., 1963) ch. 7; Robert R. Dozier, *For King, Constitution, and Country: The English Loyalists and the French Revolution* (Lexington, 1983); and H.T. Dickinson, 'Popular Loyalism in Britain in the 1790s', forthcoming in *The Transformation of Political Culture in Late Eighteenth-Century England and Germany*, eds A.M. Birke and Eckhart Hellmuth, to be published in Oxford.

3. H.T. Dickinson, *Liberty and Property* (1977) pp. 270–318; J.A.W. Gunn, *Beyond Liberty and Property* (Kingston and Montreal, 1983) pp. 164–93; and Thomas Philip Schofield, 'Conservative Political Thought in Britain in Response to the French Revolution', *HJ*, XXIX (1986) 601–22.

4. For a useful introduction to militant conservative propaganda see Robert Hole, 'British counter-revolutionary popular propaganda in the 1790s', in *Britain and Revolutionary France: Conflict, Subversion and Propaganda*, ed. Colin Jones (Exeter, 1983) pp. 53–69. Among the most readily accessible primary sources are *Liberty and Property preserved against Republicans and Levellers: A Collection of Tracts* (1973); and the huge collection of loyalist addresses in the *London Gazette* (1792–3) and among the Reeves papers in the British Library, Add. MSS 16929–31.

5. See, for example, *A Serious Caution to the Poor* (1792); William Paley, *Reasons for Contentment, addressed to the Labouring Part of the British Public* (1793); *Advice to Sundry Sorts of People, by Job Nott* (1792); and *A Few Plain Questions and a little honest Advice to the Working People of Great Britain* (1792).

6. See, for example, Thomas Somerville, *Observations on the Constitution and Present State of Britain* (Edinburgh, 1793); *The Englishman's Catechism* (1792); Arthur Young, *The Example of France, a Warning to Britain* (1793); and *Thoughts on the New and Old Principles of Political Obedience* (1793).

7. Thomas Hardy, *The Importance of Religion to National Prosperity* (Edinburgh, 1794); idem, *Fidelity to the British Constitution, the Duty and Interest of the People* (Edinburgh, 1794) pp. 33–4; and Susan Pederson, 'Hannah More meets Simple Simon: Tracts, Chapbooks, and Popular Culture in Late Eighteenth-Century England', *JBS*, XXV (1986) 84–113.

8. See, for example, *A Serious Caution to the Poor* (1792); *The Alarm, being Britannia's Address to her People* (1793); *Ten Minutes Reflection on the Late Events in France* (1793); George Hill, *Instructions afforded by the present War, to People of Great Britain* (Edinburgh, 1793); and R.B. Nickolls, *The Duty of supporting and defending our Country and Constitution* (York, 1793); and Lewis Goldsmith, *The Anti-Gallican Monitor* (1811–12).

9. Gayle Trusdel Pendleton, 'Towards a Bibliography of the *Reflections* and the *Rights*

of Man Controversy', *Bulletin of Research in the Humanities*, LXXXV (1982) 65–103. Extracts from the *Reflections* appeared in the *London Chronicle*, the *St. James's Chronicle*, the *Public Advertiser*, the *Newcastle Advertiser*, etc.

10. Pederson, 'Hannah More meets Simple Simon'.

11. Mitchell, 'The Association Movement', p.72; BL Add. MSS 16922, ff. 20, 129v, 16923, f. 132, 16924, f. 30; and Alan Booth, 'Reform, Repression and Revolution: Radicalism and Loyalism in the North-West of England, 1789–1803', unpublished Ph.D. thesis (Lancaster, 1979) p. 125.

12. *The Warning Drum: The British Home Front Faces Napoleon*, eds Frank J. Klingsberg and Sigurd B. Hustredt (Los Angeles, 1944) p.214.

13. Ibid., pp. 83, 126, 142, 164, 187, 214.

14. See, for example, Marilyn Butler, *Jane Austen and the War of Ideas* (Oxford, 1975) pp. 88–123; Betty T. Bennett, *British War Poetry in the Age of Romanticism 1793–1815* (New York, 1974); Gerald Newman, 'Anti-French Propaganda and British Liberal Nationalism in the Early Nineteenth Century', *Victorian Studies*, XVIII (1975) 385–418; John Ashton, *English Caricature and Satire on Napoleon I* (New York, 1888) esp. pp. 141–241; Herbert M. Atherton, 'The British Defend their Constitution in Political Cartoons and Literature', in *Studies in Eighteenth Century Culture*, II, ed. Harry C. Payne (Madison, 1982) pp. 3–31; H. T. Dickinson (ed.), *Caricatures and the Constitution 1760-1832*, (Cambridge, 1986), pp. 36–7; and Dorothy George, *English Political Caricature*, 2 vols (Oxford, 1959).

15. Nancy Uhlar Murray, 'The Influence of the French Revolution on the Church of England and its Rivals, 1789–1802', unpublished D. Phil. thesis (Oxford, 1975) esp. pp. 44–79.

16. Ibid., pp. 108–9, 122–3, and 259–307.

17. See, for example, the loyal addresses in the *London Gazette* in 1792–3, 1795–6, 1797, 1798, 1800, 1803, 1807 and 1809.

18. Murray, 'Influence of the French Revolution', pp. 212–58; John Walsh, 'Methodism at the End of the Eighteenth Century', in *A History of the Methodist Church in Great Britain*, I, eds Rupert Davies and Gordon Rupp (1965) pp. 303–8; and Bernard Semmel, *The Methodist Revolution* (1974) pp. 127–30.

19. Deryck Lovegrove, 'English Evangelical Dissent and the European Conflict 1789–1815', *SCH*, XX (1983) 266; and PRO, HO, 42/16/52–3.

20. Details of these and the other addresses mentioned in the text can be culled from the relevant issues of the *London Gazette*.

21. Linda Colley, 'The Apotheosis of George III: Loyalty, Royalty and the British Nation 1760-1820', *P & P*, 102 (1984) 112, 122.

22. BL Add. MSS 16922, f. 124; 16923, f. 67; 16924, ff. 46, 128v-29, 162v, 179; 16925, ff. 2, 33–4; 16931, ff. 9, 48–8v, 101, 127; and Dozier, *For King, Constitution and Country*, p. 63.

23. This correspondence is in the Reeves papers in the British Library, Add. MSS 16919-28.

24. Dozier, *For King, Constitution and Country*, p. 66. Dozier is wrong to claim that there were no associations in Cumberland or Northumberland, since the Reeves papers include loyalist addresses from associations in Carlisle, Newcastle and Berwick. He has also surprisingly ignored the details of several hundred loyalist addresses printed in the *London Gazette* in 1792–3.

25. Dozier, *For King, Constitution and Country*, p. 61; Booth, 'Reform, Repression and Revolution', pp. 110, 112–13; Alan Booth, 'Popular Loyalism and public violence in the north-west of England, 1790–1800', *Soc Hist*, VIII (1983) 295–313; and the list of Scottish groups in *Letters & c from Friends of the People: Or, the last words and dying advice of a weaver to his children* (n.d., but Edinburgh, 1793), pp. 14–15.

26. Mitchell, 'The Association Movement', p. 65; BL Add. MSS 16929, ff. 12–13, 54 and 16931, f. 81v.

27. See, for example, ibid, 16922, f. 49; 16923, f. 55; 16924, f. 46; and 16929, ff. 60-60v.

28. Ibid., 16929, f. 123.

29. HMC *Fortescue MSS*, ii, 354. Earl of Carysfort to Lord Grenville, 10 Dec. 1792.

30. *Newcastle Courant*, 29 Dec. 1792 and 5 Jan. 1793.

31. BL Add. MSS 16931, ff. 83-4.

32. Dozier, *For King, Constitution and Country*, pp. 124-5; Booth, 'Reform, Repression and Revolution', p. 113; and PRO, HO42/26/701, HO42/27/510-14 and 625.

33. Dozier, *For King, Constitution and Country*, pp. 108-12; PRO, HO42/24/526, HO42/25/35, HO42/27/131, HO42/28/88-9; and BL Add. MS 16925, f. 22.

34. BL Add. MSS, 16920, ff. 110, 129; and PRO, HO42/19/574, HO42/22/402 and HO42/22/490-1.

35. Ibid., HO42/29/285.

36. Dozier, *For King, Constitution and Country*, pp. 141-9; and J. R. Western, 'The Volunteer Movement as an Anti-Revolutionary Force, 1793-1802', *EHR*, LXXI (1956) 603-14.

37. Quoted in ibid., p. 613.

38. BL Add. MSS 16929, f. 41 and 16931, f. 149.

39. Ibid., Add. MSS 16921, f. 73; 16929, ff. 1, 14, 34v, 74, 76-7, 86, 110; 16930, ff. 25, 38-9, 51-2, 67-8, 77-8, 85-6, 99-100; and 16931, ff. 38, 61-2, 64, 81, 116v-17, 122-6, 130.

40. Ibid., Add. MSS 16931, ff. 151, 154; *Manchester Herald*, 20 Oct. 1792; *Chester Chronicle*, 20 July 1792; and PRO, HO42/23/13.

41. BL Add. MSS 16924, f. 23 v; 16929, ff. 34v, 50; and 16931, ff. 120, 155.

42. Booth, 'Reform, Repression and Revolution', pp. 144-53; *Newcastle Advertiser*, 5 Jan. 1793; and BL Add. MS 16924, f. 58.

43. R. B. Rose, 'The Priestley Riots of 1791', *P & P*, 18 (1960) 68-88.

44. Booth, 'Reform, Repression and Revolution', pp. 144-53; and Booth, 'Popular Loyalism and Public Violence', 300-1.

45. PRO, HO42/27/131v; J. Walsh, 'Methodism', p. 302; and W. R. Ward, *Religion and Society in England 1790-1850* (1972) pp. 24-5.

46. *London Gazette*, May-Dec. 1792; Dozier, *For King, Constitution and Country*, pp. 21, 33.

47. PRO, HO42/21/277-80 and HO42/22/401-8.

48. HMC *Fortescue MSS*, ii, 336-7, 344-5, 349, 352, 354-5; and Huntington Library, San Marino, Stowe MS STG, box 39(6).

49. BL Add. MS 16919, f. 111v.

50. Ibid., 16919, ff. 71 and 132.

51. PRO, HO42/33/160, 162, 232, 240; HO42/34/197-8; HO42/35/377, 385-6, 434; and Western, 'The Volunteer Movement', p. 608.

52. John Bohstedt, *Riots and Community Politics in England and Wales 1790-1810* (Cambridge, Mass., 1983) pp. 49-51.

53. Quoted by Linda Colley, 'Whose Nation? Class and Class Consciousness in Britain 1750-1830', *P & P*, 113 (1986) 114.

54. Ibid.: PRO, HO42/34/122-3; HO42/42/30; and HO42/44/23-4, 100-1.

55. William Cobbett's *Weekly Political Register*, V (1804) 33-54, 89-92; VI (1804) 218-20, 302-4.

56. J. C. D. Clark, *English Society 1688-1832* (Cambridge, 1985).

57. Ian R. Christie, *Stress and Stability in Late Eighteenth-Century Britain* (Oxford, 1984).

6.   BRITISH DIPLOMACY AND THE FRENCH WARS 1789-1815   *Michael Duffy*

1. The delighted response of the Foreign Secretary, the Duke of Leeds, is quoted in

John Ehrman, *The Younger Pitt*, II, *The Reluctant Transition* (1983) p. 4; the relief of the Home Secretary, William Grenville, in Duke of Buckingham (ed), *Memoirs of the Courts and Cabinets of George the Third* (1853), II, p. 165.

2. *Parl Hist*, XXIX, col. 826.

3. Buckingham (ed.), *Courts and Cabinets*, II, p. 224.

4. Bodleian Library, Oxford, Burges MSS: 'Transcripts of political papers of Col. Burges 1747, and Sir James Burges 1789–92, 1814–16': Burges to Thornton, 25 Apr. 1792.

5. BL, Add. Ms 28,068, Memoir of 27 Aug. 1789.

6. William L. Clements Library, Ann Arbor, Michigan, Pitt Papers: Pitt to Dundas, 15 Nov. 1792.

7. *Parl Hist*, XXX, cols 253–6. For simplicity the term Belgium has been used throughout this essay in place of the several appellations of the Belgic Provinces, Pays Bas, Low Countries, or Austrian Netherlands.

8. P. I. Bartenev (ed.), *Archives Woronzow* (Moscow, 1870–95) IX, p. 285: S. Vorontsov to A. Vorontsov, 21 Jan. 1793; Buckingham (ed.), *Court and Cabinets*, II, p. 237: HMC *Fortescue MSS*, ii, 372–3.

9. C. K. Webster (ed.), *British Diplomacy 1813–1815* (1921) pp. 265–6.

10. BL, Loan 57/107: Dundas to Richmond, 8 July 1793; P. Kelly, 'Strategy and Counter-Revolution: the Journal of Sir Gilbert Elliot, 1–22 September 1793', *EHR*, XCVIII (1983) 340.

11. For detailed examination see Ch. 1 of the author's unpublished D.Phil. thesis: M. Duffy, 'British War Policy: The Austrian Alliance, 1793–1801' (Oxford, 1971); and Ehrman, *Pitt*, II, ch. 8.

12. J. M. Sherwig, 'Lord Grenville's Plan for a concert of Europe, 1797–1799', *JMH*, XXXIV (1962) 284–93; J. Holland Rose, 'Pitt's plans for the settlement of Europe' in Rose, *Napoleonic Studies* (1904) pp. 51–61; PRO, London, FO 65/45 Grenville to Whitworth 19 Nov. 1799.

13. Webster (ed.), *British Diplomacy*, pp. 1, 389–394.

14. Rose, *Napoleonic Studies*, 64–76.

15. P. Mansel, *Louis XVIII* (1981) pp. 83, 104, 146; V. W. Beach, *Charles X of France. His Life and Times* (Colorado, 1971) pp. 90, 116.

16. Maurice Hutt, 'The 1790s and the Myth of 'Perfidious Albion', *Franco-British Studies*, II (1986) 3–15; idem, 'Spies in France 1793–1808', *History Today*, XII (1962) 158–67. Britain spent *c*. £1 million on the small *émigré* army of Condé in 1795–7 and 1800 and over £½million in payments to royalists within France (£303,000 via Wickham and Talbot in Switzerland between 1795–9; £78,000 via Windham to western France 1795–7; and lesser amounts via the London agent of the *émigré* princes, Dutheil, and via Windham again in 1798–1800). *c*. 20,000 stand of arms were despatched to western France in 1795–6, another 20,000 in 1799–1800 (most were quickly seized by the republicans on each occasion). In 1815 during the 'Hundred Days' 20,000 arms were sent to western and 15,000 to southern France.

17. PRO, FO 72/27: Grenville to St Helens, No. 19, Secret, 9 Aug. 1793.

18. See particularly Pitt's speech to the Commons, 17 June 1793, *Parl Hist*, XXX, cols. 1016–18.

19. Summary from Grenville's correspondence with Pitt, 4 Oct. 1793 in Holland Rose, *Pitt and Napoleon: Essays and Letters* (1912) pp. 256–9, and with his envoys Eden (PRO, FO 7/34: 7 Sept. 1793), St Helens (FO 72/28: 4, 22 Oct. 1793), Wickham (*Correspondence of William Wickham*, 1870, I, pp. 12–14), and Macartney (FO 27/45: 10 July 1795).

20. Rose, *Pitt and Napoleon*, p. 258; PRO, FO 72/28 Grenville to St Helens, 22 Oct. 1793; FO 67/16: Trevor to Grenville, 11 Apr. 1795.

21. Maurice Hutt, *Chouannerie and Counter-Revolution. Puisaye, the Princes and the British Government* (Cambridge, 1983), chs 7–8; Harvey Mitchell, *The Underground*

War Against Revolutionary France: The Missions of William Wickham 1794-1800 (Oxford, 1965) ch. 4.

22. This episode is the subject of W. R. Fryer, *Republic or Restoration in France?* (Manchester, 1965).

23. Marquess of Londonderry (ed.), *Letters and Despatches of Viscount Castlereagh* (1831), v, p. 455.

24. PRO, FO 64/58: Carysfort to Grenville, 27 Sept. 1800; Earl of Malmesbury (ed.), *Diaries and Correspondence of James Harris, First Earl of Malmesbury* (1845) III, p. 143; H. Hüffer and F. Luckwaldt, *Der Frieden von Campo-Formio* (Leipzig, 1907), pp. lv-lvi; PRO, FO 7/60: Minto to Grenville, 7 Sept. 1800; H. Randolph (ed.), *Narrative of Events during the Invasion of Russia* (1860) pp. 233-4.

25. PRO, FO 7/41: Grenville to Eden, 24 Apr., 10 July, 5 Aug. 1795; Ehrman, *Pitt*, II, pp. 548-56.

26. Webster (ed.), *British Diplomacy*, p. 1; A. Gielgud (ed.), *Memoirs of Prince Adam Czartoryski* (1888; repr. Orono, Maine, 1968) II, pp. 41-53.

27. HMC *Fortescue MSS*, II, p. 497. Whereas between 1793 and 1802 Britain increased her tax income from £18.1 to £39.1 million, Austria (which until 1814 consistently fielded the largest armies against France) struggled to raise her tax revenue from £8.7 to £9.5 million in 1801 and to a maximum of £16.2 million in 1808, whereas Britain's continued to rise to £77.9 million in 1815 (B. R. Mitchell and P. Deane, *Abstract of British Historical Statistics*, (Cambridge, 1971), pp. 388, 392; C. J. von Czörnig, *Statistiches Handbüchlein für die österreichische Monarchie*, (Vienna, 1861, p. 114).

28. J. M. Sherwig, *Guineas and Gunpowder. British foreign aid in the wars with France 1793-1815* (Cambridge, Mass., 1969) pp. 78, 83, 150, 153, 179, 208, 210; E. E. Roach, 'Anglo-Russian Relations from Austerlitz to Tilsit', *International History Review*, v (1983) 181-200.

29. Sherwig, *Guineas and Gunpowder*, pp. 365-7.

30. Ibid., pp. 181, 305-6, 311-12; Roach, 'Anglo-Russian Relations', 192-3, 196.

31. Rose, *Napoleonic Studies*, pp. 70-4, 148-9; Roach, 'Anglo-Russian Relations', 189-92; E. Kraehe, *Metterniche's German Policy* (Princeton, 1963), I, pp. 260-1; Webster (ed.), *British Diplomacy*, pp. 14-15, 31-3.

32. See B. Perkins, *Prologue to War. England and the United States 1805-1812* (Berkeley, 1961) chs 1-2 *et passim*.

33. *Hansard's Parliamentary Debates* (1809) XI, cols 890-1.

34. J. E. Cookson, 'Political Arithmetic and War in Britain, 1793-1815', *War and Society*, I (1983) 37-60. The poet William Wordsworth stressed more Britain's spiritual resources in his ode *November 1806*.

35. J. E. Cookson, *The Friends of Peace. Anti-war liberalism in England 1793-1815* (Cambridge, 1982) ch. 9.

36. Sherwig. *Guineas and Gunpowder*, pp. 284-342, 365-8; *Hansard's Parliamentary Debates*, XVII, col. 134; Webster (ed.), *British Diplomacy*, p. 166.

37. This confluence is brought out most clearly by Kraehe, *Metterniche's German Policy*, I, chs 6-10.

38. G. J. Renier, *Great Britain and the Establishment of the Netherlands 1813-1815* (The Hague, 1930) p. 34 *et passim*; Kraehe, *Metternich's German Policy*, I, p. 304: II, p. 310.

39. Ibid., II, p. 136; Webster (ed.), *British Diplomacy*, pp. 126-8.

40. Ibid., p. 218.

41. The efficacy of the settlement is discussed by P.W. Schroeder, 'Old Wine in Old Bottles: Recent Contributions to British Foreign Policy and European International Politics, 1789-1848' *JBS*, XXVI (1987) 22-4, and A. Sked, *Europe's Balance of Power 1815-1848* (London and New York, 1979) pp. 12-13 *et passim*.

7. STRATEGIC PROBLEMS OF THE BRITISH WAR EFFORT *Piers Mackesy*

1. *Parl Hist*, XXXIV, p. 203.
2. Michael Duffy, *Soldiers, Sugar and Seapower: The British Expeditions to the West Indies and the War against Revolutionary France* (Oxford, 1987) p. 16. I have drawn elsewhere below on this key work for the West Indies.
3. J. Holland Rose, *William Pitt and the Great War* (1911) p. 271.
4. *Parl Hist*, XXXVI, p. 165.
5. Piers Mackesy, *War Without Victory: The Downfall of Pitt, 1799-1802* (Oxford, 1984) p. 84.
6. Duffy, *Soldiers, Sugar and Seapower*, p. 25; J. Holland Rose, *Lord Hood and the Defence of Toulon* (1922) p. 17; Mackesy, *War Without Victory*, pp. 13, 84. For the advantages which accrued from the West Indian strategy, see Duffy, *Soldiers, Sugar and Seapower*, ch. XV.
7. Mackesy, *War Without Victory*, p. 227.
8. For the training problems of the eighteenth-century army, the most helpful work is J. A. Houlding, *Fit for Service: The Training of the British Army, 1715-1795* (Oxford, 1981).
9. A. J. P. Taylor, *The Trouble Makers: Dissent over Foreign Policy 1792-1939* (1957) p. 27.
10. Sir Herbert Richmond, *Statesmen and Seapower* (Oxford, 1946) p. 179; Duffy, *Soldiers, Sugar and Seapower*, pp. 54, 56.
11. Huntington Library, San Marino, California, Stowe Papers Box 173: *c.* 16 Nov. 1799, Lord Grenville to Lord Buckingham.
12. HMC *Fortescue MSS*, II, 464.
13. This contention is referred to in Mackesy, *War Without Victory*, p. 229 n.
14. Duffy, *Soldiers, Sugar and Seapower*, pp. 161, 195, 330, 333-4 and *passim*.
15. The account in Piers Mackesy, *The War in the Mediterranean, 1803-1810* (1957) is supplemented by C. D. Hall, 'Factors influencing British Strategic Planning and Execution during the Napoleonic War, 1803-14', unpublished Ph.D. thesis (Exeter, 1984), which is a valuable work.

8. PUBLIC FINANCE IN THE WARS WITH FRANCE 1793-1815 *P. K. O'Brien*

1. P. K. O'Brien, 'The Political Economy of British Taxation, 1660-1815', *EcHR*, XLI (1988) 1-32; unless otherwise stated, this article is the source for statistics cited in Parts I and II of this essay; P. Mathias, *The Transformation of England* (1979) ch. 6, contains useful data connecting taxation to national income; on the rise of Britain to great power status, see P. M. Kennedy, *The Rise and Fall of British Naval Mastery* (1976) chs 2-5.
2. P. Mathias and P. K. O'Brien, 'Taxation in England and France, 1715-1810', *Jn. Eur. Ec. H*, V (1976) 601-50; C. Wilson, 'Taxation and the Decline of Empires - an Unfashionable Theme', in C. Wilson (ed.), *Economic History and the Historian* (1969) pp. 114-27; S. Ardant, 'Financial Policy and Economic Infrastructure of Modern States and Nations', in C. Tilly (ed.), *The Formation of National States in Western Europe* (Princeton, 1975) pp. 164-220.
3. Paul Langford, *The Excise Crisis: Society and Politics in the Age of Walpole* (Oxford, 1975) pp. 2, 35, 151-62; J. W. Osborne, 'The Politics of Resentment: Political, Economic and Social Interaction in Eighteenth-Century England', in *Eighteenth-Century Life*, VIII (1983) 49-64; H. T. Dickinson, *Walpole and the Whig Supremacy* (1973) pp. 56-65; 93-112; 141-87.
4. C. Brooks, 'Public Finance and Political Stability: The Administration of the Land Tax', *HJ*, XVII (1974) 281-300; J. V. Beckett, 'Land Tax or Excise: the Levying of

272   BRITAIN AND THE FRENCH REVOLUTION 1789–1815

Taxation in Seventeenth and Eighteenth Century England', *EHR*, C (1985) 285–308; J. C. D. Clark, *Revolution and Rebellion. State and Society in England in the Seventeenth and Eighteenth Centuries* (Cambridge, 1986) pp. 52–63, 66.

5. R. A. Becker, *Revolution, Reform and the Politics of American Taxation* (Baton Rouge, 1980); J. L. Bullion, *A Great and Necessary Measure: George Grenville and the Genesis of the Stamp Act, 1763–65* (Columbia, 1982).

6. François Crouzet, *De la Supériorité de l'Angleterre sur la France* (Paris, 1985) pp. 22–89; N. F. R. Crafts, *British Economic Growth During the Industrial Revolution* (Oxford, 1985) pp. 45–7; J. G. van Dillen, 'Economic Fluctuations and Trade in the Netherlands, 1650–1750', in Peter Earle (ed.), *Essays in European Economic History 1500–1800* (Oxford, 1974) pp. 199–211.

7. Mathias and O'Brien, 'Taxation', pp. 601–50.

8. F. Chaumont, *Mémoire sur la France et l'Angleterre* (Paris, 1769); J. Nicholls, *Remarks on the Advantages and Disadvantages of France and of Great Britain* (1754); F. Crouzet, 'The Sources of England's wealth: some French Views in the Eighteenth Century', in P. L. Cottrell and D. H. Aldcroft (eds), *Shipping Trade and Commerce: Essays in Memory of Ralph Davis* (Leicester, 1981), pp. 61–72.

9. W. R. Ward, *The English Land Tax in the Eighteenth Century* (Oxford, 1953) pp. 66–85; W. Kennedy, *English Taxation 1640–1799* (1913) pp. 23–82, 95–179.

10. On the structure and incidence of taxes from 1660 to 1815, see O'Brien, 'Political Economy', pp. 14–17.

11. Modern historians of the eighteenth century rarely discuss this most intimate and important point of contact between the State and its citizens. See W. A. Speck, *Stability and Strife in England 1714–60* (1977); Ian R. Christie, *Wars and Revolutions: Britain 1760–1815* (1982). But on progression see F. Shehab, *Progressive Taxation* (Oxford, 1953) pp. 1–69. For comparison see R. Brawn, 'Taxation Sociopolitical Structure and State Building', in Tilly (ed.), *Formation of National States*, pp. 243–327.

12. W. R. Ward, 'The Administration of the Window and Assessed Taxes, 1696–1788', in *EHR*, LXVII (1952) 522–42; S. Dowell, *A History of Taxation and Taxes in England* (1888, reprinted 1965) II, pp. 41–238; III, pp. 103–10, 156–7, 159–62, 170–80, 193–209, 222–8, 235–47, 252–7, 262–4, 272–5, 288–96, 304–14, 321–33; J. E. D. Binney, *British Finance and Administration 1774–94* (Oxford, 1958) pp. 174–92.

13. J. V. Beckett, 'Local Custom and the New Taxation', *North Hist*, XII (1976) 105–26.

14. John Owens, *Plain Papers Relating to the Excise* (Linlithgow, 1879) pp. 9–10; E. Hughes, 'The English Stamp Duties', *EHR*, LVI (1941) 234–64.

15. E. Hoon, *The Organization of the English Customs System 1696–1786* (New York, 1938); W. A. Cole, 'Trends in Eighteenth Century Smuggling', *EcHR*, X (1958) 395–410; H. and L. H. Miu, 'Trends in Eighteenth Century Smuggling', *Ec.HR*, X (1958) 395–410; H. and L. H. Miu, 'Trends in Eighteenth Century Smuggling Reconsidered', *EcHR*, XXVIII (1975) 28–43.

16. J. B. Williams, *British Commercial Policy and Trade Expansion* (Oxford, 1972) pp. 345–82.

17. H. Roseveare, *The Treasury* (1969) p. 39; O'Brien, 'Political Economy', for shares of total taxes collected by revenue departments.

18. O'Brien, 'Political Economy', p. 21. To see how the costs of war are calculated, the incremental taxes raised and money borrowed through the creation of funded debt in wartime, see 'Accounts of Public Income and Expenditure 1688–1869', in *Parliamentary Papers*, XXXV (1868–9) appendix 13.

19. E. L. Hargreaves, *The National Debt* (1930) pp. 91–156.

20. E. J. Evans, *The Forging of the Modern State* (1983) pp. 6–44; J. Torrance, 'Social Class and Bureaucratic Innovation', *P & P*, 78 (1978) 58–64, 78.

21. P. M. G. Dickson, *The Financial Revolution in England: A Study in the Development of Public Credit 1688-1756* (1967).

22. O'Brien, 'Political Economy', p. 4; Mathias, *Transformation*, p. 121.

23. O'Brien, 'Political Economy', pp. 3-5.

24. L. S. Pressnell, *Country Banking in the Industrial Revolution* (Oxford, 1956) pp. 75-135, 366-440, 462-70; D. M. Joslin, 'London Bankers in wartime 1739-1784', in L. S. Pressnell (ed.), *Studies in the Industrial Revolution* (1960) pp. 156-77; Mathias, *Transformation*, ch. 5.

25. R. Peel, *The National Debt Productive of Bankruptcy* (1787); Evans, *Forging*, pp. 19-32.

26. John Ehrman, *The Younger Pitt: the Years of Acclaim* (1969) pp. 239-326.

27. J. Holland Rose, *William Pitt and the National Revival* (1911) pp. 178-95; Christie, *Wars and Revolutions*, pp. 181-214.

28. 1st, 2nd and 6th Reports of Commissioners of Enquiry into the Excise, *Parliamentary Papers*, XXI (1833), XXIV (1834).

29. 'Accounts and Papers 1688-1869', pp. 192-213.

30. C. B. Cone, 'Richard Price and Pitt's Sinking Fund of 1786', *EcHR*, IV (1952) 243-51; Ehrman, *The Years of Acclaim*, pp. 258-69.

31. This 'revisionist' interpretation of the sinking fund is fully referenced and supported in Chapter 8 of my forthcoming book: P. K. O'Brien, *War and Public Finance in Britain 1793-1815* (Oxford, forthcoming).

32. John Ehrman, *The British Government and Commercial Negotiations with Europe* (Cambridge, 1962) pp. 1-209.

33. The statistics used throughout this section will be published and referenced in O'Brien, *War and Public Finance*. They are also available in P. K. O'Brien, 'Government Revenue 1793-1815. A Study in Fiscal and Financial Policy in the War Against France', unpublished D.Phil. thesis (Oxford, 1967).

34. John Clapham, *The Bank of England: A History*, Vol. I (Cambridge, 1944) pp. 59, 124-30, 156, 169, 172, 177, 181, 204-16; Elmer Wood, *English Theories of Central Banking Control, 1819-58* (Cambridge, Mass, 1939) pp. 3-5, 20 and 26-7; F. W. Fetter, *Development of British Monetary Orthodoxy* (Cambridge, Mass., 1965) pp. 1-26.

35. These events are detailed in two reports from committees of the House of Commons and the House of Lords, set up to enquire into the suspension of specie payments – see *Parliamentary Papers*, III (1810) and III (1826).

36. Kennedy, *Rise and Fall*, pp. 137-43; J. E. Cookson, 'Political Arithmetic and War 1793-1815', *War and Society*, I (1983) 37-60; Clive Emsley, *British Society and the French Wars* (1979) pp. 5, 28-33, 82-3, 85, 95-6, 111-12, 120, 135-7, 153-6, 161-3, 167, 170-1.

37. Connections between war including wartime taxation and the economy, is dealt with in Crouzet's chapter in this volume and by Phyllis Deane, 'War and Industrialization', in J. M. Winter (ed.), *War and Economic Development* (Cambridge, 1975) pp. 91-101.

38. *Parl Hist*, XXXII (1795) p. 562; the latest study of the eighteenth-century land tax is M. Turner and D. Mills (eds), *Land and Property: The English Land Tax 1692-1832* (Gloucester, 1986).

39. Lord Auckland, *Substance of a Speech* (1799), p. 300. The debates preceding the introduction of the first income tax are summarised in A. Hope-Jones, *Income Tax in the Napoleonic Wars* (Cambridge, 1939) pp. 5-17; and Shehab, *Progressive Taxation*.

40. *Parl Hist*, XXXIII (1797) cols. 331 and 1048.

41. P. K. O'Brien, 'British Incomes and Property in the Early Nineteenth Century', *EcHR*, XII (1959) 255-67; Deane, 'War and Industrialization', pp. 96-8. For an entertaining argument that Addington was the real author of income taxation, see A. Farnsworth, *Addington – Author of the Modern Income Tax* (1951).

42. The government's management of the national debt from 1793 to 1815 is dealt with in necessary detail in O'Brien, *War and Public Finance*.

43. The *locus classicus* for the long historiographical critique of the wartime sinking fund is R. Hamilton, *An Enquiry Concerning the Rise, Progress, Redemption and Management of the National Debt*, 3 edn (1818).

44. Boyd Hilton, *Corn Cash and Commerce: The Economic Policies of the Tory Governments 1815–30* (Oxford, 1977) pp. 250–6.

45. The bullion controversy over the Government's monetary policy from 1797–1819 is summarised in F. W. Fetter, 'The Bullion Report Reconsidered', in T. S. Ashton and R. S. Sayers (eds), *Papers in English Monetary History* (Oxford, 1953) pp. 66–75. The most recent treatment of this topic is I. P. H. Duffy, 'The Discount Policy of the Bank of England During the Suspension of Cash Payments 1797–1821', *EcHR*, xxxv (1982) 67–81.

46. O'Brien, 'Political Economy', p. 13.

47. On post-war financial reconstruction, see A. W. Acworth, *Financial Reconstruction in England 1815–22* (1925); Hilton, *Corn, Cash and Commerce*, and B. Gordon, *Political Economy in Parliament, 1819–23* (1976).

9.   THE IMPACT OF THE FRENCH WARS ON THE BRITISH ECONOMY   *François Crouzet*

1. J. Mokyr and N. E. Savin, 'Stagflation in Historical Perspective: the Napoleonic Wars Revisited', *Research in Economic History*, I (1976) 198–259; and J. G. Williamson, 'Why was British Growth so Slow during the Industrial Revolution?', *Journal of Economic History*, xliv, 3 (1984) 687–712, are pioneering works with this approach.

2. Rates calculated by exponential adjustment, from figures in B. R. Mitchell and P. Deane, *Abstract of British Historical Statistics* (1962) pp. 281–82.

3. F. Crouzet, 'Toward an Export Economy: British Exports during the Indusrial Revolution', *Explorations in Economic History*, 17, 1 (1980) 61–5, for some details.

4. A. D. Gayer, W. W. Rostow and A. J. Schwartz, *The Growth and Fluctuation of the British Economy, 1790–1850*, 2 vols (Oxford, 1953; 2nd edn., 1975) vol. 1, p. 468, table 39; also Mitchell and Deane, *Abstract*, p. 470.

5. P. K. O'Brien, 'Agriculture and the Home Market for English Industry, 1660–1820', *EHR*, c (1985) 789–90, 795; G. Hueckel, 'War and the British Economy, 1793–1815: A General Equilibrium Analysis', *Explorations in Economic History*, 10, (1973) 388, table 3. The shift in the terms of trade is less marked according to O'Brien than to Hueckel's figures.

6. J. Mokyr, 'Has the Industrial Revolution Been Crowded Out? Some Reflections on Crafts and Williamson', *Explorations in Economic History*, 24, (1987) 304.

7. E. A. Wrigley and R. S. Schofield, *The Population History of England, 1541–1871. A Reconstruction* (1981) pp. 213, 529.

8. Hueckel, 'War...', 371–72.

9. P. Deane, 'War and Industrialization', in J. M. Winter (ed.), *War and Economic Development. Essays in Memory of David Joslin* (Cambridge, 1975), 97–8; J. L. Anderson, 'A Measure of the Effect of British Public Finance, 1793–1815', *EcHR*, xxvii, (1974) 616–18.

10. M. D. Bordo and A. J. Schwartz, 'Money and Prices in the Nineteenth Century: Was Thomas Tooke Right?', *Explorations in Economic History*, 18 (1981) 97–9, 103, 125, reasserts this thesis.

11. M. Turner, *Enclosures in Britain 1750–1830* (1984) pp. 17–21.

12. P. Deane and W. A. Cole, *British Economic Growth 1688–1959; Trends and Structure*, 2nd edn (1967) pp. 161–2.

13. G. Hueckel, 'English Farming Profits under the Napoleonic Wars, 1793–1815', *Explorations in Economic History*, 13, (1976) 332–6, 338, 342–3.

14. P. K. O'Brien, 'The Impact of the Revolutionary and Napoleonic Wars, 1793‒1815, on the Long Run Growth of the British Economy', unpublished paper (this writer is most grateful to Dr O'Brien for his permission to use this essay); also O'Brien, 'Agriculture and the Home Market', 784; G. Hueckel, 'Agriculture during Industrialisation', in R. Flood and D. McCloskey (eds), *The Economic History of Britain since 1700, Vol. 1: 1700‒1860* (1981) p. 198.

15. Based on N. F. R. Crafts, *British Economic Growth during the Industrial Revolution* (Oxford, 1985), p. 23, table 2.4; see his notes, pp. 22‒3, on the sources and nature of the series (not all fully reliable) from which these growth rates have been computed. Deane, 'War and Industrialization', p. 99, table 3, has figures which complete those of Crafts, but which give different results for some minor industries. Only major industries have been included in table 2.

16. H. A. Shannon, 'Bricks ‒ A Trade Index, 1785‒1849', *Economica*, N.S., 3 (1934) reprinted in E. M. Carus-Wilson (ed.) *Essays in Economic History*, III (1962) pp. 188‒201.

17. For instance, the figures of G. N. von Tunzelmann, 'The Standard of Living Debate and Optimal Economic Growth', in J. Mokyr (ed.), *The Economics of the Industrial Revolution* (1985) p. 213, table 10.1. This view also fits with what we know of technological and structural change.

18. Econometric test by Mokyr and Savin, 'Stagflation', 199, 213‒20.

19. Deane and Cole, *British Economic Growth*, p. 282, table 72; C. H. Feinstein, 'Capital Formation in Great Britain', in P. Mathias and M. M. Postan (eds), *The Cambridge Economic History of Europe*, vol. VII, part I (Cambridge, 1978), p. 91; O'Brien, 'The Impact...', table 3; Crafts, *Industrial Revolution*, pp. 46‒7.

20. Feinstein, 'Capital Formation', p. 91, table 28, also pp. 69, 92‒3.

21. Crafts, *Industrial Revolution*, p. 73, table 4.1.

22. Williamson, 'British Growth' pp. 687‒90, 697‒8, 701‒2, 709‒10, 712.

23. Mokyr, 'Has the Industrial Revolution...', 298‒300.

24. O'Brien, 'The Impact...'.

25. D. Cannadine, 'Conspicuous Consumption by the Landed Classes', in M. Turner (ed.), *Malthus and his Time* (1986) pp. 97‒100.

26. Calculation from figures in O'Brien, 'The Impact...'.

27. The indices which have been used (and recalculated on the basis 1790 = 100) come from S. Pollard and D. W. Crossley, *The Wealth of Britain, 1085‒1966* (1968) p. 184; P. K. O'Brien and S. L. Engerman, 'Changes in Income and its Distribution during the Industrial Revolution', in Flood and McCloskey, *Economic History*, p. 169, table 9.1; H. P. Brown and S. V. Hopkins, *A Perspective of Wages and Prices* (1981) p. 30; Wrigley and Schofield, *Population History*, pp. 643‒4, appendix A9.2; P. H. Lindert and J. G. Williamson, 'English Workers' Living Standards during the Industrial Revolution: A New Look', *EcHR*, XXXVI (1983) 13, table 5 (index for blue-collar workers); L. D. Schwarz, 'The Standard of Living in the Long Run: London, 1700‒1860', *EcHR*, XXXVIII (1985) 40, appendix II (2 series, based on different cost-of-living indices, have been used).

28. Wrigley and Schofield, *Population History*, pp. 408‒9, 431, 435, 440.

29. Lindert and Williamson, 'English Workers...', p. 13, table 5, also pp. 4, table 2, 10.

30. Von Tunzelmann, 'Standard of Living Debate', p. 208. However, P. H. Lindert and J. G. Williamson, 'English Workers' Real Wages: Reply to Crafts', *Journal of Economic History*, XLV, (1985) 153, maintain their view of 'dismal rates of improvement in the standard of living up to 1810'.

31. E. Cocks, 'Malthus on Population in a War-Based Industrial Economy', in Turner (ed.), *Malthus...*, pp. 223‒6.

32. Wrigley and Schofield, *Population History*, pp. 213, 414, 418, 534‒5.

33. P. Sraffa (ed.), *The Works and Correspondence of David Ricardo*, II (1951) p. 361.

10.   THE SOCIAL IMPACT OF THE FRENCH WARS   *Clive Emsley*

1. Arthur Hope-Jones, *Income Tax in the Napoleonic Wars* (Cambridge, 1939); B. E. V. Sabine, *A History of Income Tax* (1966). Sabine's second chapter is called 'The Tax that beat Napoleon'.

2. Clive Emsley, *British Society and the French Wars 1793–1815* (1979), pp. 37 and 133. See also Linda Colley, 'Whose Nation? Class and National Consciousness in Britain 1750–1830', *P & P*, 113 (1986) 101.

3. *Parl Hist*, XXXII, 1256–73, and XXXIV, 22–4.

4. Cumbria Record Office (Carlisle), Stenhouse MSS Box 3, Mrs Michelson to Catherine Stenhouse, 9 May 1798.

5. Northumberland Record Office, Delaval MSS. 2/2E.4.57/93. John Carr to Lord Delaval, 23 Dec. 1797.

6. Oldham Local Interest Centre. 'William Rowbottom Diaries 1787–1830', 9 Feb. and 17 April 1794.

7. N. A. M. Rodger, *The Wooden World: An Anatomy of the Georgian Navy* (1986) pp. 78, 150 and 164–82; Emsley, ...*French Wars*, pp. 40 and 50.

8. PRO, HO 42.132. William Margett to Sidmouth, 10 Mar. 1813.

9. J. M. Beattie, *Crime and the Courts in England 1660–1800* (Oxford, 1986) pp. 213–35; Clive Emsley, *Crime and Society in England 1750–1900* (1987) pp. 28–9.

10. Michael Lewis, *A Social History of the Navy, 1793–1815* (1960) pp. 90–2.

11. PRO, HO 42.74.30. John Bennett to Yorke, 29 Dec. 1803; HO 42.78, John Wright to Yorke, 4 and 15 Feb. 1804.

12. PRO, HO 452.27. Captain Smith-Child to Admiralty, 27 Oct. 1793. For earlier hostility to press gangs in Liverpool see Rodger, *Wooden World...*, pp. 169 and 175–6.

13. John Stevenson, 'The London "Crimp" Riots of 1794', *Internat. Rev. Soc. Hist.*, XVI (1971) 40–58.

14. Birmingham Reference Library, 510640 Garbett–Lansdowne Correspondence, IV, 25; Garbett to Lansdowne, 7 feb. 1794; and see also IV, 27, same to same 18 Mar. 1794.

15. Eric Richards, *A History of the Highland Clearances: Agrarian Transformation and the Evictions 1746–1886* (1982) pp. 147–56. In some instances the proposals for an improved lease or a better holding, in exchange for a son, emanated from the tenant.

16. Ann Kussmaul (ed.), *The Autobiography of Joseph Mayett of Quainton 1783–1839* (Buckinghamshire Record Society, vol. 23, 1986) p. 55.

17. Ibid., p. 23.

18. J. R. Western, 'The Volunteer Movement as an Anti-Revolutionary Force, 1793–1801', *EHR*, LXXI (1956) 603–14; Roger Wells, *'Wretched Faces': Famine in Wartime England 1793–1801* (forthcoming). My thanks to Dr Wells for permission to read and cite the manuscript.

19. W. Branch Johnson (ed.) *'Memorandums for' The diary between 1798 and 1810 of John Carrington* (Chichester, 1973) pp. 150–1.

20. John Bohstedt, *Riots and Community Politics in England and Wales 1790–1810* (Cambridge, Mass, 1983) pp. 173–84.

21. J. R. Western, 'The Formation of the Scottish Militia in 1797', *SHR*, XXXIV (1955) 1–18; Sandy Mullay, *Scotland's Forgotten Massacre* (Edinburgh, 1979).

22. Rowbottom Diary, 21 Sept. 1795.

23. [Thomas Carter], *Memoirs of a Working Man*, (1845) pp. 137–8.

24. John Nicol, *The Life and Adventures of John Nicol, Mariner* (1937) pp. 206–10.

25. PRO, HO 42/71. John Fleming to Pelham, 28 July 1803 and HO 42/72, same to same, 4 Aug. 1803.

26. R. I. and S. Wilberforce, *The Life of William Wilberforce* (1838), IV, p. 35.

27. J. E. Cookson, 'Political arithmetic and war in Britain, 1793–1815', *War and Society*, I (1983) 37–60.

28. Colley, 'Whose Nation?', pp. 110-11.

29. Emsley, ... French Wars, p. 32.

30. Northumberland Record Office, Delaval MSS 2 DE 4/27.30. John Bryers to Lord Delaval, 6 Mar. 1805.

31. Roger Morriss, *The Royal Dockyards during the Revolutionary and Napoleonic Wars* (Leicester, 1983) pp. 120-6; Norman McCord, 'The Seaman's Strike of 1815 in North-East England', *EcHR*, XXI (1968) 127-43.

32. For the fullest, and most recent assertion of the revolutionary nature of the nocturnal meetings of 1799-1801 see Roger Wells, *Insurrection: The British Experience 1795-1803* (Gloucester, 1983), chs 9 and 10.

33. Linda Colley, 'The Apotheosis of George III; Loyalty, Royalty and the British Nation 1760-1820', *P&P*, 102 (1984) 94-129. See, also, chapter 5.

34. F. K. Prochaska, 'English State Trials in the 1790s: A Case Study', *JBS*, XII (1973) 63-82.

35. *The Loyalist*, No. 2 (15 Aug. 1803) pp. 42-3.

36. William Burdon A.M., *Advice addressed to the Lower Ranks of Society* (Newcastle-upon-Tyne, 1803) pp. 21-2.

37. Bedfordshire Record Office, Whitbread MSS W1/3663, James Nisbett to Whitbread, 19 July 1811. My thanks to S. C. Whitbread for permission to read and cite this material.

38. 'The British Tars', in C. H. Firth (ed.), *Naval Songs and Ballads* (Navy Records Society, vol. 33, 1908) p. 136.

39. George Wood, *The Subaltern Officer* (1825) pp. vi-vii.

40. Stanislav Andreski, *Military Organisation and Society*, 2nd edn (1968).

41. Clive Emsley, 'The Impact of War and Military Participation on Britain and France 1792-1815', in Clive Emsley and James Walvin (eds), *Artisans, Peasants and Proletarians 1760-1860* (1985).

11.   'THINGS AS THEY ARE': THE LITERARY RESPONSE

TO THE FRENCH REVOLUTION 1789-1815   *Iain Robertson Scott*

1. This contrast between contemporary society, which seemed corrupt and artificial, and Rousseau's idea of a more natural state of man, was a favourite theme of the Jacobin novelists and is reflected even in their choice of titles, for example Robert Bage's *Man As He Is* (1792) and *Hermsprong; or, Man As He Is Not* (1796), and Elizabeth Inchbald's *Nature and Art* (1796).

2. See Wordsworth, 'Letter to Dorothy Wordsworth,' 6 Sept. 1790, *The Letters of William and Dorothy Wordsworth*, eds. E de Selincourt and C. L. Shaver (Oxford, 1967) I, p. 36.

3. Wordsworth, *The Prelude* (1805), Book X, ll 692-3, in *The Prelude: 1799, 1805, 1850*, eds J. Wordsworth, M. H. Abrams, S. Gill (New York and London, 1979) p. 396.

4. Southey, 'Letter to C. Bowles,' 13 Feb. 1824, in *The Correspondence of Robert Southey with Caroline Bowles*, ed. E. Dowden (Dublin, 1881) p. 52.

5. See Wordsworth, *The Prelude* (1805), Book IX, ll 294-555, in *The Prelude: 1799, 1805, 1850*, pp. 326-40.

6. See Wordsworth, *Descriptive Sketches* (1793), ll 520-5, *The Poems*, ed. J. O. Hayden, 2 vols (1977), I, p. 911.

7. See Coleridge, *Conciones ad Populum* (1795), *Lectures 1795: on Politics and Religion*, eds L. Patton and P. Mann, *The Collected Works of Samuel Taylor Coleridge* (London and Princeton, 1971) I, p. 48.

8. See Wordsworth, *Letter to the Bishop of Llandaff* (1793), in *The Prose Works of William Wordsworth*, eds W. J. B. Owen and J. W. Smyser, 3 vols (Oxford, 1974) I, pp. 44-6.

9. See Coleridge, *Lines* (1794), in *Complete Poetical Works*, ed. E. H. Coleridge, 2 vols (Oxford, 1912) I, pp. 57-8.

10. See Wordsworth, *The Prelude* (1805), Book XII, ll 179–84, in *The Prelude: 1799, 1805, 1850*, p. 446.

11. Wordsworth did not publish his radical pamphlet *Letter to the Bishop of Llandaff*, written in 1793, during his lifetime, most probably because of the changed political climate. Even *The Prelude* (1805), which reflected on Wordsworth's radical youth, was never published in his own lifetime. Southey's radical play, *Wat Tyler*, written in 1794, was not published until 1817, much to the poet's embarrassment, because he then held much more conservative views and was the Poet Laureate. William Blake published very little between 1795 and 1804, when government repression was at its most intense.

12. See Marilyn Butler, *Jane Austen and the War of Ideas* (Oxford, 1975) p. 112.

13. See Coleridge, *Recantation* (1798) in *Complete Poetical Works*, I, p. 299.

14. See Wordsworth, *The Female Vagrant* (1798), ll 118–26, in *Lyrical Ballads*, ed. R. L. Brett and A. R. Jones (1965) pp. 48–9.

15. Wordsworth, *Lines Written A Few Miles Above Tintern Abbey* (1798) ll 110 and 111–12, in *Lyrical Ballads*, p. 116.

16. Wordsworth, *The Prelude* (1805), Book III, ll 404–07.

17. Wordsworth, 'Preface' (1800), in *Lyrical Ballads*, p. 245.

18. Coleridge, *Lord Moira's Letter* (1798), in *Essays On His Times*, ed. D. V. Erdman, from *The Collected Works of Samuel Taylor Coleridge* (1978) I, p. 16.

19. Coleridge, *The Rime of the Ancient Mariner* (1798) l 63, in *Lyrical Ballads*, p. 12.

20. Blake 'Letter to John Flaxman,' 19 Oct. 1801, in *Poetry and Prose of William Blake*, ed. G. Keynes (1975) pp. 852–3.

21. Wordsworth, *The Prelude* (1805), Book X, ll 934–5, in *The Prelude: 1799, 1805, 1850*, p. 408.

22. See Coleridge, *Letters on the Spaniards VI* (1809) in *Essays On His Times*, 3 vols, ed. Erdman, from *The Collected Works*, II, pp. 75–6.

23. Southey's most trenchant criticism of Britain's social, political and economic system at this time can be found in his *Letters From England* (1807) ed. Jack Simmons (Gloucester, 1984).

24. Coleridge, *The War XVIII (contd.)* (1816) in *Essays On His Times*, 3 vols, ed. Erdman, from *The Collected Works*, III, p. 247.

25. Geoffrey Carnall, *Robert Southey and His Age* (Oxford, 1960) pp. 140–1.

26. Hazlitt, *Character of Mr. Wordsworth's New Poem, 'The Excursion'*, (1814) in *The Complete Works of William Hazlitt*, ed. P. P. Howe, 21 vols (London and Toronto, 1930–4) XIX, p. 18.

27. See Blake, *Marginalia on Dr. Thornton's 'The Lord's Prayer'*, (1827), in *Poetry and Prose of William Blake*, p. 826.

28. Wordsworth, *Westmorland Address* (1818) in *The Prose Works of William Wordsworth*, III, p. 181.

29. See Wordsworth, *The Convention of Cintra* (1809), in *The Prose Works of William Wordsworth*, I, pp. 234, 288; and Coleridge, *War XI* (1811) in *Essays On His Times*, 3 vols, ed. Erdman, from *The Collected Works*, II, p. 185.

30. Coleridge, *The Friend*, 9 Nov. 1809, in *The Friend*, 2 vols, ed. B. E. Rooke, from *The Collected Works of Samuel Taylor Coleridge* (1969) II, 161.

31. Byron, *Don Juan* (1818) in *Poetical Works*, eds F. Page and J. Jump (1970) pp. 612, 636.

32. Marilyn Butler fully investigates this proposition in *Jane Austen and the War of Ideas* (Oxford, 1975).

33. See Southey, *The Life and Correspondence of the Late Robert Southey*, ed. C. C. Southey, 6 vols (1849–50) III, pp. 183–4.

34. Coleridge, *A Lay Sermon* (1817) in *Lay Sermons*, ed. R. J. White, from *The Collected Works of Samuel Taylor Coleridge* (1972) p. 233.

35. Coleridge, *The Friend*, 21 Sept. 1809, in *The Friend*, 21 Sept. 1809, in *The Friend*, 2 vols, ed. B. E. Rooke, from *The Collected Works*, II, p. 86.

36. See Robert Browning, *The Lost Leader* (1845), in *Poetical Works, 1833–1864*, ed. I. Jack (1970) p. 429.

37. Quoted in Geoffrey Carnall, *Robert Southey and His Age*, p. 118.

Notes on Contributors

FRANÇOIS CROUZET studied at the Faculté des Lettres, Paris and at the London School of Economics. He has held professorships at the universities of Bordeaux, Lille, Nanterre and he is now at Paris-Sorbonne. Among his many books are *L'Economie du Commonwealth*, *Le Conflit de Chypre*, *Capital Formation in the Industrial Revolution*, *The Victorian Economy*, *The First Industrialists*, *De la Superiorité de l'Angleterre sur la France*, and *L'Economie britannique et le Blocus Continental 1806–1813*. He has also contributed to many books and learned journals.

JOHN DERRY is Reader in Modern History at the University of Newcastle-upon-Tyne. A Cambridge graduate, he was formerly a Research Fellow of Emmanuel College, Cambridge, a Lecturer at the London School of Economics, and Fellow and Director of Studies in History at Downing College, Cambridge. His books include *William Pitt*, *The Regency Crisis and the Whigs*, *Charles James Fox*, *Castlereagh* and *English Politics and the American Revolution*.

H. T. DICKINSON is a former student at Durham and Newcastle Universities. He is now Richard Lodge Professor of British History at the University of Edinburgh and a Concurrent Professor of History at the University of Nanjing, China. He is the author of *Bolingbroke*, *Walpole and the Whig Supremacy*, *Liberty and Property: Political Ideology in Eighteenth-century Britain*, *British Radicalism and the French Revolution 1789–1815*, and *Caricatures and the Constitution 1760–1832*; the editor of *The Correspondence of Sir James Clavering*, *Politics and Literature in the Eighteenth Century* and *The Political Works of Thomas Spence*; and a contributor of essays to many books and learned journals.

MICHAEL DUFFY is a Lecturer in History at the University of Exeter. His published works include an edition, *The Military Revolution and the State, 1500–1800*, as well as *The Englishman and the Foreigner* (one of the series, *The English Satirical Print 1600–1832*, of which he was general editor) and *Soldiers, Sugar and Seapower. The British Expeditions to the West Indies and the War against Revolutionary France*.

MARIANNE ELLIOTT is Research Fellow at Liverpool University and a graduate of Queen's University, Belfast and Oxford University. She is the author of the prize-winning *Partners in Revolution: The United Irishmen and France*, *Watchmen in Sion. The Protestant Idea of Liberty*, *Theobald Wolfe Tone* and a number of articles on eighteenth-century Britain and Ireland. She translated Richard Cobb, *The People's Armies*.

CLIVE EMSLEY is Reader in History at the Open University. He was educated at the University of York and at Peterhouse, Cambridge. He has been Visiting Fellow at Griffith University, Queensland, and visiting Professor at the University of Paris. His publications include *British Society and the French Wars 1793–1815*, *Policing and its Context 1750–1870* and *Crime and Society in England 1750–1900*.

PIERS MACKESY is a Fellow of Pembroke College, Oxford. He is the author of *The Wars in the Mediterranean, 1803–10*, *The War for America, 1775–83*, *Statesmen at War: The Strategy of Overthrow, 1798–99*, *The Coward of Minden: The Affair of Lord George*

Sackville, and *War without Victory: the Downfall of Pitt, 1799–1802*, and he has contributed essays to various books and learned journals. He is a D.Litt. of Oxford University.

PATRICK O'BRIEN is University Reader in Economic History and Professorial Fellow of St Antony's College, Oxford. He has edited several books and has written numerous articles. He is the author of *The Revolution in Egypt's Economic System, The Economic Effects of the American Civil War, Two Paths to the Twentieth Century* (with C. Keyder), *The New Economic History of Railways*, and the forthcoming *War and Public Finance in Britain 1793–1815.*

FRANK O'GORMAN is Reader in History in the University of Manchester. He was a graduate of the University of Leeds and gained his doctorate from Cambridge University. He is the author of *The Whig Party and the French Revolution, Edmund Burke: his Political Philosophy, The Rise of Party in England: the Rockingham Whigs, 1760–1782, The Emergence of the British Two-Party System, 1760–1832, British Conservatism: Conservative Thought from Burke to Thatcher*, and a forthcoming book, *Voters, Patrons and Parties: the Unreformed Electorate of Hanoverian England, 1734–1832*. He has contributed a large number of essays and reviews to learned journals and periodicals.

IAIN ROBERTSON SCOTT is a teacher of History in Edinburgh. He is a graduate of Edinburgh University where he recently completed his doctoral thesis, 'From Radicalism to Conservatism: the Politics of Wordsworth and Coleridge, 1797–1818'. In 1985 he was awarded the Jeremiah Dalziel Prize in History by Edinburgh University and a Schoolmaster Fellowship by Sidney Sussex College, Cambridge.

JOHN STEVENSON is Reader in History at the University of Sheffield. Amongst his other publications are *Popular Protest and Public Order*, with R. E. Quinault, *London in the Age of Reform, Popular Disturbances in England, 1700–1870*, and *Order and Disorder in Early Modern England*, with A. J. Fletcher. He is currently working on a study of the life and times of William Cobbett.

Index